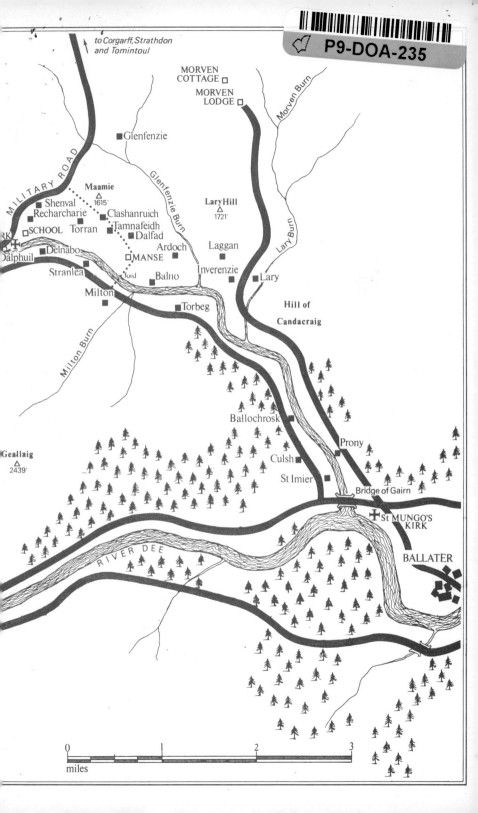

P9-DOA-235

to Corgarff, Strathdon
and Tomintoul

MORVEN
COTTAGE □
MORVEN
LODGE □

Morven Burn

■ Glenfenzie

MILITARY ROAD

Glenfenzie Burn

Lary Hill
△ 1721'

Maamie
△ 1615'

■ Shenval
Recharcharie
SCHOOL □  ■ Clashanruich
Torran  ■ Tamnafeidh
KK  □  ■ Dalfad
✝  Ardoch ■
Dalphuil  ■ Delnabo  □ MANSE
Stranlea  ...ford  ■ Balno
Milton  Inverenzie
■  Laggan

Lary Burn

Lary ■

Torbeg ■

Hill of
Candacraig

Milton Burn

Ballochrosk ■

Geallaig
△ 2439'

Prony

Culsh ■

St Imier ■

Bridge of Gairn

✝ St MUNGO'S
KIRK

RIVER DEE

BALLATER

0        1        2        3
miles

# THE
# HILLS OF HOME

Be it granted to me to behold you again,
Hills of Home!
                    Robert Louis Stevenson


This is my country,
The land that begat me,
These windy spaces
Are surely my own,
And those who here toil
In the sweat of their faces
Are flesh of my flesh
And bone of my bone.
                    Sir Alexander Gray

# THE
# HILLS OF HOME

Amy Stewart Fraser

## Routledge & Kegan Paul
London and Boston

*First published 1973*
*by Routledge & Kegan Paul Ltd*
*Broadway House, 68-74 Carter Lane,*
*London EC4V 5EL and*
*9 Park Street,*
*Boston, Mass. 02108, U.S.A.*

*Reprinted 1973 (twice)*

*Printed in Great Britain by*
*T. & A. Constable Ltd,*
*Hopetoun Street, Edinburgh*
© *Amy Stewart Fraser 1973*
*No part of this book may be reproduced in*
*any form without permission from the*
*publisher, except for the quotation of brief*
*passages in criticism*
ISBN 0 7100 7414 X

For my children and grandchildren
and their grandchildren

# CONTENTS

# PREFACE

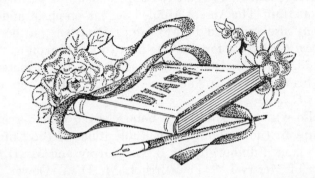

This is not a work of fiction; it is the simple annals of a happy family living a contented life three-quarters of a century ago. All the characters are real people with their real names. Many of the people are real 'characters'.

In the spelling of Gaelic place-names, with one or two exceptions, the spelling is that used on the Ordnance Survey Maps.

> There's a clean wind blowing
> Over hill-flower and peat,
> Where the bell-heather's growing,
> And the brown burn flowing,
> And the ghost-shadow's going
> Down the glen on stealthy feet.
> There's a clean wind blowing
> And the breath of it is sweet.
>                                    Will Ogilvie

My grateful thanks are due to Susan, Lady Tweedsmuir, and the family of John Buchan for permission to quote the lines he wrote on his father, and the reference to *Witchwood*;

to Mr John Gray for allowing me to quote his father's lines which appear on pages ii and 5; to the family of Will Ogilvie for permission to quote the lines which appear on p. ix; to Miss Lavinia Derwent for allowing me to quote her lines on pp. 146, 201 and 225; and to Mrs George Bambridge and A. P. Watt & Son, London, for permission to quote from 'The Absent Minded Beggar' on pp. 39 and 40.

I am also indebted to Mr James Drawbell, author of *The Sun Within Us*, for allowing me to quote him on pp. 100 and 158, and to Mr Douglas C. Mason for the use of material from his articles on St Andrews University which appeared in the *Courier*.

I also wish to acknowledge help received from Dr Alan Thompson; the Committee on Publications of the Church of Scotland, Edinburgh; Mr B. G. Murray and Mr D. M. Bailey of Messrs J. S. Fry, Bristol; Mr D. A. Dewar and Mr J. Armstrong of Messrs Cooper & Co., Glasgow; the Aberdeen Journals, Ltd, and Messrs D. C. Thomson & Co., Ltd. In spite of careful enquiry I have been unable to trace the owners of certain copyrights, and beg forgiveness from anyone whose rights have been overlooked.

A. S. F.

# CHAPTER ONE

# INTRODUCTION TO THE GLEN

> There's a valley in the Nor' East
> And a river rippling free,
> Ever singing in the sunlight
> As it hurries to the Dee;
> And I think of it with longing,
> I remember it with tears,
> For the echoes of its music
> Brings me back the vanished years.
>
> Adapted from
> Clifton Bingham's *Coming Home*

Everyone has roots somewhere . . . mine are in the Glen. Glen Gairn, Aberdeenshire, may be found on an Ordnance Survey map . . . not Glencairn, mind you, which is in Dumfriesshire, but Glen Gairn with a G, less than a mile from Balmoral as the eagles soar and the grouse fly, but Geallaig Hill lying between makes it a bit farther by road, over the steep Stranyarroch or round by Deeside.

This book is written to record, before old landmarks vanish and there is no one left to remember them, the manner in which people lived in a remote Scottish parish nearly a century ago.

Glen Gairn has been described by one well-known Scots writer as 'just as bonnie a Highland glen as ever I have seen'.

If this were fiction it would be pleasant to say with a sentimental sigh that unchanged are the little patchwork crofts and the roads that were so deep in dust that a passing car sprayed white the juniper bushes by the wayside, but this is not so.

The once well-populated glen is nearly empty of farming folk. Heaps of stones and clumps of birches show where once were larachs, and a twisted rowan, planted long years ago, to keep off evil spirits, still may brave the winter's blast. Now the thatched cottages are a ruckle o' stanes, with, in summer, a wild rose or two clinging to the rubble; here and there on the moors are signs of 'ferm-touns' that were occupied by generations of hardy, industrious, long-lived folk.

There is beauty in the Glen at any season of the year, but the colouring is most lovely when birches and larches are in their freshest green; and again, when the trees change, the wealth of colour is indescribably beautiful. Rowans, geans, alders and birches against the dark green of Scotch firs, with great stretches of brown heather and golden bracken, make an impressive patchwork.

Today the Manse of Glen Gairn is a desolate heap of stones; the once-gracious avenue is moss-grown, the garden a wilderness. Over-grown shrubs encroach more and more as the years go by; the ubiquitous rose-bay willow-herb and rank grass flourish where once there was a lawn. Gean-trees blossom by the old croquet-green, but those by the woodland gate are dead. In the undergrowth one may still find a clump of snowdrops or primroses; yellow daisies and poppies have spilled into the woods below, but the stone-crop has gone. It covered the wall by the bleaching-green, making with its golden-star flowerets a solid patch of colour. At the main entrance 'the honeysuckle spreads its trailers fast, and the old palings sag'.

Yet, when I mooned around the deserted scene one sunny

day in June I could see in my mind's eye a moving cloud, could imagine the air filled with a high-pitched hum and a faint echo of children's voices excitedly shouting, 'The bees have come! The bees have come!' They came every year, from whence we never knew. They may have been wild bees for no one ever reported a lost swarm. To watch one in action was exciting, almost hypnotic. We children would sprawl on the grass and watch the cloud hover over the house, gradually dissolve and disappear under the rafters above a certain window. There the bees busied themselves throughout the long summer days. They could be seen coming and going from their workshop under the eaves to the heather-bells heavy with nectar, and their gentle humming could be heard indoors at the bedroom window. In late autumn came the time to smoke them out, a drastic operation that appals me now, but we knew of no other way to harvest the honey. We humbly regarded it as one of Nature's gifts, and thought no more of smoking out the bees than cottagers thought of killing their specially-fattened pig and curing it against winter months of isolation and privation.

Preparations were elaborate; first, the bedroom floor and furniture were shrouded in sheets; then my father, with head and arms well protected, unscrewed the ceiling-board of the dormer-window which gave access to the rafters. He cautiously lowered it and thrust in on a shovel pieces of flaming, sulphur-impregnated brown paper and held the board closely in position till the fumes had achieved their deadly purpose. When it was again lowered, down came a shower of bees which were quickly swept up and removed. My father then reached up with a carving knife and hacked the golden combs from the well-filled rafters. We children stood well back while my mother held in readiness, one after another, her largest ashets and basins to receive the dripping treasure. What a harvest it was! Pounds and pounds of delectable heather-honey delicately flavoured with wild thyme! Everybody in the vicinity got a generous portion, select cuts were packed with care and dispatched to distant friends, some pieces were drained into jars, inferior bits of comb made into beeswax for polishing furniture. Not a scrap was wasted, for in that household a much-quoted maxim was 'Waste not, want not!' When the last sticky plate had been cleared, and the last delicious crumb consumed, we looked forward with complete confidence to a visit from questing scouts in the following May or June, and the arrival of another swarm of bees to honour us.

Now let me tell you of my father's early years and his call to the ministry.

# CHAPTER TWO

# THE LAD O' PAIRTS

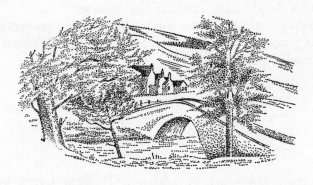

Labour by day and scant rest in the gloaming,
With Want an attendant not lightly outpaced.
          Sir Alexander Gray

James Anderson Lowe was one of a family of fourteen boys
and girls, eight of whom died in childhood in the terrible
epidemics of diphtheria that frequently wiped out whole
families. Within one month six children were taken; twice
it happened that two children died on the same day. The
overwhelming sadness in that stricken family must have left
a deep impression on the four schoolboy sons and two
daughters who miraculously survived.

Their mother, Elizabeth Williamson, daughter of a family
well known in Scottish pulpits for some generations, had
been disowned by her parents for marrying below her
station, a not uncommon attitude for parents of substance
to adopt in those days. When she announced her intention
they stormed at her in a stream of Victorian clichés. Despite
echoing phrases like, 'We wash our hands of you. Never
darken our doors again', one morning she put on her best
blue-flowered silk gown, her bonnet, and her new cashmere

shawl (six yards long, with a silvery stripe running through it, like the one the Queen had recently made high fashion) and serenely set forth to marry her gallant young crofter.

'Where thou goest, I will go,' she murmured, and went with him to a small house adjoining Wyndford Smithy in Laurencekirk, in the Howe o' the Mearns.

She was a plucky young woman, and if she ever regretted leaving her comfortable home at Muir of Lunan no one was made aware of it.

> Substantial steadfast man was he
> Who shod the horses, forged the ploughs,
> Who tilled the glebe that kept his cows,
> Stern in his ways as ought to be
> The father of a filling house.

I never knew my grandfather, William Lowe, but I believe the above lines by James Stoddart, a former editor of the *Glasgow Herald*, would describe him fairly well, with his glebe, his forge, and his filling house. It was the day of large families.

My grandmother had all the old Scottish reverence for a good education, coupled with a fervent wish to see her sons wagging their heads in the pulpit.

She had three brothers in the ministry. They stood by their sister, and encouraged her in her ambition, which she proudly saw fulfilled. William, George and James (my father) became parish ministers. The youngest, Tom, qualified as a solicitor, specialized in municipal law, and held a position in the office of the Town Clerk of Arbroath.

From the village school the boys proceeded, one by one, to graduate at St Andrews University; the girls stayed at home to help their mother.

It was early instilled in Scots lads in that day and generation that the main thing in life was to work hard and get on in the world by their own unaided efforts.

Before he went to the university my father acted as a pupil-teacher for some years. He had probably been no

[6]

farther from home than Edzell, Fordoun, or Fettercairn, on the annual Sunday School trip to the Clatterin' Brig, or on a family outing to St Paldy's Fair, which commemorated a bishop called St Palladius; so when at the age of eighteen, having won an entrance bursary of £80, he took the road to St Andrews, the old town with its medieval colleges must in itself have been an education to the country lad, as he wandered through its pends and closes, treading its cobbled streets, absorbing what it had to offer.

The choice of subjects was more limited than it is now. The course was largely the same for all students, consisting of four years' study. Latin and Greek were taught throughout. Mathematics and Logic were added in the second year, Moral Philosophy in the third, and Natural Philosophy in the fourth. My father started to keep a diary, a habit he was to keep up for the rest of his life. He briefly recorded current events, an outline of his work and leisure, and personal expenditure. These old diaries have been invaluable to me in disclosing facts relating to his life and work. His accounts were meticulous, stating with almost pedantic accuracy where his money went each week. Books were a heavy item, but a haircut only cost 3d.

He lived in modest lodgings in Abbotsford Place on a frugal and monotonous diet. When college days were over he thankfully renounced cocoa forever, having consumed gallons of that humble beverage over the years, rather than hurt the feelings of his well-meaning landlady with whom he stayed for four years. Her charge for board and lodging was fifteen shillings per week. (Paraffin was extra, and no doubt he did his share of burning the midnight oil.)

It was possible in those days to enjoy an active and varied life outside the lecture-room and my father, though always studious, took part in the life of the community by attending concerts and public lectures by visiting notabilities. There were also meetings of the university Classical and Literary Debating Societies to attend. He revelled in the Gaudeamus and similar gatherings and, though tone-deaf, joined heartily with his friend, Millar Patrick, in the choruses of student songs.

He played an occasional game of golf, and had congenial friends who accompanied him on long tramps in the beautiful countryside, and on the sand-dunes which were then accessible only to keen walkers.

He was essentially a modest man, and from him in later life, we, his family, learned nothing of his scholastic achievements. We guessed he was a scholar because of his fondness for reading books in Latin, Greek and Hebrew which he did with facility, and his eagerness to share his knowledge with others; but only after his death, when we found copies of his testimonials, did we discover that he had gained at the university several of the highest prizes, and that when he went on to study theology he came top in the entrance examination, gaining another bursary of £90.

He graduated Master of Arts in 1885, and oft recalled the capping ceremony and the custom, long forgotten, of students chanting 'Old Soldiers Never Die' when there trooped up to the dais one or two well-known characters who had taken more than the normal four years to get their degree. Such happy-go-lucky fellows whose sole object was to enjoy the social amenities of university life, apparently unhampered by financial worries, lazed away the months and years and are now only a legend, but there were many at universities before the First World War. Failure to graduate was not then a very serious matter, and many students did not worry about it unless they intended to go on to study divinity and enter the Church. Between dullards and wastrels there were bound to be some examination casualties.

My father completed his Arts course in the prescribed period and went on to spend a further three years at St Mary's College.

The ancient trees under which he strolled in the precincts of St Mary's College are still there, upheld by strong iron supports, including the thorn which is said to have been planted by Mary, Queen of Scots.

The dining-hall is the austere chamber it was in past ages, with its table marked to show where sat those below the salt and those who occupied an exalted position above it.

The Theological Society, believed to be the oldest student society in Europe, provided a forum for the divinity students to discuss topics of religious importance.

Towards the end of his course my father, according to his diary, was much occupied in the preparation of endless sermons, homilies, discourses, and expositions which were, I imagine, variations on the theme of religious composition.

The parish minister of Laurencekirk, the Rev. Charles Morrison, took a genuine interest in his progress and on several occasions invited him to preach. There stood the young man in the pulpit of the church in which he had been brought up, with his mother, fresh from her Sunday School class, sitting doucely with her husband in the pew they occupied Sunday after Sunday, their listening faces upturned to the pulpit intent on every word, and in the congregation many critical sermon-tasters who had known the preacher since he was a child.

At the close of his theological course my father won several prizes including the Chancellor's Prize open to all students, and in 1888 graduated Bachelor of Divinity. His youth was therefore spent in the true Scottish tradition . . . the lad o' pairts went into the ministry.

He had put himself through college by competitive scholarships and by spending part of each summer vacation in tutoring various young men with a university course in mind, for a monthly fee of a guinea. He had also continued to work on farms as he had done as a boy; the help of every hardy boy and girl had always been required in Laurence-kirk fields when crops, root and grain, were ready for harvesting.

On leaving St Andrews my father reckoned up his expenditure during his seven years at college, and found the sum total to be £244 17s 1½d. He had supported himself, and helped his mother, mainly out of his vacation earnings, and no doubt felt a great sense of satisfaction at having achieved what he set out to do, without costing his parents or the State a penny. By way of celebration, he went out shopping and bought himself a pair of new shoes which cost him ten shillings, and ordered his first clerical suit of clothes for the sum of £4 18s 6d.

His first appointment was as Assistant Minister to the Rev. George Muir Smith in the West Church in Stirling, at a salary of £8 a month.

He undertook chaplain's duties to the soldiers stationed at the Castle, including those in the military prison, and every Sunday visited the Royal Infirmary, as well as taking part in morning and evening services, fitting in a Bible class and a visit to the Sunday School. Weekdays were occupied with a continuous round of sick-visiting, visiting the bereaved, praying at the bedsides of the dying, and attending evening meetings of Guilds and Young People's Classes. He loved his work, and inscribed on the front page of his diary his own choice of Rules for Guidance through Life, including the advice of Thomas à Kempis, 'Never be entirely idle, but either be reading, writing, or meditating, or endeavouring something for the public good'.

Two maxims he followed all his life, mistakenly, for his health suffered because he endured pain too long in silence . . . these were: 'I must never be late'; 'I must never be ill, or, if I am, I must not show it'. When in Stirling he fell ill, he dosed himself with a proprietary brand of lung tonic which did no good and fever made him take to his bed. There he lay for two months, dangerously ill with typhoid fever with a doctor in attendance twice daily. His temperature rose to 104° and was seldom below 102°. In those days isolation and hospital care were not thought to be necessary, nor was the welfare of contacts taken into consideration. His mother came at once to nurse him, and sat in silent prayer tending him every daylight hour and, with the gas-jet turned low, by night for many weeks, snatching sleep when she could. On his recovery she took him home to recuperate. After a short convalescence he was back in harness for he could not afford to do without his salary any longer and had no sickness benefit.

In July 1891 he was ordained to the Quoad Sacra Parish of Glen Gairn in the Presbytery of Kincardine-o-Neil, where he ministered for twenty-seven years; then he went to Southwick in the Presbytery of Dumfries, where he ended his ministry after fifteen years, thus completing, on his retirement, forty-two years in the ministry.

Glen Gairn Church was dedicated to St Mungo, and united with Glenmuick in the early part of the seventeenth century.

After the Disruption the little church, which seats 100 people, was erected, and celebrated its jubilee in 1913.

Several acres of land, known as the glebe, and a scattering of farm buildings were attached to the Manse. My father, though knowledgeable on such matters as the rotation of crops, did not wish to farm the glebe, possibly because he lacked capital to stock it, so it was turned over to the farm of Balno and has remained part of it ever since.

During his period as an Assistant Minister, out of his meagre salary my father had managed to save £30. This sum he trustfully handed to a business friend in Stirling, requesting him to furnish the Manse as best he could with the money. The friend complied with wisdom and imagination. My father lost no time in starting pastoral visitation, part of his ministerial duties on which all his life he laid great stress.

His parish extended far beyond the Glen, over to the clachan of Micras in Crathie and down to the Braes o' Cromar. In his first week he trudged a day's journey over Morven to reach the Braes. Next day six miles in the opposite direction to baptize a shepherd's children. The following day he conducted a funeral in Crathie which involved two hours hill-climbing each way, and next day was up bright and early to cover ten miles of hilly tracks to baptize a baby at Morven, an outpost of the once great estate of an impoverished marquis. Judging by entries in his log-books this was fairly typical of his parochial visitation in the years to come, but he was young, strong and thought nothing of it. For the next seven years he footed it blithely till in 1898 both he and my mother were able to buy bicycles and joyously began to explore the wider countryside.

My father found the Glen folk warmly friendly; kind-hearted women called at the Manse with gifts of cream, pats of freshly-churned butter, new-laid brown eggs, and sometimes the pale-green duck eggs of which he was specially fond. The Manse had been built on the site of an old thatched cottage, and the original gable-end had been retained. It was found to be in sad need of repair . . . the church and vestry, too, had to be re-floored and new windows put in. There was a great stir in the Manse, for slaters, carpenters and paper-hangers had been called in. Masons worked all through one night, finishing the job at 5 a.m. They then had breakfast with the minister and his mother and left at 9.

In November my father received his first cheque . . . it must have been a Great Day! It was blandly assumed that he had something to live on till then. His full stipend of £100 per annum, received in two instalments, was made up thus:

|  |  | £ | s | d |
|---|---|---|---|---|
|  | Endowment Committee | 80 | 0 | 0 |
| Heritors | The Marquis of Huntly | 8 | 11 | 5 |
|  | Alexander Farquharson of Invercauld | 11 | 8 | 7 |
|  |  | 100 | 0 | 0 |

The heritors also contributed towards the fabric of church and manse. The Marquis of Huntly shortly afterwards sold his estate to James Keillor of Dundee, who became a heritor in his place. Doubtless a grant was sought from the Smaller Livings Fund of the Church of Scotland which had not long been established.

In Stirling my father had fallen in love with Agnes Smart who had a fine soprano voice and often sang at church concerts and conversaziones where the young minister met her from time to time, but he did not reveal how much he admired her till he had a home and a position to offer her; he then wrote and asked her to marry him. She consented and the wedding was fixed for the spring. In the interval they exchanged visits and presents, and long letters almost daily, addressing each other simply as 'Dearie', an endearing habit which they preserved for twenty-four years, after which, by wordless consent, they changed to 'Grannie' and 'Grandpa'. The young minister, meantime, was in the process of learning certain duties which hitherto had not come his way, and his first log-book contained references to several cases which required church discipline. Church law at that time decreed that for a first offence the offender must be suspended for three months, for a second offence suspension was for one year, and a third offence had to be referred to the Presbytery.

In Coldstone, he recorded, a young woman appeared before the Kirk Session, and after professing penitence was restored to church membership and privileges. Another girl at the Braes who had been of good conduct while on probation for a twelve-month, was absolved from censure and restored to the privileges of the church. Her child was *then* baptized. About the same time a girl at Cromar was brought before the Session, being guilty of bearing a second illegitimate child to the same man. On being formally admonished, her justifiable comment was, 'He should be here, too'. She was suspended for a year; he, having moved to another parish, was summoned through its Kirk Session, to appear before it to answer a charge brought by the girl that he was the father of her two children. He was warned that if he refused to appear he would be deprived of church privileges as being contumacious. What eventually transpired is not recorded.

I remember that couples who married so that their child should be born in wedlock were *both* brought before the Session and admonished for committing 'prenuptial fornication'. I heard of it happening on numerous occasions, and in 1902 a rule was enacted by the General Assembly that Kirk Sessions must keep a separate book of records of church discipline.

As his wedding day approached the young minister planned, with consent of Presbytery, a short leave of absence, and arranged with a brother-minister to occupy his pulpit for one Sunday.

The wedding took place, according to custom, in the bride's home. She was married in her travelling costume, a dress of fine wool with a short cloak of the same material, and a bonnet to match. (I never saw the dress and bonnet, but I wore the cloak to school for many years!) The honeymoon was spent on the Angus coast and just over a week later, homeward bound, they alighted from the train at Ballater and drove in a hired waggonette up the Glen road which began its twisting course at the top of the Culreoch Brae. There, my father, naming all the farms and cottages they passed, pointed to the Roman Catholic Chapel across the water at Candacraig, seen through the trees, and the house of the priest with whom he was on very friendly terms. When the horses had toiled up another stiff brae they came to Torbeg. It used to be a common feature in the Highlands to train rowan trees over cottage gates as a safeguard against witchcraft. In the distant past someone had done that at Torbeg. A seedling must have been planted on either side of the gate; in due course the saplings had had their slender tips plaited to form an arch so that all who passed under it would receive protection from evil spirits. When the blossom is in full bloom, and when the berries are red, the arch is still a fine sight.

Presently, they crossed the Gairn by a stone bridge which

was soon to be swept away in a storm of wind and rain. (They never forgot the tremendous rumbling noise made by the stones hurtling down the Gairn in spate, and this led to their instigating a plan to have another cart-bridge erected; but the money subscribed was sufficient only for a footbridge, and carts had to ford the river, as tractors now do.) At last they arrived at the Manse, and on that beautiful spring day, arm-in-arm they took an evening stroll round the garden and found the first snowdrops peeping through.

# CHAPTER THREE

# THE MINISTER'S WIFE

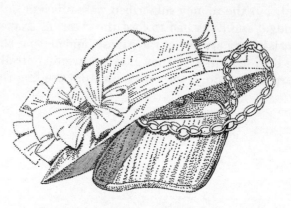

Flowers in the garden, meat in the hall,
A house with lawns enclosing it,
A living river by the door.

Robert Louis Stevenson

Hardly had the newly-weds settled down when the minister, as a courteous gesture, took his bride to call on some Ballater acquaintances. By their reception they were instantly aware of that breach of etiquette which decreed that newcomers to a district must wait till they received a formal call from people of longer residential standing in the neighbourhood, and, after a suitable interval, should then return the call. They had not realised that in a small country place, as Ballater then was, the conventions would be observed as closely as in towns.

During the nineteenth century, and for about a quarter of the twentieth, the etiquette of 'calling' was a firmly observed rule of society. The visiting-card was essential.

The Lady of the Manse soon learned that she must expect a strict observance of the formal afternoon call, and the leaving of the correct number of cards on her card-tray.

When Annie Forbes, her first young maid, a sonsy lass from Clashanruich, became accustomed to receiving cards on the tray, she, on one occasion, greeted some callers with a brusque 'Whaur's yer ticket?', which they afterwards related in great amusement.

It was not hard to get domestic help in those days. Annie was paid £1 per month, and her mother starched the minister's clerical collars and cuffs for two shillings. The roadman's wife gave help in the house at odd times for 1s 6d, and for an extra 1s 6d did the family wash.

The minister's wife, though an incomer, settled down very happily to life in a country parish. She missed the bustle and social life of the town, but it was not in her nature to admit to home-sickness, though she was sometimes heard to remark wistfully to visitors who liked to hear the sound of the Gairn urging and pushing its way to the Dee, that she found its ceaseless murmur strangely comforting . . . it reminded her of the sound of distant railway-trains.

She was a courageous, if inexperienced, woman, and it was not long before she was making her influence felt in the parish. At the earliest opportunity she accompanied her husband on a visit to every house in the Glen. He had already absorbed a great deal of local history which added interest to their journeys. She had to cultivate a country stride in order to cover the ground with ease, and it was generally agreed that she was 'gey swack'. From the Manse a pleasant river-path meandered by Balno and Inverenzie. It was Captain Macgregor of Inverenzie who mustered his little band of followers on the Haugh of Balno, and marched them off to join Lord Lewis Gordon's regiment in the '45; two other Inverenzie Macgregors perished in the Gairn within sight of their home when they were returning from a cattle-raiding expedition.

Another road led to Dalfad where, in the spring of 1746, there was a gathering of Macgregors from which they marched over the Glas-choille to join their fellow-clansmen and fight for Prince Charlie at Culloden. To the west was Old Meggie's cottage at Clashanruich, Tamnafeidh, the Torran of the Round Hill, where the Laird of Drum once had a hunting lodge, and Glen Fenzie, within sight of the Allt-dubh-iasgan, the Burn of the Black Trout. Across the Gairn was Stranlea, a little white cottage cupped in a wide green saucer of a croft, serene among the cradling hills, with a great boulder like a crouching elephant brooding over it; and along the waterside there was Delnabo, with its wood nestling at the foot of Geallaig where capercailzies came down to nest in the tall pines.

By devious by-ways and heather-tracks the travellers wended their way to Belnaan, to the Clachan of Loinahaun where Queen Victoria used to visit relatives of John Brown, to Tullochmacarrick, the former Manse, and on to Sleach.

Another road took them to Renatton, Riemicras, and Blairglass, beneath the hill called the Broon Coo, where snow lies late in a corrie and is known as its White Calf. The Macdonalds of Renattan claimed descent from the Lords of the Isles, and were distantly related to the Farquharsons of Invercauld. A simple stone sepulchre, the family burying-ground of the Macdonalds, is hidden by a clump of pine trees behind the house. Ian Roy of Skellater, who became General John Forbes, a Field-Marshal in the Portuguese Army, as a child was sent over the hill from Strathdon to live with the Macdonalds of Renatton, where there was a good school. He left this country when he was quite young, and years later turned up in the Netherlands. Honours and decorations came thick and fast after his marriage to a Portuguese lady of high rank, and he spent forty years as Military Governor of Rio de Janeiro. His exploits have passed into tradition on Donside.

The footsore travellers from the Manse also went to the isolated shepherd's cottage at Daldownie, and to the shooting lodge at Corndavon, the last inhabited dwelling in the Glen, beyond which lies the little-known lochan called Builg. A recital of these names, and many others I have omitted, would appear to be valueless as few of the houses still stand, but it does show how many were still occupied in the 1890s. Visits to them took many days, but the warmth of the welcome at each homestead made it all worth while.

The minister found his young wife a great help and comfort to him in his work. Together they laboured, and inspired others to labour with them, to improve both church and manse.

Because there was no water laid on in the Manse it had to be fetched from the Gairn in a barrel on a farm-cart, at infrequent intervals because the brae was hard on horses. The barrel sat upright on the cart and was filled by the bucketful from the top. It had a bunged hole at its base, and when the bung was removed water gushed forth into sundry pails and tubs. The alternative was a muddy little well at the roadside, near the back door.

By special efforts over a period of two years sufficient money was raised to have plumbing and indoor sanitation installed; some years later a hot-water system was added.

In their early days in the parish my parents found that any suggestion of improvement in church practice brought from the older members of the congregation nothing but opposition, for to them the old ways were best . . . any change could only mean a change for the worse; what had been good enough for their forebears was the only right way to follow. However, the incomers gradually overcame the opposition; they opened an organ fund to which a large number of personal friends contributed, and had an American organ installed in the church. It cost £28 and gave valiant service for over thirty years. They also bought half a dozen choir chairs for 22s 6d, and introduced the *Church Hymnary* which had recently been authorized and published.

My mother did not speak much of her early life. She told us that when she was a mere toddler, well below school age, she accompanied her brother to school one day, just for the fun of it. She was given a slate and told where to sit. When the teacher came round to examine the children's work there was, naturally, nothing on the tiny girl's slate except a few experimental squiggles. She was hauled to the middle of the floor and thrashed unmercifully until she collapsed and was carried home. She lay seriously ill for many weeks, it may have been months, and the schoolmaster came and wept at her bedside where her parents watched night and day. There was no thought of taking action against the sadistic master, nor was my mother of the opinion that the experience had done her any permanent harm. The rest of her school life was uneventful. The cane was, apparently, still part of the scholastic scene, for she remembered a rhyme which the pupils chanted, an irreverent parody of a well-known hymn:

> Here we suffer grief and pain
> Under Mr. Campbell's cane.

She had two brothers and three sisters who died in childhood, probably from diphtheria or scarlet fever; both diseases were rampant in that era and there was little that could be done in the way of prevention or cure. Their mother followed them while still a young woman. A picture shows her wearing a high-necked black silk dress with a touch of white at the neck. In her cap of white net and lace with its velvet bow, and her tight-fitting bodice, she appears mature, serene, and sedate, though only in her early forties. My mother often recalled with affection how her mother spent hours brushing her daughters' abundant hair which fell to their waists. 'I could sit on my ringlets when I was your age', she would tell us. While her hair was being brushed she worked at the crochet which her mother taught her, a craft of which she later made good use as mistress of the Manse. She and her surviving sister, May, were brought up as Young Ladies by their father, their beloved 'Da', to whom they were devoted. Neither received training in any profession or occupation outside their home; in their day

Young Ladies stayed at home. They studied music, painting and needlework, and learned the homely arts of house-wifery in which both were very proficient. Their father was indulgent and gave them everything their hearts desired. They had gowns for every occasion. Their dress-maker, Miss Johnstone, made each a new walking-dress every autumn and another in the spring, with frills and furbelows all sewn by hand.

They had incredibly small waists. Every young woman of that era aspired to have a waist that measured no more inches than her age, the height of their ambition being to marry at eighteen with an 18-inch waist. The Smart sisters, Agnes and May, had beribboned hats and feathered bonnets, and flounced parasols of silk and lace with very long handles. They had fans of lace and mother-of-pearl, and vanity bags which, as part of a dress, hung by ribbons from the waist.

My mother wore a long gold chain round her neck with her watch tucked into her belt. Its face was the size of a penny and the case covered with engraving.

I remember, too, her chatelaine with its tiny button-hook, scissors, and other appendages. She had brooches and bracelets, a large silver locket containing a miniature of her mother, which hung on a silver collar, and a belt which simulated antique silver, its linked cameo-type discs fastened with a clasp of the same beaten silver.

She treasured these souvenirs of her girlhood, and often declared, 'Keep a thing for seven years and you'll find a use for it', a theory she proved in practice, for her carefully-hoarded ribbons were used over and over again, and her dresses of cream wool delaine were made over for our wear at boarding-school, and were much admired because of their unusual embroidery.

In her young days choir picnics were a form of entertain-ment that was very popular. The choir members drove in horse-drawn waggonettes to some pleasant spot in the country where they spread their picnic cloth and eatables.

There the choir's male voices, gallants sporting large moustaches, straw boaters and blazers, waited on the young ladies who adopted languishing attitudes on the sward, wearing neat sailor hats with their leg-of-mutton sleeved blouses and ankle-length skirts.

In the brakes on the homeward journey they indulged in community singing. In one brake, Scots songs would be favoured, in another, the popular choruses of the day, and in the brake with the precentor, douce man, there would be hymn-singing.

In those days every young girl had a bottom drawer in which she stored items of napery and sets of embroidered underwear, and added to them from time to time, in readiness for her trousseau, which she fondly hoped would sooner or later be required. My mother did not marry till she was thirty; I have a list in her clear pointed hand of the contents of her bottom drawer which she took to the Manse as a bride. A very large chest of drawers, and the usual commodious marriage kist, of which she had two, must all have been well filled. Here, then, is her list:

| | |
|---|---|
| 6 pairs blankets | 10 pairs sheets |
| 3 tapestry bedspreads | 8 pillows |
| 4 honey comb ,, | 4 bolsters |
| 8 print ,, | 6½ dozen towels |
| 2 quilts | 12 tablecloths |
| 3 dozen pillow and | 12 breakfast napkins |
|     bolster cases | 12 dinner napkins |

Her personal trousseau consisted of

| | |
|---|---|
| 12 cotton chemises | 12 cotton nightdresses |
| 12 pairs cotton drawers | 12 cotton slip-bodices |

and for winter wear

| | |
|---|---|
| 12 flannel chemises | 6 house-dresses |
| 6 flannel petticoats | 2 morning-gowns |
| 6 pairs flannel drawers |    (house coats) |
| 6 underskirts | 2 dressing-jackets |

About this time a famous Regent Street linen house was

advertising real Irish linen sheeting, fully bleached, at
1s 11d a yard, but my mother's linen sheets had been
woven on a hand-loom in narrow widths which were later
hand-seamed together. I remember how on washing-days
she spread her linen in the sun, on the bleaching green,
and sprinkled it with water from a small red watering-can,
a job much to my liking when I was very small. I loved the
rain-like patter on the linen and was apt to overdo it. In
later years, I helped her to stretch and fold the dry linen,
clutching it at one end, rugging and tugging while grasping
tightly the four-fold sheets and table cloths, pulling them
evenly into shape. The fragrance of the sweet-smelling linen
is with me still.

My mother's underwear, as her list reveals, consisted of
several layers of cotton or flannel. Her cumbersome, stiffly-
boned stays fastened at the back with laces, and in front
with steel busks which gave her the fashionable wasp-
waist.

Over her corset she wore a garment called a slip-bodice
which was shaped, tucked and embroidered like the tops
of her nightdresses and chemises. As well as flounced cotton
petticoats, she had alpaca and moirette underskirts, and
once had one of shot-silk which changed colour from green
to crimson as she moved, with a soft, whispering sound.

Considerably later, knickers closely buttoned at the back
were designed; till then, women and girls wore open
drawers which were tied round the waist with tape and had
no other fastening.

Indoors, my mother wore black slippers with buckles. For
walking she wore black lacing-boots, and in cold weather
added calf-length gaiters which had to be patiently fastened,
button by button, with a special hook. She possessed one
smart black hat at a time and wore it for years, so they are
easily remembered. One had a small stuffed bird perched
on the brim; another was a Dolly Varden intended to be
worn well tilted forward. It was weighted with red cherries
and green leaves bunched at the back, each glossy cherry

C

stuffed with cotton-wool and every leaf wired firmly to its stalk.

Those were the days when ladies wore fine net veils over their faces on almost every outdoor occasion. The gentry wore them to church; the Laird's wife wore one when she came to call. My mother had some adorned with chenille spots but kept them for town wear. She once received a present of a handsome casket of toilet requisites. It contained bay rum, pomade, glycerine and rose-water, Vaseline, Florida water, smelling-salts in a little green bottle with a fancy glass stopper, and a pot of unscented cold cream. It lacked vanishing cream, lipstick and face-powder for these had not then been acknowledged as necessities. Women sometimes allowed themselves the discreet use of a booklet of powdered leaves designed to cool a flushed cheek. This was all the make-up a Nice Woman was permitted, but when another minister's wife showed it to my mother she was slightly affronted. She could never be persuaded to use make-up in even the mildest form, and never in her life did she smoke a cigarette.

For many years she kept up an unwearying correspondence with the friends of her girlhood and they all wrote in the delicate, pointed hand of the period, using the long 'ess' in words that ended in two 'esses', like princess, mistress or miss. The terminal letter was written in the ordinary way, but the preceding one with a long loop above and below the line of writing. Writing-paper was sold only in double sheets. Friends numbered their pages, writing first on the front, then on the back, finishing pages three and four on the inside. When all four pages were filled and with still more news to impart, they turned the sheet sideways and continued the letter over the existing writing . . . more from custom than for reasons of economy, for a letter weighing four ounces could be sent for a penny. Many words must have been quite indecipherable, and, probably for that reason, criss-cross writing, together with the long 'esses' went out of fashion.

Loved of wise men was the shade of my roof-tree,
The true word of welcome was spoken in the door,
Dear days of old, with the faces in the firelight,
Kind folks of old, you come again no more.

It was said of a worthy lady that it was hard to imagine one
more completely fitted than she to preside over the hospitality of a country manse, and to undertake the none-too-
easy duties of the wife of a parish minister. The same might
have been said of my mother. She was a good hostess with
the gracious ways of yesterday, and thrifty as befitted a
housewife who had to manage on the stipend of a Quoad
Sacra pastor. With her thrift went a deep sense of the
importance of maintaining the dignity of the Manse.
Despite economies practised in private, she contrived to
present a comfortable front, and there was genuine warmth
and kindliness in the welcome extended to all who came to
the Manse, and a sympathetic ear to those who came for
advice and help. She had no patience with ministers' wives
in similar circumstances who moaned at straitened means,
and adopted a dejected, self-pitying appearance . . . what
she called 'making a poor mouth'. She was of the opinion
that few people were justified in being, like Wednesday's
child, chronically full of woe. On the other hand, she was
full of genuine sympathy for those who were suffering
actual poverty, and had already met and helped many in
her charitable work in Stirling.

Both parents kept careful accounts of what was spent
on food, fuel, clothing, and footwear, buying nothing for
which they had not ready cash. They had to budget carefully, for the stipend was paid only twice yearly. If an item
had to be temporarily entered to their account, the bill
was paid as soon as rendered and they had peace of mind
once more. Even taking into consideration the change in
the value of money and the cost of living as it then was, I
marvel how they managed to maintain the home in comfort
and dignity. They ignored all offers of 'easy monthly

instalments', and were never a penny in debt. They had, indeed, the serenity to accept what cannot be changed, courage to change what should be changed, and were given the wisdom to distinguish the one from the other.

They kept open house, believing with Mark Twain that nothing helps scenery like ham and eggs. Passers-by on walking and fishing expeditions were invited in and given refreshment, even if there was time only for 'a cup in your hand'.

Guests at the tea-table were offered scones and drop-scones fresh from the girdle, two kinds of home-made jam in twin dishes on a silver stand, butter curls on plates from which to help themselves, for, according to an old saying, 'in Scotland we trust you wi' the butter', and sent on their way with a cordial 'Haste ye back'.

Every quarter, the Ballater policeman, in smart navy blue puttees, called at the Manse, propped his bicycle against the wall, his neatly-rolled waterproof coat strapped to the crossbar, and produced his book for my father to sign. Sometimes the Corgarff policeman met him there as the Manse was roughly half-way between their police houses. Theirs were not strenuous lives, but routine had to be followed, so they compared notes, had their books signed as proof of duty done, then each bicycled home to his own 'patch'.

# CHAPTER FOUR

# EARLY RECOLLECTIONS

It's a frail memory that remembers but present things.

Ben Jonson

How far memories of nursery days are reliable is sometimes a matter for doubt. There is on record the case of a personage who said he remembered lying in his cradle, seeing his nurse take a swig from a brandy bottle, and thinking, 'I shall tell my Mama of this when I am old enough to speak'. This story, however, was intended as a joke at the expense of that great Victorian statesman, William Ewart Gladstone, who boasted that he remembered being set on a chair at the age of two to make the first of countless speeches beginning with the words 'Ladies and Gentlemen'. Given such an early start is it any wonder that Queen Victoria once crossly begged him to refrain from addressing her as if she were a public meeting?

Once again it is fashionable to announce one's ability to recall incidents in one's very early childhood; Osbert Sitwell had a fantastically retentive memory and could have filled volumes with his childhood recollections. Compton Mackenzie claims to remember lying in his pram and the stifling, terrifying darkness produced by the dark walls of its hood. Following such august examples what then are my own earliest recollections?

I must have been barely three years old when I recall being lifted on to my grandfather's bed in Stirling. He had kind eyes, a snowy beard, a white night-shirt and a tasselled nightcap. He had been something of a pioneer in photography. I remember wandering into his deserted studio with its large skylight windows draped in stone-grey curtains, its painted backcloths, plaster pillars and 'rocks' for seaside pictures. There were velvet-covered armchairs, my grandmother's buttoned nursing-chair for child-sitters, and an escritoire, all of which appear in sundry family pictures.

On that visit to Stirling there was bought for me in Miss Jeanie Gardiner's exclusive shop, which would now be called a boutique, a white fur muff which hung from my neck on a silk cord, a crimson coat with fur-trimmed capelet, and a fur-edged, satin-lined bonnet with broad satin ribbon-strings. Oh, but they were bonnie! They were delivered by a young apprentice carrying an oval band-box with wide straps through which she thrust her arm. This was for delivery only . . . the girl returned it to the shop. I remember how my mother whisked away sheets and sheets of white tissue paper and lifted out the garments in a cloud of fragrance. How luxurious they felt with their elusive scent! Possibly the silk-lined band-box was delicately perfumed. Things that were said to look as if they had come straight out of a band-box were indeed immaculate. At the same time I acquired snowboots trimmed with fur, and patent leather buckled shoes. I do not recall actually *wearing* any of these braws but the splendour of their newness left a deep impression. In after years I was frequently reminded of my mother's chagrin when, on that Stirling visit, I found a pair of scissors and cut adrift a scattering of bobbles from a curtain before I was discovered and disarmed. She was 'black affronted'.

I remember my juggie, a nursery mug with wild roses

painted on it, and was reminded of it when not long ago I read the true story of a grandmother who travelled half-way across the world to find her grandchild whose parents had lost their lives in a national disaster. She carried with her a wild rose mug which had belonged to her daughter as a bairn, having heard that a similar one had recently been acquired for the baby. She had no idea how she would recognize the child among the many orphans of the disaster but thought the juggie might help. It did. As soon as she displayed it a tiny girl thrust chubby hands towards it, cooing 'Rosie, rosie', and a tearful grannie thankfully claimed her daughter's child.

Snowstorms figured largely in my early life. One was raging when I was born; the doctor had to leave his gig behind and make his way on foot to reach the Manse. A nurse was already installed as was the custom.

At the age of three I went with my parents to Tomintoul, then a sleepy, friendly village among the high hills, to attend a parish concert at which my mother had been invited to sing. The invitation ought never to have been extended; it was, as the saying goes, 'tempting Providence'. In far-off times, to travel over the notorious Lecht hill-road at any time was not for the nervous, even eighty years ago it was little more than a stony track, and in winter it was a positive death-trap. Experienced travellers hesitated to cross it between November and the end of April. Deep snow made wheeled traffic impossible and it was considered foolhardy to risk the journey on foot unless the road was clear and weather promising. It was also well known that winter weather might set in even earlier with little warning, and so it was that night in late October. A storm arose in the night and we were snowbound for several weeks.

My father went home alone to continue his pastoral duties, and no chronicle was made of his solitary trek across the treacherous Lecht, but when my mother eventually returned with me much later she described in detail on innumerable occasions in after years how in the deep snow she had to lift her feet knee-high at every step to place them in the tracks of the brawny elder who had undertaken to escort her on her homeward journey, ploughing ten hilly miles through deep drifts to Cock Bridge, with a brief rest at Corgarff Manse, then a further eight miles across the Glas-Choille to Glen Gairn, he carrying me pick-a-back because almost at the outset his horse and gig had to be abandoned at a farmhouse. Tomintoul is said to mean 'the knoll of the hollow', surely a misnomer for the highest village in the north, no longer sleepy, but sharing the bustle of tourist traffic. With the first heavy snowfall great ploughs move into action and prevent its old isolation, but tales of travellers who lost their lives in olden days are frequently re-told; one, Margaret Cruikshank, is specially remembered. The ballad, 'The Lass o' the Lecht', which tells her tragic story, used to be sung to the tune, 'The Haughs o' Cromdale', in many a Donside bothy and farm kitchen, especially on stormy nights which called to mind the century-old tragedy. Margaret was the daughter of Lewis Cruikshank, a contractor at Lettoch, near Advie. She was in domestic service at Milton of Allargue, in Corgarff, and had spent a free day in early February with her former employers at Auchriachan, near Tomintoul. She was convoyed a mile or two on her way home by Young McHardy, the son of the house. When he left her the weather was fair, but shortly afterwards a sudden storm arose. The lass succeeded in crossing the worst part of the Lecht, but with a howling wind against her and snow ever growing deeper she must have been weary and unable to think clearly. It is supposed that she missed the turn which led on to Corgarff, wandered off the road on to the moors, lost her way and succumbed close by the Earnan Burn. In sixteen graphic verses the ballad describes how for months the wind-swept hills were searched, but it was not till May that the body of the lass was found by Luke Grant, a shepherd boy. He was led to the spot by one of his sheep-dogs which set up an eerie howl.

In a quiet corner of Corgarff churchyard Margaret was laid to rest, and there on her headstone one may read how that 'blooming lass in her eighteenth year' lost her life in the year 1860. A native of Speyside, Gillies Lobban, of Bridge of Earn, once told me:

I first heard the 'Lass o' the Lecht' from Mrs May of Achgourish, whose father farmed Inchory before it was turned into a deer forest, and whose mother was a Grant of Croughly, near Tomintoul. I can remember when gaun-aboot bodies sold copies of the ballad from door to door, which they obtained from John Thompson, a printer in the High Street of Grantown. They could not have made much profit, but it was an excuse to beg a wee pickle sugar or a maskin' o' tea. An old man used to sing the ballad and, while singing, twirl his stick like the distaff of a spinning-wheel. In February 1860, at the time of the Lecht tragedy, my father was engaged in floating logs from the mouth of the Nethy to Garmouth for ship-building, and later walked home, a mere 50 miles. The floaters of timber on the Dee and the Spey had an adventurous life. The floating could only take place in times of spate which made the work all the more dangerous.

The method was to prepare the trees and lay them at convenient places on the river-banks, and when the floods came, push them off in rafts for Aberdeen. It was a local industry that was completely killed by the coming of the railways.

At a later date my father was employed in the reconstruction of Invercauld House, and often told us how he sent his tools home by the newly-constructed Deeside Railway, and walked home to Nethy Bridge over the Stranyarroch, the Glas-Choille, and the Lecht, sampling, as all travellers were expected to do, the fine spring water at the

Well o' the Lecht, where a crude inscription tells
part of the story of the making of the road.

Another tragedy which took place in 1860 is commemorated in a ballad called 'The Lads lost on the Hill'. It
tells how seven militiamen on Christmas leave from Edinburgh, attempted to cross from Braemar by the Lairig an
Laoigh (east of the Lairig Ghru and not such an arduous
hill-pass) to visit friends on Speyside, and how all were
overwhelmed by a blizzard, except two hardy lads who
managed to reach a croft on the Braes o' Abernethy. In the
old churchyard may be seen the five graves, including that
of one who lay out on the hills for eighteen months before
his body was found . . . 'down in a low green his red coat
was seen'.

Another of my childhood memories is going to bed by lamp-
light. My crib had rails painted blue, brass knobs, and no
dropside. It was placed behind a screen in what was then
called the parlour, so that I might have the benefit, after my
tub, of the bright fire burning in the small grate. I can see
in retrospect the flickering flames on the ceiling, the oil-
lamp casting a yellow aura on the spot where my mother
sat reading or knitting, while the rest of the room was in
shadow except for the gleams caused by odd fragments of
wood crumbling off and flaring briefly. Often I fell asleep to
the clicking of her needles.

Most mornings I would sit at the parlour fire on the little
stool of yellow pine which my grandfather had made for me.
It had a pattern of flat brass nailheads set round a hole in
the middle by which my small fingers were able to
manoeuvre it from one spot to another.

My high chair had a half-moon tray in front, on which I
banged my spoon as babies will. The chair could be lowered
and made to rock, but the rockers took up too much room so
the height was seldom altered.

In 1893 I was given my first doll. 'Miss Thomson'. She

was made of strands of white wool with red and black trimmings. As time passed I acquired dolls with kid bodies and waxen faces, and dolls with china heads fixed on canvas bodies, straw-filled, without clothing but endowed with glossy black china boots on their stuffed leg-ends, and china hands on the ends of stuffed arms; my father brought me from Norway a china doll in gala costume, but 'Miss Thomson', object of my baby affection, remained my most beloved.

A wooden Dutch doll with a flat body and strangely-jointed limbs and painted extremities in lieu of hands and feet, often made her appearance in a Christmas stocking. Black hair was painted on her round head; eyes and mouth were also painted and a wee chip of a nose stuck on. From the same source came Japanese dolls in kimonos with tiny dangling legs, sawdust bodies and china feet and arms. They smelled of camphor which gave them a touch of the orient.

I never saw a baby doll. Mine were all dressed as adults but invariably had long brown or golden hair and round wide-eyed faces. A sleeping doll was a novelty. Except for their shoes and socks my dolls were not meant to be undressed. I could only admire their pretty dresses and lace-trimmed petticoats, and satisfy my maternal instinct by wrapping them bodily in make-shift shawls, as I had seen babies happit in many a mother's arms when I trotted at my mother's side to visit and admire new arrivals in the Glen. I believe I may have owned one of the last wax dolls; china dolls ousted them and they disappeared in the early 1900s.

Inevitably as I write I am aware of a misty something which is partly daydreams and partly the dawn of an actual recollection. From out the bright mist emerges a day which, had I known it, conferred on a four-year-old the responsible role of Elder Sister. That morning my mother bustled from room to room, trimming lamps, making beds, preparing sundry jugs and basins in readiness for the new arrival, while I traipsed after her, wondering why she was in such a hurry. My father had gone on foot to Ballater to fetch the doctor, returning later with him and the nurse in the doctor's gig, but nobody thought of telling me what was afoot. Later that day, sitting on my father's knee in the room adjoining the best bedroom and hearing strange noises through the wall, I recall patting his cheek and saying, 'Give Mama a sweetie and tell her not to cry'.

My father had been in Norway earlier in the year and had brought home two china mugs inscribed in gilt lettering with the Norwegian equivalent of 'For a Pretty Girl' and 'For a Good Boy'. He did not, however, get a Good Boy but another daughter that May evening in 1897.

I shall never forget the stir caused by having a baby in the house; the trays of covered jugs, the scent of scalded milk, the feeding-bottles with glass screws, long glass tubes inside, even longer rubber tubing outside from which dangled a rubber teat. The teat was inserted through a bone washer designed, one supposes, to prevent the baby getting more than the teat in her mouth and strangling herself with tubing. How the whole contraption was sterilized was a miracle. I have no recollection of lines of nappies but I saw plenty of baby garments . . . long day-gowns, nainsook petticoats, flannel barricoats, fine lawn vests and flannel squares which covered the napkin of turkish towelling. Nightgowns were shorter and plainer, but the barrie and flannel square were still worn at night. Everything was handsewn and embroidered, even the flannels. A head-shawl was worn indoors, and for the briefest airing a bonnet tied on with a net veil for protection from the wind or sun. The baby was then swathed in a knitted shawl, and for good measure my mother would wrap a fringed plaid round herself and the baby, making a cosy sling, gipsy fashion, in which to cradle the child, and would pace the avenue with her till she fell asleep.

The fashion was for the day-gowns and long robes to have low necks and short puffed sleeves, and my mother added knitted sleeves and little jackets to keep the baby cosy.

At three months the baby was 'shortened', long gowns being discarded; the day outfit then consisted of a pinafore over a short dress (which nevertheless reached the feet), two petticoats (one being of flannel), a flannel pilch over the nappie, and knitted bootees. When the baby began to 'feel its feet' she was promoted to knitted socks and soft shoes. Nightwear remained unchanged.

To town dwellers, the postman is on the same level as the paper-boy and the milkman . . . somebody who delivers the goods at the same hour every day, and it is possible that in some country districts these days he may be regarded in much the same light, but when I was a child things were very different. Postie was a personality, the dignified bearer of tidings of special interest. 'Come awa' in! Fit's yer clash?', was a familiar invitation. The function of a daily newspaper was merely to supplement verbal clash. Once, when the goodwife of Balno was given some item of news by a neighbour, she exclaimed in surprise and some indignation, 'Is that a fac'? Postie had nae word!' (Postie had slipped up that time.)

The day after my sister was born, Postie greeted me with 'Aweel, Emma, sae ye're in the stirkie's sta' noo!' He and others among the older folk frequently mis-pronounced my name. Amy did not come readily to their tongue; it was, as they said, 'no' a here-aboots name'. The reference to the stirkie's stall meant that I had been up-graded . . . I was no longer a calfie.

In June our baby was baptized. She wore the christening-robe which had belonged to our great-great-grandmother. It is seventy inches long, as fine as a lawn handkerchief, the tiny sleeves, bodice and front panel exquisitely hand-embroidered. Now in occasional use for the seventh generation of babes, it is fragile but still cherished.

A few days later the Diamond Jubilee of Queen Victoria was celebrated in every part of her Empire. There was a procession through London on 22 June, the hottest day in a very hot summer, followed by a fête in Hyde Park when 30,000 children had a feast of pies, buns, oranges and 'temperance beverages', with games and prizes, and the Queen herself helping to distribute souvenir mugs. We, in the Glen, also had a procession, from the school to the Haugh of Tamnafeidh, and a fête, which was called a picnic, with tea served to everyone seated on the grass, with cup in one hand and in the other a poke containing buns and cakes with carvies in them. Women in their Sunday best made the tea and men carried round the big tin tea-pots. Every child was presented with a souvenir mug, even the Manse baby, whose feeding-bottle was heated that day by immersion in the large urn in which tea for the multi-tude was prepared over a wood-fire.

On the previous day several young men had climbed to the summit of Maamie, about 1,600 feet, and built a cairn, fixing a pole from which a flag flew bravely on Jubilee Day. No one had a Union Jack big enough, so my mother made a flag from a huge piece of white Bolton sheeting with bands of 'turkey red', a stout version of cotton generally used for lining patchwork quilts. I can see her now, kneeling on the floor tacking the material into place, then stitching it on her treadle sewing-machine.

John Kilgour, one of the young men, wrote to me from Bulawayo when he was over eighty, recalling the building of the cairn and the inscription which Duncan Davidson, Postie's son, chiselled on one of the stones. He remembered that it was a fine sunny day for the picnic, that the flag on the hill-top looked well from the Haugh, that there were games and races for the children, dancing for all to the music of the pipes on a board set up on the grass, and a grand show of fireworks to round off the day.

When our smiling Queen arrives at Balmoral with her husband and family for a well-earned rest among her beloved hills, a crowd of well-wishers at the castle gates sees her alight from a saloon car which is inconspicuous, except for the fact that it flies a miniature Royal Standard and

[36]

carries no number-plates, and there she inspects her Guard of Honour selected from a Scottish regiment.

How well I remember the days when her great-great-grandmother used to arrive in the royal train at Ballater! (This much-publicized small station, which unrolled its red carpet for six generations of Royalty, and offered a hearty welcome to hundreds of their distinguished guests, was closed in February 1966 within a few months of its centenary.) After receiving the Lord Lieutenant of the County and other personages, including Sir Dighton Probyn, Keeper of Her Majesty's Privy Purse, Queen Victoria drove off in an open carriage to which were harnessed the famous Windsor Greys. These beautiful horses always arrived at Ballater a few days in advance of the Queen. Throughout the long years of her summer-into-autumn residence at Balmoral, her arrival never failed to attract a loyal, cheering crowd.

The whole spectacle was unforgettable; the kilted Guard of Honour, the magnificent Scots Greys . . . four ridden by postilions, accompanied by smart out-riders, all in white breeches, coloured jackets, and jockey caps. On the box beside the top-hatted coachman sat a liveried footman, and two others stood on a ledge directly behind the Queen. Sometimes the latter place was occupied by kilted Highland attendants, or by turbanned Indian servants in bright-coloured native dress. It was in her Jubilee Year 1887 that the Queen decided she would have Indian attendants, and the two who were chosen stayed with her to the end of her reign.

Sir Dighton Probyn was a venerable figure with a long grey beard who lived at Birkhall and drove over in a landau to meet the Queen on her arrival. His mode of dress never varied . . . a John Bull hat and dark grey Inverness cape. When the Queen had driven away there was usually a rush to see the royal train, which was in every way an outstanding piece of railway workmanship. It had two large locomotives with white-painted wheels and a string of gleaming coaches providing sleeping, dining and sitting accommodation for the Queen and her retinue. At night the train drew into a suitable siding *en route*, for the Queen never 'slept' aboard a train . . . she 'retired'; nor did she care to eat while the train was in motion. At mealtimes, the train stopped and a picnic basket was unpacked. There were no corridors on the royal train, and the Queen did not like the speed to exceed forty miles an hour. Incidentally, the first lavatory to be installed on a train was on the royal coach in Queen Victoria's day.

It was a leisurely drive to Balmoral in those days. From the age of five I was taken to a vantage point high among the pines at Fit o' Gairn to see the Queen drive past, a little old lady in a black bonnet and dolman. All along the road groups of people gathered to wave to her as she went by sitting very erect, bowing in her serious, formal way.

Ballater Barracks, where the men of the Royal Guard of Honour are still housed, have a curious history. Their style of architecture is so different from that generally chosen by the War Office that there were good grounds, at the time they were erected, for the belief that there had been a mix-up of the plans for military quarters at an Indian hill station and those for Ballater, with the result that in Ballater the buildings are of the bungalow type, and in India . . . but where has never been revealed . . . there is, presumably, a regular barracks of a place. In Queen Victoria's reign, the Guard was stationed in Ballater for six or seven months of the year, and many of the men, by all accounts, were dissolute types. A lassie who went out with a sodger was considered to be 'no verra particular'. It was customary for Ballater folks to ask, when the Guard arrived for the royal season, 'What like are the sodgers this year?', and the villagers, whose homes were in the vicinity of the Barracks, would reply, perhaps, 'A nice, quate lot o' lads', or, more probably, 'A gey roch lot'.

When in 1899, at the outbreak of the South African War, the men of the Guard were ordered overseas, the Queen

drove from Balmoral to bid good-bye to her Gordon Highlanders, and returned to the castle with a lump in her
throat. One heard then a good deal about the Volunteers,
who eventually became the Territorials; in 1900 I was taken
to Ballater to see the local company depart. I remember
seeing the Marquis of Tullibardine, later the 8th Duke of
Atholl, who, on the command of Lord Kitchener, had raised
the Scottish Horse, familiarly known as Tullibardine's
Horse. We saw him striding across the square to join his men
who were all lined up. Soldiers' uniforms had always been of
brilliant colours, as dress uniform still is, but at the outbreak of the South African War the gay colours were
abandoned and drab khaki was substituted to make men less
conspicuous on the veldt. The young Marquis was wearing
the new uniform of khaki overcoat reaching almost to the
ankles so that on horseback it would cover the legs, and a
wide-brimmed hat of khaki felt turned up at one side.

As time went on, I heard the names, and was shown
pictures, of the British Generals . . . French, White, Hector
Macdonald, Redvers Buller and Kitchener. There was also a
Colonel called Baden-Powell and a veteran Field-Marshal,
Lord Roberts, affectionately called 'Bobs'. The names of the
Boer leaders, Cronje, Joubert, Botha, de Wet and Kruger,
nicknamed 'Oom Paul', and place-names like Spion Kop,
Majuba Hill, Mafeking, Ladysmith and Kimberley continually cropped up in conversation. My father took a weekly
periodical called *Black and White*, which was devoted
entirely to war news; he also took the *Graphic* and the
*Illustrated London News* and closely followed their pages.
There were war correspondents, but no war photogra-
phers; the papers were mainly illustrated by drawings made
by 'Our Special Artist at the Front'.

We became familiar with the popular songs of the day . . .
'The Soldiers of the Queen', 'Private Tommy Atkins',
'Goodbye, Dolly', and 'The Absent-minded Beggar'. The
latter, with words by Rudyard Kipling set to music by
Arthur Sullivan, swept the country. The proceeds of its sale

D                    [39]

were in aid of the wives and families of soldiers and sailors
of all ranks on active service. Some of the lines I remember . . .

When you've shouted 'Rule Britannia', when you've
    sung 'God Save the Queen',
When you've finished killing Kruger with your mouth,
Will you kindly drop a shilling in my little tambourine
For a gentleman in khaki ordered south.
He's an absent-minded beggar and his weaknesses are
    great,
But we and Paul must take him as we find him.
He is out on active service, wiping something off a slate,
And he's left a lot of little things behind him. . . .

Duke's son, cook's son, son of a belted earl,
Each of 'em doing his country's work
(And who's to look after the girl?)
Pass the hat for your credit's sake, and Pay, Pay, Pay.

Sweets were a rarity at the Manse, but I readily recall the
lime flavour of some boiled sweets, coloured green, which
were sold in the shops as 'lyddite shells', named after a type
of ammunition then in use. Button badges were worn, with
pictures of generals and other war-time personages. In
black and white they cost a penny; naturally, they were
tuppence coloured.

The sorrows of the war pressed heavily on the aged
Queen, and at the turn of the century it was noticeable that
she was failing in health. A few days before she was due to
leave Balmoral and return to Windsor, she drove round the
cottages at Bush and Piperhole to bid good-bye to the women
who, over the years, had enjoyed her visits, treasured her
gifts and grown old along with her. She was then too frail to
leave her carriage, but she was driven up to the doors and
they came out to greet her and wish her God-speed. It was
their last farewell.

When the Queen died at Osborne House in January 1901
Madame Albani sang 'Come unto Me' and 'I know that my

Redeemer liveth' in St George's Chapel, Windsor, for the comfort of the Royal Family. The pulpit in Glen Gairn Church for the special service was draped in black, as were pulpits all over the kingdom. A snowstorm was raging in the Glen, and the black dress my mother had ordered from Stirling was left in its box at a house in Ballater, because Postie could not carry it through the snow. He actually forgot all about the abandoned parcel which lay unclaimed for weeks, while my mother frantically tried to trace it. In those days it was respectful to wear full mourning for Royalty. In subsequent reigns, a black hat for women and a black tie for men were considered sufficient. I do not recall putting my dolls into mourning garments at the time of Queen Victoria's death as did some children, but I heard that lamp-posts, hoardings and every conceivable corner in the streets of London, were draped in black and purple; shops displayed only black, purple and white goods and only black footwear was on view. Men wore black armbands and women as much black in the way of dress as they could afford.

In private families, respectable grief dictated all black for full mourning, even black flowers on hat or bonnet; purple was for half-mourning, shading out to delicate parma violet and grey. In every case, special garments had to be purchased from the mourning departments in stores. Black-bordered handkerchiefs and black-bordered writing-paper and envelopes were used during the period of family mourning; the width of the border on the paper being very wide at first, decreasing in width as time passed, and the family mourning period was decreed to be nearing its end when only a thin black line showed round the edges. Widows' weeds at the turn of the century were not discarded for at least two years.

My mother had inherited a wooden cradle from which she removed the rockers. She did not believe in rocking babies; in this and other ways she was in advance of her generation.

Those were the days when it was customary to 'hap an' row the feetie o't'. We saw many a baby in its rocking-cradle, swathed in blankets like a cocoon, with a criss-cross pattern of cord which held it firmly in position while being rocked. A carpenter at the Timmer market used to take orders for cradles on the quiet, and it was a favourite game of farmlads to gang up on him and try to find out who had ordered a cradle. Crude jokes were rife and woe betide an unsuspecting lass who happened to stroll by at such a time.

A Glen mother once confessed in my hearing that she had often wept from sheer weariness coping with housework, with little ones scrambling round her feet and a baby in the cradle. With both hands occupied at the baking-board she rocked the cradle with her foot, while tears rolled down her cheeks, and the baby, bless it! securely battened down, 'roar'd an' grat' and refused to sleep. The rocking-cradle with its wooden hood has had its day and is now a collector's item.

My mother had no talcum powder but she vigorously applied Fuller's Earth to our infant bottoms with a large swansdown puff. She kept her babies' milk warm at night in a covered jar which fitted into a metal stand and was held in position over a night-light.

She had simple remedies for childish ailments; a spoonful of honey or a small piece of black sugar for a sore throat, for a head-cold friar's balsam for inhalation, a drop or two of eucalyptus on a handkerchief to sniff during the day, and black currant tea at bedtime.

Vaseline in penny jars was used as a soothing salve; dill water for the baby was tuppence a bottle and Fuller's Earth cost sixpence.

When I was a baby, recovering from whooping-cough in Stirling, my mother was advised by well-meaning friends to walk me round the gasworks; I doubt if she put much faith in gas-fumes as a tonic. She was a great believer in the potency of camphorated oil, and liberally anointed our chests with it, rubbing it in with her strong fingers each night. Castor oil was her medicine for all tummy upsets.

Mellin's Food for Babies was then beginning to attract attention in the advertisement pages, and there were plenty of proprietary brands of medicine such as Mother Seigel's Syrup, Owbridge's Lung Tonic, 'the Mighty Healer', Beecham's Pills, 'worth a guinea a box', and Lever's Glycerine, which was recommended for curing earache, sweetening tea, preserving eggs and preventing steamy windows.

Of my babyhood in my pram I remember nothing, but in later years my sister and I had riotous fun in it. It was roomy and hooded, and was variously referred to as my coach, my go-cart or mail-cart because it resembled the small horse-drawn carts that brought mail to Victorian mail-coaches at set points all over the country. It had long shafts and could have been harnessed to a goat or small pony. In our play, one of us between the shafts pulled the other downhill, but our most successful game was to dispense with a 'pony' and, holding up the shafts with rope, career together down our favourite grassy slope till our chariot got out of control and we were coupit out, whereupon we plodded uphill for a repeat performance.

One of the occupational hazards of writing any form of memoirs is the tendency of the mind to wander; one thing brings another to mind. Sometimes one is lagging behind one's story, sometimes leaping ahead into forgotten by-ways. Who can now remember the winter of 1894-5? That, I was told, was one to out-winter all winters. Ten miles of Loch Lomond were frozen over; there was curling on the White Loch at Colvend and when it grew dark they fetched candles from the Manse and went on with the game by candle-light to the traditional cry of 'Soop'er up! Soop'er up!' After a spell of disappointing winters curlers often played all day and well into the night in case the dreaded thaw came in the morning. The Dee was frozen over at

Ballater and my mother, carrying her skates, walked to Fit o' Gairn and joined the skaters in their revels. This happened again in 1899 and an ice carnival was planned for a date early in February but it never took place, for the thaw came and the ice broke up.

Snow came suddenly as a rule; after a few days of wind and rain which whirled away the last reluctant leaves, we would wake one morning to find that it had fallen in the night and 'stroked the window with quiet soft fingers', covering bushes, paths and trees. The unpleasant side of winter was getting up on such a morning, facing the cold rooms and frosted window-panes. There was no glamour in bleak, poor light and draughts under the doors. We would give our faces 'a lick and a promise' and hurry downstairs to dress by the newly-lit fire, hasty fingers fumbling over buttons and tapes. We were always pleased to see on the panes ferneries fashioned by Jack Frost, but when we tried to outline their delicate tracery our fingers grew numb, so we made little peep-holes with our breath so that we could look out at the feathery flakes that continued to fall so gently, with every blade of grass stiff with dazzling frost and branches of leafless trees hung with diamonds.

Snow to us was a miracle of beauty, a clean, delightful substance which flew in the wind like spray. We loved its fluffy softness, and the wonderful stillness it brought. There is no more silent thing in all the world than a remote countryside under snow.

Warmly clad, wearing mittens and muggins, we would race out to play in the avenue which my father had cleared leaving a ridge of snow on either side. He would tuck us in the sledge he had made from a box on runners and pull us along. With his help we made a snowman while the snow was new-fallen and soft, packing it tightly so that it would not collapse too soon. We gave our snowman pebbles for eyes and nose and a twig for his mouth. We put an old hat on his head and gave him a besom to hold in the crook of his arm.

Indoors we would go, excited and glowing, to a welcoming

fire and warm slippers, first scraping lumps of hard, encrusted snow from the heels of our boots which were
dubbined daily with a hare's foot to make them wet-proof;
to sit on creepies and make toast, holding the bread on a fork
with a yard-long handle close to a red fire, and to eat it hot,
oozing with salt butter.

When we were older we each had a home-made sled
which we pulled to the crest of a steep field and, sitting
erect, held fast to the guide-rope and tobogganed gaily
down the slope. We did not grudge the long pull uphill,
anticipating another glorious 'hurll'. This caper was carried
out under supervision after my sister, who called herself
Little Ellie, nearly shot over a wall with a ten-foot drop. We
insisted on sledging however slushy the snow might become
after a thaw, and were amazingly adept at tumbling into
the wettest patches, but my mother willingly coped with a
collection of wet muggins, mittens, coats and knickers.

There were always wonderful log-fires to go home to . . .
crackling, oozing resin, and hissing in a lively fashion, they
had at all times to be carefully watched on account of the
tendency of larch, fir and pine to emit sparks.

But when a blizzard came it was a serious matter. It often
raged for days on end. When it ceased to blow my father
had to go out to cast the snow. After a heavy fall drifts were
so high that it was a hard morning's work to free the doors
and to dig paths round the house. Postie, who lived at
Rinloan, was frequently unable to travel to Ballater to fetch
the mail. When he eventually managed to get through he
brought letters which had been lying at the post office for
days, and newspapers that were more than a week old. Then
would come a thaw; the snow would all but disappear, but
in a day or two, as sure as fate, there would be a fierce
renewal of the storm. A gale would lash stinging grains of
snow against our faces and when it died down snow would
again fall heavily. Even the river was frozen over, and
miniature stalactites hung from the edge of the barn roof.
My father had to break the ice on water-pails and bedroom

[45]

jugs, and my mother spooned slivers of milky ice into our tea-cups.

At that time few houses in the Glen had running water or indoor sanitation. Some had stroups not far from the door, but privies were usually a considerable distance from the house, a tedious journey in all weathers, and a cold job on a morning when snow had to be shovelled before the placie could be reached.

At Stranlea snow often reached the eaves and my father would go across the water to dig out the old body, Lizzie Gordon, who lived there alone. He would clear a path to the burn so that she could get more water. Till he filled her water-pails and cleared the snow from her small windows she lived in darkness, for snow blotted out all light, and she could only open her door a crack and take a handful of snow to melt in her kettle to make a cup of tea. My mother, too, visited her frequently to make sure she was not in want . . . and so life went on. As the months went by there was unspoken anxiety that the supply of fuel might not last the winter and only one fire was lit at a time. Ignoring the kitchen range it became the practice to cook on the dining-room fire with a second pan simmering on a trivet at the side, and always someone had to sit by the fire and feed it. 'Keep up a good fire' was the constant injunction. To leave the cosy dining-room was to enter a refrigerating atmosphere, so my father deserted his study and brought his books and papers downstairs.

Sulky fires had to be encouraged with steady puffing of a pair of large creaky bellows. If logs were damp my mother sat patiently blowing them, first into white foamy smoke, then feeble flame, and at last a cheerful blaze.

One match per day was used to light the fire . . . tapers did the rest. We children provided a steady supply by folding strips of newspaper. Before the invention of safety matches which strike only on the box the matches used in the Manse were Bryant and May's wooden matches, longer and thicker than those now in common use. They had large pink heads and could be ignited by rasping them on the bars of the grate. In the farmhouses we often saw a big, orange-coloured box with a tiger on the lid and were quite accustomed to seeing a smoker rasp a match on the seat of his corduroy trousers.

Winter, with its succession of blizzards, gales and brief thaws passed at last, and when the long-awaited true thaw came we had a practical demonstration of the speed indicated in the expression 'melting like snaw aff a dyke'. We knew the thaw was coming when our snowman's head fell off and lay like an ungainly ball at his feet. His body disintegrated, and at last only a heap of dirty snow, a limp rag of a black hat, and a few twigs showed where he had stood.

The spruces in the avenue, which held the snow better than other trees, let it fall in soft thuds. We heard it slide off the roof with slithering noises and thuds; soon, we knew, there would be the excitement of seeing the great break-up of the ice on the Gairn. We ran down to the haugh by the black briggie at the first resounding crack as the fettered river broke loose from its months of bondage. Rapidly, huge pieces of thick ice came crashing down on the tide of roaring, peaty-brown water. When the river broke its banks it left behind great blocks in the fields. We stood at a safe distance gazing at the boiling torrent; it was an awe-inspiring sight. Then, one morning, we would wake to see remnants of snow lying here and there in sparkling patches on the dark-brown hills, touched by the pale glow of early sunshine and a clear blue sky above, and our hearts would be lighter because the winter was over and gone and the time of the singing of birds had come.

# CHAPTER FIVE

# FUN AT HOME

There is beauty all around
When there's Love at home;
There is joy in every sound
When there's Love at home.
J. H. M'Naughton

Unlike many children today, my sister and I were not given expensive toys, glamorous holidays, extra privileges, and a lot of pocket-money, but we were the recipients of the most precious commodity any parents can give their children . . . time. Lots and lots of time . . . and fun! When I remember the love and happiness that filled our home in spite of the lack of luxuries I feel immense gratitude to my parents and a deep sense of admiration.

In an age when children were supposed to be seen and not heard we were not by any means kept in the background, but it was understood that when strangers were present we did not join in the conversation, nor at any time interrupt when our elders were speaking, nor answer back when being admonished.

My mother dandled us when very small to the words of an old rhyme,

> Hey diddle dumpling, my son John
> Went to bed with his trousers on,
> One shoe off and the other shoe on,
> Hey diddle dumpling, my son John!

Then she would toss us in the air, or part her knees and let us slip down the gap in her lap while we chortled with glee; or she would chant

> This is the way the ladies ride, jimpin' sma', jimpin' sma'
>> (gently bobbing up and down)
> This is the way the gentlemen ride, trottin' an' a', trottin' an' a'
>> (jogging a little more actively)
> But OH! THIS is the way the cadgers ride, creels an' a', creels an' a'. (bouncing us right off her knee and down again several times in a most lively manner)

She would tickle a solemn baby under the chin and thus induce a chuckle from the most determined sobersides.

With two fingers lightly 'walking' over a baby's head she would gently touch, in turn, the brow, eyes, nose and mouth, while reciting

> There was a wee man came over the hill,
> He knocked at the door,
> He keeked in,
> He lifted the latch
> and walked in!

or, as a variation, with the lightest of touch, she would repeat

> Brow, brow, brinkie,
> Eye, eye, winkie,
> Nose, nose, nebbie,
> Cheek, cheek, cherry,
> Mouth, mouth, merry,
> Chin, chin, chumpie, and BORE A HOLIE.

chucking the now-laughing baby under the chin.

[49]

A ride on my father's foot while he swung it back and forth to 'Ride a Cock Horse to Banbury Cross' was a sure winner; and a plea for a story invariably met with the reply, 'I'll tell you a story of Wee Johnnie Nory', Then he would set us, one on each knee, and show us pictures in a volume of prehistoric creatures, dinosaurs, pterodactyls and the like, or, in a small book with blue covers, pictures of unusual types of fish, in which we demanded to be shown, before all others, the John Dory and the Swordfish.

One of our favourite rhymes was about Wee Joukie Daidles, such a pet!

> Wee Joukie Daidles toddlin' oot an' in,
> Eh, but she's a cuttie, makin' sic a din!
> Aye sae fu' o' mischief, an' minds nae what I say,
> Ma verra hert gaes loup! loup! fifty times a day!

and there was the ever-new finger game

> Two little dicky birds sat upon a wall,
> One named Peter, the other named Paul;
> Fly away, Peter! Fly away, Paul!
> Come back, Peter! Come back, Paul!

My mother sang to us the old songs and rhymes in Walter Crane's attractive books, *The Baby's Opera* and *The Baby's Bouquet*, which were illustrated by charming pictures in the Randolph Caldecott manner. From their quaintly-decorated pages we learned 'The Frog that would a-wooing go', and a medley of lullabies and ditties; some of the repetitive ones were good memory training. There was, for example, The Old Woman and the mischievous Pedlar who, while she slept by the wayside, cut her petticoats right above the knee, so that she on waking cried in dismay, 'This is not I!'

We were enthralled by the sing-song stories of *Chicken Licken, The Old Woman and the Pig* that would not get over the stile, and *The House that Jack Built*, the latter so old a tale that it is believed to have been contrived from some lines in an ancient Jewish Service Book.

We learned about other piglets while my mother played with baby toes. She had shapely hands with long fingers and often made shadow pictures for us on the nursery wall. We had a nightly game when days were short, lamps lit early and curtains drawn. When my father came downstairs at teatime he would exclaim 'High Jinks!' and obligingly take a long time to find us, two little figures chortling in the dark behind the curtain, clinging together on the organ-stool which was barely wide enough to accommodate us on its sloping surface.

On the whole, Ellie and I played amicably together. In her toddler days we had fleeting, high-pitched arguments like all children, possibly about the ownership of toys, and when we were overheard there was never any doubt as to who was at fault!

'Be good to Little Sister, now', my father protested mildly to me.

'We got a little sister for you to play with, and now you quarrel with her', scolded my mother. I was never consciously jealous of her; I accepted the precedent that she, being the younger, must be cherished and protected, and never scolded or chastised. I gladly undertook to look after her at all times, and this, at boarding-school, must have become very tedious for her, for without a shadow of doubt, my zeal and devotion made me irritatingly bossy.

We had no 'comics', but Canadian friends dispatched at intervals bulky copies of the exploits of Buster Brown, which we spread on the nursery floor and read the captions over and over again. In later life we realized the origin of little boys' buster suits. We had clockwork mice, life-like in size and colour, complete with long tails. At the Manse, unfortunately, we were seldom without the real thing, and were constantly in a state of war with them. We heard them scuttering round the house behind the skirting-boards, and many were the methods employed to catch them, the easiest being a multiple trap which could take six mice at a time, each hole baited with toasted cheese. We disliked mice, but accepted them as one of the trials of living in an old house, and pursued them relentlessly whenever we caught sight of them.

Unlike Budge and Toddy in *Helen's Babies*, we *did* like 'buyed toys', and derived pleasure, too, from those we contrived for our own amusement. We had endless fun from a lump of 'potty'; we made walnut shell cradles for the baby dolls that came in Christmas stockings but could be bought in toy-shops, four-a-penny.

We busied ourselves with empty cotton-reels and wool oddments, first hammering four brass tacks into one end of the pirn and twisting the wool round the tacks. With a strong pin, well worthy of the name of preen, we drew the wool over each tack in turn; gradually a slender tube of primitive knitting emerged from the hole. Later, perhaps, we might coil the tube, tack it to a piece of material and call it a kettle-holder. Whatever the end-product, it kept us out of mischief on a rainy day and when we were tired of that ploy it was pleasant to turn the pages of my mother's big album of Christmas cards, some hand-painted on thin, polished wood, others containing pressed leaves and flowers. The pictured children looked so quaint, dressed in the fashion of my mother's childhood, and there were many cherub-heads with curls and tiny wings. From unknown admirers, too, in her girlhood, she had dainty valentines, consisting of lace-framed pictures which could be lifted by means of a ribbon. Under the picture on a cushion of satin, were sentimental verses. Some valentines opened like a book and contained a hand-painted scene.

On other wet afternoons we were happily occupied with a box of crayons and a couple of John Noble's dress catalogues, colouring the fashionable ladies pictured there, using dark brown freely for velvet, and pale blue for silken gowns and frilly parasols.

From time to time we had toy mouth-organs, drums, tin trumpets, bamboo whistles and a primitive form of xylophone consisting of a set of graduated metal bars fixed to a frame; when hit with a minute hammer a tune could be played in a high metallic key. When very small we had home-knitted reins. The 'horse' thrust her arms through padded quoit-like rings covered with fabric. The rings were attached to a breast-plate adorned with kittens' bells. The 'driver' held the reins (long knitted strips) and the bells made a tinkling sound when the little horse trotted.

We often saw pictures of a horse's head on a stick which ended in two small wheels, but we made our own hobby-horse by riding astride my father's walking-stick, which trailed along leaving a most satisfactory furrow in the dust.

Small, dapple-grey horses and woolly lambs with stick-like legs were mounted on little green platforms on wheels to be pulled along by string. They broke easily and were found to contain a curious white powder.

We were quite accustomed to getting a 'hurll' in spring-carts and it was a bone-shaking experience to travel occasionally in a farm-cart, lying on a horse-blanket, jolting along to a dawdling clip-clop. The back of the cart had iron pegs which fitted into holes in the floor, and could be lifted off for loading and unloading. At lowsing time, the cart was tilted back to tip out the load of turnips or whatever it was, and possibly remained in that position, with the shafts in the air, till next it was required; or it might be backed into the cart-shed and left with the shafts down. In that position, we used them for climbing games. They smelled of chaff, oil-cake and lime.

Carts of every description had iron-bound wheels which grated on the road. A high dog-cart would start off with a jolt, a scrape of wheels, and a clatter of hooves. One passenger sat beside the driver, two more mounted by a projecting iron step to sit back-to-back with the others, in an open-fronted seat. On the back seat we clung frantically to the side of the cart when going uphill, for it was tilted at such an angle we were afraid we might fall off. Sometimes we were given a ride on the broad back of a cart-horse; the glossy brown hide moved with the horse, and it seemed to roll from side to side.

At Lumphanan Manse, where we often visited, there was a magnificent rocking-horse, pony-size, and rides on it were even better than the real thing. Mounted, we took the reins in our hands and at once, as if it were alive, and not being zealously pushed by our hostess, the horse dipped forward and back, slowly at first, then faster and faster. Our hearts bursting with joy, we swayed in time with the horse. It was so exhilarating we could have kept it up for ever.

Celluloid balls and rattles were common gifts; these my mother destroyed after the well-meaning donor had departed. She, in advance of her time, recognized their potential danger. A baby's ball was made of tinsel-covered cloth as a rule, and dangled from thin elastic; a more substantial version was quartered in bright felt. It could be thrown in the air but did not stot. When we were given balls of painted rubber we stotted them out-of-doors, threw them against the gable-end of the house, executing twirls and turns before catching them ere they reached the ground.

We had ceramic carpet bowls, blue, white and rose-coloured, patterned with stars. They were heavy enough not to crack when they collided. Larger than a cricket ball but not so large as a wood, they were, as the name implies, intended for indoor play. Our rooms, however, were too small for a game, so we rolled them in a haphazard way, being warned not to damage the furniture.

Summer days found us on the croquet green playing our own version of the game. We carried on season after season, till every mallet was broken and every ball had lost its distinctive colour.

My father made amusing peeries, using slender-waisted empty pirns cut in half. Having sharpened the cut end to a fine point, he inserted a short stick in the hole, which we held between finger and thumb to send the peerie spinning.

The knack lay in causing it to spin steadily on the spot, not to ramble all over the table and tire after a brief spin. I remember picture-blocks, an elementary introduction to the jig-saws of later years; and I was much attached to my tin ladybird, realistically shaped and painted, about three inches long, with a spool of thread on her underside. The thread, brought through a hole in her spotted back and held upright, made her run quickly along the floor while I carolled 'Ladybird, Ladybird, fly away home'. Rubber animals in those days had a metal ring inserted on the underside which provided a squeak when the toy was squeezed. The squeaker was a menace, apt to work loose, and my mother had no peace of mind till the novelty palled and the thing could be removed.

Ca'in' a gird was one of our chief delights in summer . . . not the slow-moving wooden hoop which had to be struck intermittently with a stick till it fell lifeless at the roadside, but a lively iron gird spurred on by a cleek to guide or stop it at will. There was skill in the hand that pursued a clattering gird down the winding roads and braes. Common substitutes were the rim off a barra-wheel, or the hoop off a barrel, and these, being unsymmetrical, bounded downhill on courses of their own choosing, bouncing over stones and ruts till they fell with a tuneful clatter in a ditch; but it was fun to pursue and retrieve them, and start all over again.

On summer Saturdays we ran barefoot, and when tired of play would throw ourselves down on the grass to watch our little maid at her wyvin', for in those days it was thought right and proper that she should, when not otherwise engaged, have 'a stocking in her hand', She could cast on and off, or turn a heel with an ease we envied and later had to achieve, for to be able to knit socks and stockings at an early age was part of our education. My mother started us off on long, narrow strips in garter-stitch, so-called because the finished strips were originally used as garters . . . not that my mother wore these. Her garters took the form of leather straps, half an inch wide, like a flexible dog-collar, lined with red flannel and buckled above the knee.

She taught us, too, to knit rag-rugs with strips of cloth, fine string, and long steel needles, in convenient widths, later sewn together.

The Manse garden was large and, doubtless, untidy. It contained no formal beds, but in summer bees 'bizzed' all day in its profusion of flowers. Snowdrops, 'Fair Maids of February' farther south, were here under a blanket of snow till early March. Sometimes they pushed through the snow, outrivalling it in purity. The first snowdrop ranked in importance with the first call of the cuckoo at Whitsuntide and, by then, snowdrops lay like a drift of foam on the grass, and crocuses had made little pools of blue, gold and white beneath the trees.

Ellie and I thought it no ordinary garden. To us it was a fairyland of magical delights. In the shrubbery, the bushes in their springtime green enclosed us and made lovely hidey-holes where we 'kept house' and played hide-and-seek.

From the vegetable garden would come the metallic sound of my father's spade as it clicked against a stone. All the heavy work, digging, sowing, planting and harvesting, was his personal responsibility. Every year he studied the new seed catalogues but seldom made any perceptible change in his annual order. He dug the garden completely over in the autumn, sometimes used the earth thrown up by moles to enrich his seed-beds, and patiently carried countless pails of liquid manure to the fruit-bushes.

He took pride in growing potatoes. Using a home-made dibber when planting and a three-pronged graip when raising, he specialized in Blacksmith, a dark, thick-skinned potato which had a characteristic flavour and was always boiled and served in its jacket, Rosebery, which had a delicate pink skin, Edzell and Early Regent. He exchanged seed potatoes with neighbouring farmers, but mostly used seed from the best of his own crops.

When we were small he gave us each a little garden, then scratched our names in large letters with a sharp-pointed stick allowing us to scatter in the shallow trenches corn-flower seeds like minute paint-brushes, sweet-peas, and the fragile Shirley poppies first raised with loving care by a brother-minister, the Rev. W. Wilks at Shirley. Later, we had the pleasure of seeing our names picked out in green seedlings.

His great friend, the Rev. W. C. Fraser, who, in his latter years was Warden of Queensberry House in Edinburgh, often came over from his parish at Straloch.

Ellie and I took him on all our favourite walks and he encouraged us to collect stones of interesting shapes and roots of ferns from moist places; with these he helped us to construct a rockery near the summer-house, overlooking the sunken garden.

A flight of rustic steps led to the garden; these we used soberly on Sunday. On other days we romped down the grassy slope which in summer was covered with ox-eye daisies and ladies' bedstraw. It was down that slope, bordered by beeches, that we rolled our dyed eggs at Easter, and ate our hot cross buns among the daisies.

Sturdy and thick like a miniature hedge grew the dwarf boxwood which divided the garden into sections, and at the four corners of each section in splendid profusion, grew bushes of the old-fashioned yellow, white and pink Scotch roses, with their entrancing scent.

The straggling borders were gay with sweet old favourites . . . pansies, bachelors' buttons, columbines, Canterbury bells, monkshood, scarlet poppies with great frilly flowers that flamed in the sun and fluttered in the breeze, and peonies, which we called 'peeny roses', with huge satin petals. There was Sweet William, said to have been named after the Duke of Cumberland (Highlanders, remembering Culloden, preferred to call it 'Stinking Willie') and there was Solomon's Seal, which we thought very graceful with its arching stems and butterfly leaves, and its dangling bunches of pale, elongated bells.

Nestling in the shelter of the boxwood hedge, along with blue periwinkles, were the white double violets which Francis Bacon commends for their scent, and for the fact that they bloom twice a year. They are very uncommon in Scotland, but it is said that the stone jetty of Dundrennan House bears a heavy crop in the spring, in memory of Mary, Queen of Scots, who set sail from there on her ill-fated journey to England.

In the Manse garden, too, were powerful tiger-lilies, heavy and dusty with pollen, but never cut; and bushes of flowering currant, which some people dislike, but we cut great sprays, arranging them in our own interpretation of the Japanese manner. Cowslips in the garden were much larger than those in the woods, and their bells were a deeper amber colour touched with red. In the wild part of the garden snowberries flourished, as well as foxgloves, wild violets, persicaria with short pink spikes, and the golden glory of the tasselled laburnum.

There was a wooden gate and a painted fence at the front entrance of the avenue, and there I recall the sweetness of eglantine and the fragrant honeysuckle frothing from the palings which encircled the adjoining plantation.

There was a similar gate at the far end of the garden, at the top of a flight of rough stone steps leading to the wood through which we ambled on our way to church and school. There grew the apple trees, the gooseberry and currant bushes, the raspberry canes, and the wild cherry trees . . . the geans, so called because they were brought to Scotland from Guignes in France. Towards the end of May the trees were a mass of delicate white blossom.

Friends on a tour of the garden, after complimenting my father on his abundant crops of peas and potatoes, would admire the roses, the clumps of pheasant-eye narcissus and double lilies, and were sent on their way with their arms full of fragrance. Flowers . . . flowers everywhere . . . masses of colour and scent . . . in the garden, in the fields and woods, on the moors . . . that, I believe, is the most lasting impression of my childhood. Flowerless months are forgotten . . . memories of endless summer days and flower-scented evenings remain.

As children we were free to roam where we pleased, not that we roamed far . . . perhaps as far as Maggie Cumming's cottage in search of pancakes, over to the Milton to see the Cameron bairns, or up to Dalfad to play with the Spences. There was no need to warn us of the dangers of talking to strangers . . . there were no strangers, and all the Glen bairns were our playmates.

The Spences lived in the house which had once been occupied by the Lairds of Dalfad, and once when we slept there we were awed by the sight of Alex Spence's shot-gun which rested on a rack of wooden pegs projecting from the wall above our bed-head. Every cottager owned a gun and used it to ensure that his family had plenty of appetising rabbit-stew and hare-soup.

I recall, too, sleeping in Maggie's but-an'-ben in a box-bed, which during the day was enclosed by folding doors, on a caff mattress under hand-loom blankets which were harsh against my chin. Her hot-water bottles were stone jars which had once held some imported brew. One day I found a crusie at the bottom of her parkie; she said it had belonged to her father. She told me of the fir candles which her parents often made from strips taken from a fir-log from the peat moss, which burned like candles, being full of *rozzen*. These logs, she explained, lay embedded many feet below the surface of the mosses where they had once grown as trees. A fir-candle gave better light than the crusie, which often had only two or three peeled rashes lying in the crude oil to serve as wicks. The rashes, Maggie said, had to be gathered when the moon was full as they were at their best then. The wick floated in the oil in the upper saucer and this gave the light, such as it was. The lower one contained water, partly to keep the upper one cool and minimize the risk of fire, and partly to lessen the smell of burning oil. This was long before the days of paraffin lamps. Maggie spoke, too, of her father tanning raw hides and making house-slippers for his family. Every household had its spinning-wheel, and hand-loom woven cloth and blankets were the only kind they knew.

At the Manse, part of our daily autumn routine was to go for sticks. Bleached twigs from the hillside, heather and juniper, were known as cowes and made excellent kindling. Seeking kindling we took a large square of hessian to the wood, filled it with dry brushwood, knotted the four corners and carried it home on our backs. It was bulky, had awkward, spiky contents, but was light in weight. We gathered quantities of fir-cones to store for winter fires. They were quickly consumed but made a bright, scented blaze. We dragged home fallen branches, and occasionally felled birches which were sawn into logs in the barn.

Pine wood gave slow, lasting heat and dry willow gave quick fires. They were our main standby, obtained free by sweat of brow and strength of arm, and being acquired by such toil, were never wantonly wasted.

Our childhood was, in the eyes of today, uneventful. In an age when gramophones were a novelty, and radio, tele-vision and tape-recorders were unknown, we had to provide our own entertainment. It was, as one writer commented,

A world, hardly to be imagined by young people
today, before the Age of Speed, faster and faster,
towards an unknown goal, perhaps in Outer Space.
Beyond the railways, the pace of man was no faster
than that of the horse. The British Empire seemed
all-powerful, permanent and glorious, as acknowledged by all the world on the day of Queen
Victoria's Diamond Jubilee.

When we felt like dancing, as we often did of a winter evening, my mother would diddle for us. Modelled on the only steps we ever saw, those of the Highland Fling and the Schottische, our efforts consisted of ungainly hopping on one foot, waggling the other, and twirling round in imitation of the dancers we saw at soirées. With bright eyes and flushed cheeks we pounded on till, breathless and laughing, we collapsed in our chairs.

*The Scottish National Dictionary* gives several meanings of the word 'diddling', all of them linked with rhythm and music. One interprets it 'to sing in a low-pitched key without words, as an accompaniment to dancing'. It is literally mouth-music. My mother must have devised her own variation of one of the traditional tunes which are diddled in the Western Isles, and have been revived for dancing at some Highland Gatherings. Her diddling went something like this:

Ta, de diddle dow, diddle dow, da de diddle dow dow,
Diddle dow, diddle dow, da de diddle dow,
Ta, de diddle dow, diddle dow, da de diddle dow dow,
Dow, dow, diddleum dow, dow de diddleum dow.

These words sung in strict tempo to a Highland Schottische tune will soon have listeners' feet tapping!

We seldom saw a motor-car. Signposts being few and far between, motorists from time to time got lost on their way from Speyside and came knocking at the Manse door asking for directions. Those who ventured down the stony track generally ended up in the ford which was deceptively shallow two-thirds of the way across. My father would then go to Balno and beg Johnny Kilgour to bring a horse and rope to pull the car out of the hole at the far side.

It made a diversion for Ellie and me. We hovered on the bank, frankly staring at the goggled lady passengers shrouded in chiffon veiling, in flat tweed hats and voluminous coats to protect them from the dust which was an inevitable part of the joys of early motoring. They must often have sensed the antagonism of people who rode in pony-traps and had to dismount to hold a pony's head every time a motor loomed noisily in the distance, for many ponies shied violently at the early motors they encountered. As cars became part of the common scene there was a popular song which enquired, 'O Flo, why do you go, riding alone in your motor-car?' Flo must have been at the head of a long line of women-drivers.

I distinctly recollect seeing the first A.A. scouts on the Darrach, and being informed that they were employed to warn motorists of police-traps to catch the unwary who were exceeding the official speed of 12 m.p.h. in their 6 h.p. cars.

In 1907 I sat at the roadside to watch a number of cars struggling up the Shenval Brae on their way to Cockbridge and Speyside. They were taking part in the first of the great reliability trials arranged by the R.A.C. The petrol engine had by that time established its superiority over steam and electricity as a prime mover, and road-tests created a tremendous amount of interest. We witnessed many trials in our time for the roads in our vicinity were eminently suitable for the purpose. Very few main roads were tarred; the majority were gravelled. Cars ground the surface into dust, and in wet weather made them into thick mud which was very unpleasant for the pedestrian, and drove the motorist to despair.

When picture postcards came into fashion they were known as pictorials and there was a universal craze for collecting them. My sister and I acquired albums in which to display our collection to friends as an earlier generation had displayed the contents of the family photograph-album.

Postage on a card was a ha'penny and an enormous number were exchanged and circulated. Coloured cards usually cost a penny, glossy ones were tuppence. There was a time when cards decorated with glittering frost were popular, but were discontinued because they adhered to letters in the mail and were a trial to postal workers.

That was the era of the picture postcard beauty. Some were society beauties, but most were stars of the Edwardian stage. There was Mabel Love seated at her photograph-laden, shawl-draped piano; mandolin-playing Gertie Millar, who married Lionel Monckton; Edna May as The Belle of New York, Marie Studholme on a floral swing, and Gabrielle Ray, her shoulders rising from billowing chiffon. I remember the baby face of Billie Burke, seventeen-year-old Gladys Cooper with a tammy on her long fair hair, and the beautiful sisters, Zena and Phyllis Dare, who smiled sweetly on all their admirers, yet managed to remain aloof. I had glossy pictorials of them all.

Comic postcards appeared in 1905, or thereabouts; fortunately, we never saw any. My mother thought rather vulgar an innocuous card received by a friend who was staying at the Manse. It referred to the current fashion of the hobble skirt, which limited movement to a series of little jumps. Pictured was the dismay of a lady who could not step on a tram-car because of her narrow skirt, and the caption ran:

> There she goes! There she goes!
> All dressed up in her Sunday clo'es,
> Nobody knows, nobody knows
> Whether she wears any underclo'es!

Although postal rates have risen from the ha'penny stamp of my childhood to a fearsome two-and-a-half new pence, an avalanche of picture postcards is still pushed through letter-boxes throughout the country, mainly in the holiday season. In the beginning, only five words of greeting were allowed, in addition to the date and sender's name and address. From those days must have originated the perennial message, 'Wish you were here'.

Birthday books are out of fashion, but when I was young such a book was a treasured possession. In it were entered

the names and birthday dates of friends and relations . . .
even casual visitors were invited to inscribe their names in
the appropriate frames, which were garlanded with flowers
and foliage. Birthday-cards, as we know them, were not
then widely used, nor were there, as now, greetings cards
for every conceivable occasion.

Twice a year all the Glen children came to tea. My mother
was prepared to seat any number, by adding more leaves to
the table. When tea was over, room had to be made for
games, so the table was reduced to its normal size. It would
have been an easy matter, previous to the party, to oil the
immense screw that penetrated the table, but that would
have silenced its squeaks and deprived us of part of the
entertainment. Mother always said, 'Listen to it singing'.
Duncan Spence, aged eight, impressed with this unusual
form of amusement, told his mother that the minister's wife
had 'ca'd a hannle an' the table sang syne', and also
reported that there were 'ingans growin' in a bottle'. These
were my mother's hyacinth bulbs in beautiful blue glasses.
When the sweet spikes of blossom were out they scented the
room.

At the party we played musical chairs, hunt the thimble,
blind man's buff, and spin the platter. Then my mother
would turn the lamp low and send everyone out of the room
save one child whom she arrayed in turban and shawl and
set on a throne, impersonating the Queen of Sheba. One by
one the children were brought in to the dimly-lit room,
which was now filled with an eerie humming. Each had to
kneel on a mat and do obeisance to the Queen. As they
knelt, the mat was tugged away, prostrating them at the
feet of the Queen. This provoked good-natured laughter,
which mystified those waiting outside the room. The
humming increased in volume as the number of kneeling
figures increased, and the game went on till everybody had
been fooled . . . it was elementary, harmless fun. At their
first party, the Glasgow children, who were boarded out in

the Glen, sang several songs that were new to us. One was 'Sixteen come Sunday', a courting song which ended with the appeal, 'O, Mither, can I mairry him? Mither, can I mairry?' and the complaisant reply was 'Oh, ay, on Monday'.

Another was:

> Sweet Rosie O'Grady, my beautiful Rose,
> She's my little lady as everyone knows,
> And when we get married how happy we'll be,
> For I love Sweet Rosie O'Grady
> And Rosie O'Grady loves me.

This was a pop-song of the times, ground out on countless street-pianos.

They also introduced us to a song for two which began:

> O Lassie, leave yer milkin' pail
> Lassie, leave yer fee,
> O Lassie, leave yer milkin' pail
> An' gang alang wi' me!

The refrain, accompanied by soft shoe steps and the flouncing of an apron from side to side, went:

> Wi' a rooden-tow, rooden-tow, rooden-tooden-tow.

The lassie's reply was:

> I wadna leave ma milkin' pail,
> I wadna leave ma fee,
> I wadna leave ma milkin' pail
> Tae gang alang wi' ye.
>
> Wi' a rooden-tow, rooden-tow, etc.,

But I think she went in the end.

It was a mystery how a song with such a rural flavour should have become well known in the back streets of Glasgow.

We always had great fun at Hallowe'en. The making of turnip-lanterns was essential, as it still is, for the correct observance of the festival. Scooping out the inside of a large swede, eating a good deal of raw turnip in the process, carving eyes, nose and mouth, occupied a considerable part of the day. When we had fixed a handle of string, and put a piece of lighted candle inside, which revealed the grinning mask, we strutted round exhibiting our lanterns to admiring adults.

A supply of rosy apples was laid in. We used them in a variety of ways. There were rafters in the kitchen from which we conveniently suspended apples on long strings while we tried to get a bite with our hands held behind our backs. This continued till jaws were aching and the apples were cut down. For the traditional dookin' we knelt beside a tub of bobbing apples endeavouring to seize one in our teeth.

Children of my generation never wearied of examining photographs in family albums; the subjects were usually posed self-consciously . . . men standing by an aspidistra on a pedestal, or leaning against a Grecian column; the women seated, holding an open book, a fan, or a flower. No clue to character or temperament could be gathered by gazing at them, for natural expression had been wiped from their faces. They had all been instructed to fix their attention on a given object while the photographer, under a black velvet cloth, manipulated shutters and plates, and told to hold that position while he removed and flourished a cap, or pressed a bulb. No photographs of my father's family exist, save a miniature of his revered Uncle William, but my mother's father turned a fascinating hobby into a profitable occupation. He was a contemporary of David Octavius Hill though I am not aware that they ever met, and, like him, scorned the stiff poses of the day, aiming at and achieving natural pictures. Like him, he used the Calotype process, and his materials must have been of excellent quality, for the family portraits which he executed over a hundred years ago are today clear, unspotted and unfaded. He mounted his prints on thick, bevelled cards with gilded edges and, as was the custom, emblazoned his name on the reverse side in gilt lettering. Clients expected to have one photograph in every dozen hand-coloured; my mother did the colouring with special paints. Her father's other hobby was modelling. Patiently he kneaded the clay which became soft under his fingers and modelled the figures very delicately. It has been said that 'to give life to the model involved a subtle use of the hands comparable to the touch of a good musician'. Two groups of figures modelled by my grandfather I remember very distinctly. One represented 'The descent from the Cross'; the other 'By Babel's streams we sat and wept'. In the latter group a patriarch held a silent lyre, and a mother clasped her babe to her breast. The most difficult part of that composition, I was often told, had been to nestle the baby's head on the mother's bosom. If, indeed, my grandfather's hands created these biblical scenes in clay with the touch of a musician, his finished masterpieces were as eloquent as the Psalms of David.

What pictures form when I conjure up the Christmas of my early childhood! A magic blend of bright fires, winking baubles, the feel of a rustling stocking in the dark and the excitement when its bulges were explored at daybreak!

No matter how severe the weather, Christmas at home was always merry!

Preparations began in good time. Cards were bought and posted early. Our parents had cards selected from a catalogue; we children had a fine selection of twopenny packets of six cards, complete with envelopes, from the general merchant in Ballater, and they were by no means of poor quality. We sent and received a great many cards. Postage was a ha'penny per card. We helped to wrap Christmas parcels using brown paper and string; decorative wrappings had not then come our way.

Armfuls of greenery were brought in; sprays of larch, ivy, and holly were placed behind every picture. Mistletoe we never saw, but we garlanded every room with paper-chains and an occasional Japanese lantern. Had we thought of a Yule log it would undoubtedly have been of sweet-smelling birch, but birch-logs were no Yuletide novelty. My father cut a fresh tree from the plantation every Christmas. Sometimes it was a little fir, sometimes a young Norway spruce, the tree which is said to have grown in Scotland before the Ice Age. We trimmed it with fragile glass ornaments similar to those available today. Handled with extreme care, and packed after use in cotton-wool, they lasted for years; they became a little shabbier each year but shone with all the magic of the season and were part of our traditional Christmas, as were the spiral candles in holders of painted tin in the shape of squirrels and birds, which clamped firmly to the tree.

On Christmas Eve we hung up our stockings on the brass knobs of the big double bed which Ellie and I shared. While still very young we had learned the verses by Clement Clarke Moore, which begin,

> 'Twas the night before Christmas
> When all through the house
> Not a creature was stirring,
> Not even a mouse.

We looked for Santa's arrival in his miniature sleigh with eight midget reindeer, and knew all their names . . . Dasher, Dancer, Prancer and Vixen; Comet, Cupid, Donner and Blitzen.

We lay awake as long as possible, hoping to hear small noises that would indicate that our stockings were being filled by Santa but invariably fell asleep till the blissful dawning of Christmas morning, then came the first fumbling in the dark and the triumphant announcement to sleepy parents, 'He HAS come! He HAS come!' The contents of our stockings lacked novelty, but always gave us pleasure. Every year there was an apple, an orange, a watch on a chain (you could wind it and move the hands), a handkerchief, a little red jumping-jack or a monkey on a stick, crayons and a painting-book, and a new penny in the toe.

Handkerchiefs were printed with a coloured border and a

fairy-tale picture. The picture practically disappeared at the first washing, but we had a new hankie for every special occasion. They were bought in the general merchant's shop for tuppence.

A bought stocking of red and white net stitched with scarlet wool, hung alongside our own. It, also, had familiar contents; a variety of doll's house toys, such as scales, grater and rolling-pin, tiny pasteboard dominoes or playing-cards, inch-square picture-books, life-like tortoises in glass boxes which moved head and legs when gently shaken, and sticky pink sweets in the toe. Christmas dinner comprised a chicken with savoury stuffing, and a dumpling rich in fruit and candied peel, followed by figs, dates, almonds, and juicy raisins.

The feather-weight plastic fruit of today is the modern counterpart of the wax fruit which was the pride of many a Victorian hostess. My mother produced for the Christmas side-board a bowl containing an apple, pear, peach and tangerine. Each had a leaf attached, and a ring by which it could have been hung on the tree.

We had great fun with inexpensive crackers made of coloured transparent paper called gelatine paper, fringed at the ends and decorated with a scrap. Inside were musical toys such as miniature bagpipes, bird-warblers, and har-monicas; others contained the usual mottoes, paper hats, trinkets, and ugly grey snakes which uncurled in the creepiest way at the touch of a lighted match.

There were also parlour fireworks at half-a-crown a box. Each cracker promised a comical head-dress and an amusing novelty such as 'electric light, Japanese scintillettes, fire balloons, and shooting pictures'.

In later years many merry Christmas Days were spent at Crathie Manse when the Rev. S. J. Ramsay-Sibbald was parish minister and Chaplain to the King. He was made a Member of the Victorian Order by King George V in 1911, and received his Doctorate of Divinity in 1926. He and his wife were close friends of my parents. They were the soul of hospitality and there was generally a large house-party for the festive season.

We went to church on Christmas morning for a carol service, and after lunch watched the trimming of the tree in the cosily-carpeted hall, and the placing of the angel on its highest point.

It was tall and glittering, wonderful beyond words, illuminated by candles which burned throughout the afternoon. The angel was re-wound from time to time so that she continued to revolve slowly, the musical box inside her giving forth Christmas music. She wore white tulle shot with silver, and a star in her hair. In one hand she held a scintillating wand, in the other a trumpet close to her lips. She had yellow hair, and blue eyes forever staring into space. The mingled scent of spruce and candle-wax was part of the atmosphere. After tea, we assembled for the dismantling of the tree, a ritual in which the maids were always included. How they managed to spare time from the preparation of Christmas dinner I cannot tell, but as soon as they had received their presents they disappeared again. They wore, at that time of day, black dresses, starched aprons trimmed with Swiss embroidery, and fly-away caps. Caps with streamers had gone out of fashion and muslin aprons not yet in vogue. When a maid woke us in the morning she wore a sprigged print dress, a plain cap, and a starched apron with a wide bib, and went crackling from room to room carrying brass cans of hot water, pulling up blinds and wishing us a bright 'Good morning'. In those days, maids provided their own uniform so when each heard her name called at the stripping of the tree, she was delighted to step forward to receive the conventional gift of a length of pretty print or of good black 'stuff' for a new dress.

Ellie and I were all a-quiver when our turn came to receive a mystery parcel, wrapped in white tissue paper and gaily-beribboned.

Welcome gifts from our parents at this season, as on birthdays, were books, but at Crathie Manse all sorts of

charming trifles came our way, and how we cherished the
bonny bangles and beads! Once I received a miniature
replica of the white feather fan favoured by Lily Langtry.

The Christmas dinner table at Crathie Manse was a
splendid sight, with gleaming goblets and silver, crackers in
profusion, and bon-bon dishes filled with sweets, chocolates,
and crystallized fruits. No crackers were pulled till the
remains of the turkey, plum pudding and mince-pies had
been removed and a toast drunk to the King. The crackers
were a delight to the eye. They were known as cosaques,
fashioned in richly-coloured paper and decorated with
favours like a wedding-cake. All the children in the party,
wearing paper-hats, made a point of returning to the dining-
room when it was deserted. The grown-ups were relaxing in
the study, a cosy room preferable to the drawing-room on
winter evenings, the maids were enjoying their own
Christmas dinner, the table not yet cleared. Acquisitive little
scavengers, we retrieved trinkets left lying among the nut-
shells, novelties discarded by unthinking adults, gelatine
paper which made stained-glass windows for dolls' houses,
and flower-sprays from the cosaques.

Next day, after lunch, we Glen folk set off for home,
walking over the Stranyarroch, up to the year 1904. The
journey between Ballater and Braemar was made by stage-
coach till that year, but when the Great North of Scotland
Railway Company inaugurated a service of motor-coaches
we found it convenient to board the railway bus at Crathie
Manse road-end, travel to Fit o'Gairn, and from there had
only four and a half miles to walk.

Never shall I forget the nightmare journey we took on
Boxing Day 1906. My father had conducted the Christmas
service in Crathie Church, we had been absorbed in the usual
lively party at the Manse, and had, as always, stayed overnight. It was snowing heavily when we left in the early
afternoon, and a gale was blowing up. When the bus
deposited us at the Gairn-side road-end the wind was so
strong we could hardly remain upright. My father led the

way, trying to shield us from the force of the wind, I
followed at his heels; then came my mother sheltering
Little Ellie in the folds of her cloak. We ran into blin' drift;
battling against it for less than two miles left us almost
breathless. Our tired eyes peered into the white wilderness;
we bent our heads to meet the frozen intensity of the wind
which continually hurled great flurries of snow in our faces,
and moved as if in a trance. Ballochrosk was not even half-
way, but we were thankful to crave shelter there for a brief
rest. It was the roadman's cottage. He and his wife were
kindly and hospitable, and their children gazed in wonder
at our Arctic appearance. Bedraggled and snow-encrusted,
we relaxed at a blazing peat-fire, relishing mugs of scalding
tea and thick slices of bread and jam. When the storm
showed no signs of abating, we had to continue the struggle.
By this time the high wind was forcing the snow into deep
drifts. There was practically no visibility. Landmarks were
blotted out and the blizzard raged on. The rest of that
hazardous uphill journey is mercifully forgotten; we reached
home safely, though almost exhausted. Lamps and a fire
were lit in the cold, dark Manse, and, thawed at last, we
tumbled thankfully into bed. From an account of the storm
(published in *The Annual Register for 1906*, Longmans,
1907) which intensified and raged for three days, I quote:

Snow fell heavily over England and Scotland
[from December 26 to 29]. In many places,
especially in the east of Scotland, many trains were
snowed up, and Aberdeen was all but isolated for
four days. A collision, partly attributable to the
snowstorm, occurred on the North British Railway
at Elliot [Junction], near Arbroath, between a
stationary Caledonian train and a North British
train. Fourteen persons were killed at once, eight
more died of their injuries, and about fifty were
injured.

In later years, when we recounted our story, which we

frequently did, with or without encouragement, we referred to it as 'the day of the Elliot Junction disaster, and recalled how we were sheltering in the roadman's cottage at the time it actually happened. My mother, who had a well-developed sense of drama, would tell her listeners how we plodded on, uttering no word, weighed down by the urgency of reaching home before darkness fell, for then we could have found ourselves floundering in a featureless landscape, hopelessly lost.

A. J. Cronin brought the Tay Bridge disaster into his novel *Hatter's Castle*, and Frederick Niven in *The Four Marys* used the Elliot Junction disaster to effect the death of his hero.

My mother liked winter evenings round the fire when the room had a couthie look, and while she was still a strong and comparatively young woman, but, as the years went by, she dreaded each approaching winter and the prospect of being snowbound for months on end.

I feel sure that her morbidity regarding it dated from that terrifying experience in 1906, with the recurring memory of her feat of endurance on the Lecht some twelve years previously.

Of all the Red Letter Days in the Scots calendar, Hogmanay, the last night of the year, is perhaps the most beloved. Hearts are opened, warm friendship and kindly deeds abound. It is supposed to have had its origin in the flitting of the Little People, the expulsion of all bad things and the moving in of a new set of fairies with a load of Good Luck.

The traditional First Foot, the first dark man to cross the threshold brought gifts representing Plenty in fuel, food, and drink. In the old days he carried in his pocket his personal First Footing cup, in shape like a whisky glass in copper or brass. The stem unscrewed and fitted into the reversed cup when not in use . . . unhygienic, but very handy when offering or receiving a dram. First Footing doubtless took place in the Glen in my childhood, with visiting neighbours bearing gifts of shortbread and black bun, and drams continually re-filling First Footing cups, but we saw none of that at the Manse.

In Ballater, in the early 1890s and possibly later, the chief excitement on Hogmanay night was the arrival of the village lads with blackened faces and wearing weird costumes, who called at every house to perform a traditional play, which had among its characters Galashan with his sword and pistol, Sir William Wallace, and good old Doctor Broon, 'the best auld doctor in the toon'. In countless forms this play is known all over the British Isles and is of great antiquity.

At the Manse Ellie and I arrayed ourselves in our notion of fancy dress and put on home-made masks, our so-called 'false faces'. First, we went to the study door to serenade my father, and then to carol to my mother, amid explosive giggles, the old rhyme she had taught us . . .

> Rise up, good wife, and shake your feathers,
> Don't think that we are beggars,
> We are children come to play,
> Rise up and give's our Hogmanay'
> Up sticks! Down stools!
> Don't think that we are fools,
> We are children come to play,
> Rise up and give's our Hogmanay!

Our Hogmanay consisted of an apple, sweet biscuits, cake and sweeties.

At the turn of the New Year we dismantled the tree, put away the ornaments, took down the greenery, and folded the paper-chains, bells and lanterns concertina-wise ready to hang another day.

We had no balloons left for their brief glory invariably ended with a pop on a sprig of prickly holly.

# CHAPTER SIX

# THE MANSE

A nest of little chambers . . . a well-loved house,
Its image fondly dwelt on by many travellers.
Robert Louis Stevenson

Somewhere I read that memories of childhood are as frail-
fingered as maiden-hair but mine of the Manse are as
strong as saplings. There is no room, no picture, no piece of
furniture that I cannot see clearly, though I left it for ever
over sixty years ago. In the entrance hall a weighty
chimney-pot made a capacious umbrella-stand. The lobby
was ill-lit and narrow, and there were four steps from the
kitchen premises, down which hot dishes had to be cautiously
carried to the dining-room.

The drawing-room was nearest the front door. The inner
panels of its door, a press, and the door leading to the
morning-room were all decorated with tiger-lilies, blue
irises, and scarlet poppies painted in oils by the former
daughters of the Manse, an art advocated by the *Girl's
Own Paper* in 1887. The bay-window was lace-curtained,
and by the hearth lay a white hair-rug backed by scarlet
cloth which projected a few pinked inches all round the

[75]

skin. There stood a long fender-stool in needlework, a comfortable seat for toddlers.

The fender and fire-irons were steel; the coal-box had its hinged lid embellished with hand-painted arum-lilies. Over the fireplace was an over-mantel reminiscent of a family tree, with offshoots of the main stem branching out in unexpected places. Its central mirror was flanked by tiers of small brackets, each with a miniature balustrade and backed by a mirror. Each bracket held an ornament for at that time rooms were crammed with possessions, and every sentimental knick-knack had to be displayed. The mantel-piece also held a number of figurines, and was almost hidden by a drape of fringed, painted velvet. My mother's cherished Wedgwood tea-set, on a lace cloth, stood on a side table, and behind it a few peacock feathers in an Oriental vase. There had once been a Manse peacock and superstition regarding its feathers was ignored. In one corner sat a handsome lamp set on a Corinthian column of brass, with an engraved globe protecting the chimney which shielded the flame.

On the walls were steel engravings of 'Stirling Castle', 'Wagner at Bayreuth', and 'The Ladies Waldegrave', the latter after Reynolds's portrait-study of three beautiful sisters at their embroidery. The room was furnished, in my early years, with folding-chairs and spindly bamboo tables with fringed silk covers, on which rested leather-bound albums with brass clasps, and sundry photographs framed in plush. These were later replaced by more sub-stantial furniture including a sofa, a rocking-chair, a piano with brass sconces holding spiral candles, and a rosewood 'what-not' with barley-sugar-twist supporting columns. The latter held my father's picture-albums of faraway places with strange-sounding names, my mother's pile of sheet-music, and her collection of portraits of contemporary musicians, Albani, Patti, Signor Foli, Clara Butt, and Madame Suggia with her 'cello.

Callers at the Manse were received in the drawing-room,

but tea was served in the dining-room with comfortable chairs drawn up to the table. Matching these, on either side of the fireside, with its steel fender and fire-irons, were easy-chairs; one a little larger than the other was intended for the master of the house. They had short arms on pillared frames, and the leather upholstery was fixed with buttons which sank deep into thick padding. (Tenniel drew Alice curled up in such a chair.) The dark red wallpaper was eclipsed by gilt-framed, softly-tinted portraits of members of my mother's family.

In one corner stood her American organ with high back, carved music-rack, side-brackets and candle-sconces.

A press held china and glass; the massive sideboard was laden with household silver . . . the cream and sugar stand, the cake-basket, tea-caddy and biscuit-barrel. All had to be kept shining with Goodall's Plate Powder moistened with water.

The four-bottle cruet-stand was a finicky object to clean; a separate dish, heavy as a paperweight, held the salt. Everything in common use at that time was fashioned on a grand scale . . . sugar-basins, cream-jugs, cutlery . . . all were large and heavy. Tea-trays were huge papiermâché affairs with painted decorations and mother-of-pearl inlays. In summer the bow-window, like that in the drawing-room, both facing the daisied lawn, was curtained with Nottingham lace, but in winter heavy crimson curtains with bobbled edges hung on wooden rings which rattled noisily when pulled along the mahogany pole, and were caught back in daylight hours by tasselled cords.

The dining-table was so solid it could hardly be raised from the floor and was pushed around on castors. It could be extended by the insertion of breadths of polished wood laid between the opened halves of the table; short projections fitted into corresponding holes. The whole thing was opened and closed by a huge winding key. As a child I never heard the expression 'taking a leaf out of someone's book', but I was familiar with the process of putting a leaf in the table, and when all the leaves were in place the table filled the room.

Occupying the place of honour on the mantel-shelf was my father's presentation clock of black pillared marble, surmounted by a bronze knight-in-armour seated on a charger, couching a lance on which many a time I pricked a finger when dusting. There was a brass plate affixed to the clock. This I polished and knew the wording by heart.

In those days it was customary for the chief bridesmaid to give the bride a tea-set, and my mother's gift from her sister had been her china set of white and gold design.

Her silver tea-spoons were an heirloom, thin and delicate, made by hand; one a trifle larger than the rest and intended for dispensing sugar proves they were in use before tongs were designed for handling cubes.

Stress is frequently laid on the functional excellence of modern styles in household articles, but much can be learned from the past. My mother's bullet-shaped tea-pot was of eighteenth-century design, a model of simple elegance with a spout ideally shaped for pouring.

My father had a bushy moustache and used, in common with other moustache-wearers, a special cup which had a built-in shelf to keep tea or coffee from wetting the facial adornment.

In the morning-room was a mahogany chiffonier which was similar to a sideboard and duplicated its function on a smaller scale. It had a cutlery drawer and a china cupboard, and on it sat a tea-caddy of inlaid wood, with two lidded compartments, and a lock and key.

I never saw the Timmer market so dear to the heart of Aberdonians. It was timber and timber goods brought to the city from Glen Tanar and Strathdee that started it as far back as 1637. It had a great reputation when it was held several times a year but lost its original glory when the demand for hand-made implements gave way to a craving for fairings of plastic. The 'Timmerer' served its day, and the wooden objects for which it was famous lasted a lifetime.

On our breakfast-table were wooden egg-cups and bread-board; in the kitchen were the wooden beetle for mashing potatoes, the theevil, rolling-pin and salt-backet, butter-patters, butter-print maker and the wash-tub, all products of the 'Timmerer'.

In most rooms there was a china-knobbed bell-push which jerked at one of the six dangling clapper-bells that hung, bat-like, on their S-shaped springs in a row, high up on the kitchen wall. When Ellie and I, for fun, worked the handle in any room one of the bells in the kitchen waggled violently and made a terrible din.

It was an age of cast-iron . . . even the surrounds in the upstairs fire-places were of ornamental cast-iron.

On the cast-iron kitchen range sat cast-iron kettles, one always singing on the hob. Cast-iron cooking-pots even when empty seemed to weigh a ton.

House-cleaning was done with the aid of scrubbing-brush, soap and water and a vast amount of elbow-grease; a dustpan and brush, a soft hair broom, a long-handled carpet whisk, and a carpet-sweeper also helped. There was no liquid black lead, only lumpy stuff which had to be softened with water.

The family wash was done in zinc tubs, using a ridged washing-board and plenty of yellow soap. This was bought in long bars costing about a shilling, cut up while soft into usable pieces and stored till it hardened. Sunlight soap was also very pleasant to use. It came in four-bar packets.

My mother tried a hand-operated washing-machine . . . a galvanized tub on legs, in which a type of 'dolly' was twirled to tumble the clothing and give a reversing action, but, on the whole, she preferred to wash by hand. She had no mangle, but a wringer clamped to the kitchen table squeezed the water from heavier articles and pressed them when dry.

Stranded wire stretched from tree to tree served as clothes-lines. It never rusted or sagged. A line of washing on a winter day froze in no time but when a slight breeze arose it soon became dry. There was a current belief that

a touch of frost did the washing good. The linen certainly
sparkled with frost, whiter than white. In general use was
the flat-iron, which was solid and had to be heated on a
fire or stove. The custom was to use a little spit, or even a
wet forefinger rapidly snatched away, to test if the iron
was hot enough to use. The box-iron which preceded the
flat-iron we often saw in use in cottages, when a red-hot,
solid, triangular piece of metal was brought glowing
between long tongs from the heart of the peat-fire and
placed inside a door at the broad end of the iron.

My mother had a charcoal iron, the first in the Glen. It
was a comparatively new model, and caused a good deal of
interest among Glen housewives. In an iron saucer, pierced
with holes, lumps of charcoal were made red-hot over the
fire and slid into the wide end of the iron. A little shutter
then came down and made all safe. The iron worked very
smoothly and kept hot for a considerable length of time.

On the kitchen wall were plated dish-covers of varying
sizes, ranging from one large enough to keep hot a haunch
of venison to one small enough to cover the breakfast
bacon. They were a legacy from my grandmother, and too
big for common use, but they and other metal articles,
including the brass door-knobs throughout the house, were
kept bright by the regular use of a fourpenny cake of
Brooke's soap, known as 'Monkey Brand'. It was advertised
by a picture of a monkey holding a frying-pan which
reflected his grinning face; or showed him sitting on a
crescent moon, singing:

What a capital couple, the moon and I!
I polish the earth, she brightens the sky,
And we both declare, as half the world knows,
Though a capital couple, we WON'T WASH CLOTHES!

A damp rag rubbed on the cake and on to the articles,
when dry and polished with a soft cloth, gave shining
results; so 'Monkey Brand' claimed to be 'the world's most
marvellous cleaner, makes tin like silver, copper like gold,

paint like new, brassware like mirrors . . . it brightens the world like a baby's smile!', a lyrical outburst which can hardly be beaten by 'commercials' of today.

The first of all the soap-powders, I feel sure, was Hudson's soap. It came in quarter-pound packets at tenpence per dozen, and was liberally used in washing up.

Paraffin was delivered in 10-gallon containers. Lamps had to be trimmed and re-filled every day. Unfortunately, they left their mark on the low ceilings; first they yellowed, then browned, and finally blackened them. When the glass chimneys were new they were placed in a pot of cold water and brought very slowly to the boil. They were allowed to cool, then lifted out, dried, and polished. This rendered them less liable to crack when in use. A lamp flame was never blown out; the wick was turned low till it flickered and died.

'Up the stair', with brass rods holding down the carpet at every step, there was a landing lit by two skylight windows, and two more steps leading to the bathroom and nursery. The landing and lobbies were covered with hard-wearing waxcloth. The window at the foot of the stairs had a wide ledge on which stood pot-plants and oil-lamps ready for use.

In each of the bedrooms and nursery was a double bed, and each room had a dressing-table, and a marble-topped washstand with a jug and basin, a straw-handled slop-pail to match with a hole in the lid, and under the bed a pot (given its French pronunciation).

Every bed was modestly skirted with valances of white dimity, and spread with a patchwork quilt. Each had bolster and feather pillows, and hand-woven blankets, recognizable as such by their texture and the joining of narrow widths.

My mother had inherited a dressing-case fitted with silver-topped bottles and jars, ivory-backed brushes and hand-mirror. On her dressing-table were also fancy bottles of 'White Heather', 'White Rose' and 'Jockey Club' scent, presents from friends. She never used the word perfume for the contents of these stoppered bottles; they sat permanently beneath the swinging looking-glass which she never called a mirror.

Little Ellie and I, when we had outgrown our cribs, shared a double bed and the parlour became our nursery, with home-made rugs on the floor, a chest of drawers, a washstand, and a painted chest for our toys. On the walls were framed pictures of 'The Organ-Grinder and his Monkey' and Louis Wain's 'Cats'. My mother once papered the nursery with pages from the *Illustrated London News*, a custom recently revived among trendy young people. Robert Louis Stevenson also liked his nursery

> Best of all
> With pictures pasted on the wall;
> And pleasant there to lie in bed
> And see the pictures overhead;
> Guns and ships and bleating sheep,
> And happy children ankle-deep
> In buttercups . . .

I used to weave for Ellie serial stories about the pictured people, a fresh instalment every night. We were very sad when the nursery was re-papered. In the adjoining bathroom the lavatory pan was a new model. It had a shaped tip-up seat and a handle projecting from the cistern behind, which had to be pressed down to release the water, like operating a pump. On holiday in towns we had often seen the older type in which the lavatory pan had a wide mahogany surround which extended from wall to wall of the ill-lit cubicle. Embedded in the polished wood was a brass handle attached to a chain which had to be pulled straight up to flush the pan and was very hard for a child to manage. It was easier all round when chains were made to pull down, but the noise was still unbelievably loud and embarrassing. In most town houses the bath was also enclosed in polished wood, but the Manse bath stood on claw feet, and was of iron painted green, the interior enamelled to produce a marble effect. House guests had to be cautioned not to lie soaking in hot water too long or a stream of cold water would pour from the overflow pipe which careless plumbers had fixed to project over the bath instead of through the outside wall. Shrieks of dismay were heard when the warning was forgotten.

In cold weather we children had our bath in front of a blazing fire instead of in the unheated bathroom, with our scarlet flannel nightdresses warming near us. The tin bath was deep and oval, painted yellowish-brown outside and cream inside. It had a moulded handle at each end by which it was lifted.

Toilet soap came unwrapped in boxes of twenty-four tablets . . . buttermilk, oatmeal, brown windsor, glycerine and cucumber, rose, and lavender, all at tuppence a tablet. Pear's soap was sixpence. Advertisers did not constantly change their approach to the public in those days, and some advertisements became very familiar. Pear's soap was kept in the public eye by a reproduction in colour of Sir John Millais's painting of a boy in a green velvet suit with ruffles, blowing bubbles from a long-stemmed pipe. His mop of fair curls was widely copied and became known as a Bubbles Cut. Also well remembered is the picture of a screaming child in a shallow bath being forcibly scrubbed by a muscular nurse. The caption, 'He won't be happy till he gets it', referred to the soap which lay out of reach of the child's outstretched hand. There was another of a grimy tramp in the act of writing a testimonial. 'Two years ago I used your soap, since when I have used no other'; and one of a boy being scrubbed at the village pump. The caption read

> This little fellow hadn't washed,
> He wishes now he had,
> But once he's used Pear's Soap, why then
> He won't think washing bad.

Ivy soap was always captioned 'It floats'; Swan soap also floated and was advertised as 'A Friend for Fair Forms and Faces'.

On hair-washing nights my mother made us kneel on the floor bending over the steaming water. I dreaded the moment when she would place one hand firmly on my neck and push my face down till it almost touched the water, while she lathered and rubbed vigorously with the other. Afterwards we knelt at a bright fire and had our hair plaited while it was still damp. When the plaits were undone in the morning our hair had the crimpy look which was then much admired.

Up to bed we went carrying our saucer-like candlesticks with snuffers like clowns' hats, sheltering the flame from the draught on the stairs, and playing at our bedside with the melting wax, so that grease-spots were often found in unaccountable places.

We cleaned our teeth with kitchen salt, later were promoted to tooth-soap, which was horrid . . . later still, to gritty tooth-powder. The casement windows were opened by pushing out a bar in which one of several holes was placed over a knob on the sill. Sometimes we would open the window wider, leaning out to listen to the night-sounds. The smothering curtain of darkness hid all but the faint presence of trees and the dark bulk of Geallaig; then with a skip and a jump and a twanging of bedsprings we leaped into bed.

My mother came to hear us say our prayers, and to remove the candles. We must have been very young when we were left with a Price's night-light which burned in a blue saucer with an inverted shade of orange glass and cast a comforting glow in the darkened room.

My father agreed with Sydney Smith that there is no furniture so charming as books. His study was lined with book-shelves; flat-topped desks along one side were laden with books, which were also piled in corners. The room should have been his *sanctum sanctorum*, but I never knew him to be resentful of interruption. It was a fascinating place for children, not only on account of the books, but because of the multitude of objects to be found on his writing-table. There were little boxes of pen-nibs . . .

The Waverley Pen for easy writing;
The Flying Scotchman instead of a quill;
The Flying Pen which writes 200 words per dip . . .

so claimed the advertisers.

I remember a pen-holder made from a porcupine quill, coloured pencils, small bottles of gum, trays which held an array of penny bottles of ink—blue, black, violet, green and red. The last-named he used for underlining points in his sermon-notes and reports to Church of Scotland Head-quarters. Even in those days there were numerous schedules and questionnaires that demanded attention. He had infinite patience with children, and retained a child-like ability to be amazed at all the wonders the world contains. He would take us on his knees and produce for our diversion an encyclopaedia lavishly illustrated, or a book entitled *Wonders under the Sea*. For himself he asked little, but he secretly longed for a rolltop desk, and after many years achieved this desire.

My parents spared no trouble to give of their best to their guests in the way of plentiful country fare and homely comfort. I recall my mother's hurrying steps in the lobby at the sound of the doorbell, the door thrown open wide, her outstretched hands, and her gay cry, 'Come away in!' There was cheerful chatter as they were led upstairs . . . 'Take off your things . . . you'll feel the benefit when you go out', and, seated at table, they were urged to 'make a long arm and help yourselves'. Several friends came from a distance to my mother's famous tea-parties which she held on the day following the Synod Meeting, when my father brought from Aberdeen spiced buns and delicious little iced cakes which actually cost about tuppence each. After tea they returned to the drawing-room and sat cosily chatting, and listening to the talented ones who had brought their music to entertain the others. I remember the lady who sang

> O how delightful, O how entrancing
> From (something-or-other) soon to be free!

and declared that her heart was dayncing

> Dayncing, dayncing now-ow-ow with glee!

Another assured us that

> Spring is caw-aw-ming!
> Spring is caw-aw-ming!
> Spring is coming for the swallows
> Have come ba-ack to tell me so!

A third rendered the ballad of the crossing-sweeper who fell in love with a poor little rich girl. This ended

> Ah, Rags and Tatters, sadly now you sigh,
> Fortune little matters when Love goes by!

I sat enthralled throughout the singers' performance.

As a finale, the *Students' Song-Book* was produced and we all joined in singing about the village maiden riding down from Bangor, and of the man who came to a river and couldn't get across, singing Polly-wolly-doodle all the day.

Glen folk were encouraged to step in to the Manse at any time for a rest and a cup of tea, especially on their way home, walking from Ballater. My mother was glad to provide a fly cup at any odd time. She often recalled the occasion when a wealthy caller dropped in the avenue a valuable ring which she had been wearing over her glove. A Manse house-guest found it and, believing that the owner would be distraught when she discovered her loss, she and my mother set out at once to walk the five miles to Ballater to restore it. No reward was expected or offered. They hoped, I think, to be driven home in the lady's carriage and pair, but were allowed to trudge back the way they had come, ready to drop, in the dusty heat, without *even being offered a cup of tea* to refresh them . . . and THAT to my mother was the height of ingratitude!

My father's stipend was undoubtedly augmented by many gifts from parishioners, who from time to time brought twa-three eggs, a suppie milk, a bittie home-made cheese, or a rabbit. In return, they were happy to accept seed potatoes and baskets of fruit in season. Their children were invited to pick as much fruit as they could carry home.

'Food', A. A. Milne once said, 'is a subject of conversation more spiritually refreshing even than the weather, for the number of possible remarks about the weather is limited, whereas of food you can talk on and on and on.'

I have been privileged to examine price lists for the year 1903 of Cooper's, the well-known Glasgow firm with whom my parents dealt for many years. To turn the pages gives one an astonishing insight into the cost of living at the turn of the century, and the prices provide an interesting contrast to those now prevailing.

For example, granulated sugar cost tuppence a pound; at the Manse it was bought by the hundredweight, and was delivered in a hessian sack. Tea came in 7-lb black-and-gold canisters with geisha figures posturing on every panel, and cost 2s 6d per lb but when a chest containing 100 lb was bought the price was considerably reduced. Symington's pea flour, which made excellent soup, cost one shilling for a 7-lb tin. Tins of thick kidney soup served four people at a cost of tenpence. Tinned fruit, for summer Sunday lunches, cost 7s 10d for a dozen large tins. When cows went dry and fresh milk was unobtainable, a tin of condensed milk from a dozen at half-a-crown, was a godsend. My mother used a fair amount of candied peel in her recipes; her custom was to buy a 7-lb box of mixed peel for 2s 10d and do her own chopping. My sister and I relished the piece of flavoured sugar that nestled in each half-fruit. At Hallowe'en a case of the best eating apples cost twelve shillings. At Christmas came raisin clusters at tenpence per lb, crystallized ginger in 4-lb wooden boxes at sixpence per lb, and a variety of excellent 2-lb cakes at prices not exceeding two shillings for a cake. We consumed any number of mincemeat pies, of fine, flaky pastry and a delicious flavour. At $3\frac{1}{2}d$ each they were ample for four people. Scotch bun was also bought at Christmas . . . not the very rich black bun, but a fruity mixture like a currant loaf encased in thin paste. Every Christmas a good friend sent us from Keith and Ralston, a famous Stirling patisserie, a large rich fruit cake. 'A slice of Mary's cake' was issued sparingly as a rare treat.

There used to be a saying that if you appreciate good cooking you should breakfast in Scotland, lunch in England, and dine in France. Long ago, Scots brought the art of breakfast to perfection with fresh herring, finnan haddies, Arbroath smokies, baps, scones, and oatcakes, with marmalade from Dundee, not forgetting porridge which never tastes quite the same south of the Border, possibly because it has not the advantage of being made from freshly-milled oatmeal with its distinctive peaty tang. Free gifts from trading companies are nothing new; eighty years ago consumers of rolled oats were being offered a best quality enamelled porridge-plate, for which the goodwife was required to send a certain number of coupons. In the Glen, however, rolled oats were not eaten. Oatmeal was comparatively cheap, especially if it was milled locally, and mothers, who as yet knew nothing of vitamins, set porridge before their families twice daily, thus providing a substantial, nourishing meal.

My mother kept a three-legged goblet exclusively for porridge. Using the best quality meal, with pure spring water which had its source on Maamie, she took a handful of meal for each person, letting it trickle through the fingers of her left hand into fast-boiling water, stirring briskly with a theevil in her right. As soon as we were old enough we were trusted to sit by the fire on our creepies. In turns we stirred and stirred, taking care that no black specks from the stick-fire fell in the pot. Porridge was referred to in the plural; they must always be thick and creamy. Salt was added in the last five minutes. We never ate sugar with them; true Scots know that sugar adds nothing to good porridge. Porridge made with milk was a special treat, and 'milk to milk-porridge' the height of luxury. Skirley with the breakfast bacon was another treat. My mother made the dripping smoking hot, adding as much oatmeal as the fat would absorb, and served it so hot it was apt to burn your mouth.

When she made eggeree she beat the yolks with a fork and whisked the whites on a plate with the blade of a knife. Her cloutie dumplings were rich in currants, sultanas, and orange peel and were eaten hot at the tea-table on birthdays and other important occasions such as home-comings.

Ellie and I were seldom ill, though a dietician might have expected us to suffer from certain deficiencies.

Green vegetables were obtainable only in summer, when we had an unlimited supply of home-grown peas, beans, cabbage, and lettuce. My mother probably never heard of mineral salts, but she was aware that nutriment lay directly under the skin of potatoes, so made certain they were pared thinly, or boiled in their skins. Imported fruit had a very small place in our diet. We had oranges at Christmas when they were three a penny, and bananas (a penny each) when we were on holiday.

Fruit from the garden was plentiful . . . apples, currants, gooseberries, rasps . . . we wandered among the bushes and feasted blissfully while the season lasted, and still there was an abundance to give away, and to make into jam. A peeled stick of rhubarb was good to chew . . . our doctor approved it and called it a splendid gum-stick for teething babies. Yellow gooseberries were large, sweet, almost transparent . . . they burst in the mouth; the green hairy ones made good jelly and gooseberry fool, the red ones a very special jam. My mother's blackcurrant jelly was a most beautiful colour, and high on my memory's list of good smells I place her rasp jam ready for potting. Wild rasps gathered at Fit o'Gairn made delicious jam as did the blaeberries we gathered on the roadside near Dalfad, returning with lips, fingers, and pinafores purple-stained. Jam was made over an open fire in the big brass pan, stirring with a long wooden spoon. Ten pounds of fruit were boiled at a time with the same amount of sugar. The fire had to be fed steadily with dry sticks lest the jam go off the boil. When ready, it was ladled, boiling hot, into stone jars, white, brown and putty-coloured, and covered with gummed paper circles with dog's tooth edges. Marmalade was not made at home; it was bought from Cooper's, and guests at the breakfast-table found a talking-point in the recollection of its romantic origin in 1797. That year a Spanish vessel arrived in the Tay with a cargo of bitter oranges. Unsaleable they may have been, but Mrs Keillor, the wife of a Dundee fruiterer, resourceful woman, had the happy thought to make a preserve of the strange fruit rather than let it go to waste. Thus she started at her own kitchen-stove what became a renowned industry. The special interest to Manse guests lay in the knowledge that one of her descendants owned Morven estate in my father's parish, and lived near Ballater in what some people described as a marmalade-coloured house.

My mother's old account-books are revealing. In one it is noted that she once bought at pig-killing time, 14 lb of fresh pork for 3s 10d. At the butcher's a leg of pork cost tenpence per lb, a jiggot of mutton the same, but a sirloin of the best Scotch beef cost one shilling per lb. Fresh fish was scarce in Ballater, but William Coutts, son of the old Dominie, when invited to tea during his summer vacation, would fish the Gairn all the way down from Dalphuil to the Manse and present my mother with his catch of speckled trout. We feasted royally in the salmon-fishing season when Sir William Brooke of Glen Tanar sent to the Manse a beautiful whole fish. A brace of grouse also arrived once or twice in the shooting season from Gairnshiel Lodge . . . the Shiel . . . and from Glen Tanar. Gifts of venison also came occasionally.

My mother had not first to catch her hare (advice attributed to Mrs Glasse in 1747) but, being faced with it, she had to skin and clean it, and kep the blood in a basin, which must have been an obnoxious task the first time she tackled it. She also had to draw a chicken's neck, and later pluck and dress it, for, as a new-made wife, the animal or bird was generally thrust into her hand, and from that point, the business was entirely up to her. She learned by trial and error, and it was as well that she was practical and not inclined to be squeamish. She bought rabbits locally for sixpence and hares for a shilling.

For many years hens were kept at the Manse, and surplus eggs sold to the baker, but when these were given up, my mother bought eggs, pickling a large quantity at sixpence per dozen in enormous wide-mouthed brown crocks.

The partitioned interior of the well-scrubbed girnal was filled for the winter with new meal and flour, the larder stocked with jars of salted butter, barrels of potatoes, bladders of pure lard, perhaps a small cask of bloaters or red herring, Cooper's groceries and her own preserves, all amassed in late autumn to sustain the household till the season of fruitfulness came round again.

Like all Scots housewives, she spoke of a jiggot of mutton (from the French, *gigot*). She referred to the ash-backet, a small tub fitted with a riddle in which ashes and cinders were carried out-of-doors, the latter to be sifted and used again, the former to be scattered on the garden. This word was derived from the French *bacquet*, the kitchen dresser from *dressoir*, ashets from *assiettes*; our favourite stovies came from *étuve*, and the girnal may have had its origin in *gernier* . . . all scraps of evidence of Scots-French affinity which is frequently met in Scotland.

Normally, the event of the week was the visit of the bread-van, known simply as 'the cairt'. The driver, given the honorary title of 'the baker', worked on the barter system, accepting butter and eggs from those who had them to sell, giving in exchange loaf-bread and baps. New bread was crusty and delicious. Unluckily, by the time it was delivered to us it was no longer new, nor had it been new when the cairt set off from the bakery that morning. There was a well-founded theory that the bakery staff put aside unsold loaves for sending on the cairt up the Glen.

A man was once overheard in the shop, when buying a loaf, to insist firmly, 'An' no' aff the Gairnside shelf!'

The cairt was drawn by a drowsy horse who, on the tracks he had to cover, could never enjoy a good trot, but he knew his way and needed little in the way of direction from his driver. A double door at the back of the van opened to display on shelves several kinds of loaf-bread . . . plain, pan, French, lodgers' loaf, and others. In a drawer were cookies, softies, baps, queen cakes and German biscuits, which were thin rounds of shortcake sandwiched with jam, iced, and topped with a cherry. Every dark Thursday evening, instead of waiting at the ford, we sat in Maggie Cumming's cottage to await the arrival of the baker.

It was a cosy but-an'-ben, with walls whitewashed inside and out, black rafters that shone with peat-reek, and a thatched roof. Her father had built it with his own hands nearly a century before. We sat by her peat-fire on the low hearth, listening to her tales of long ago. Sometimes she would beg my mother to sing, or to diddle for us, and this she would do while her busy needles flashed. I never saw my mother sit with folded hands. She knitted up an immense quantity of wool, which she bought by the cut. A cut of worsted equalled approximately an ounce of wool and cost her about ninepence.

Her double-lidded market-basket had a broad ash handle

and a strong ash band running from end to end. It was thus very suitable for carrying butter to market, for which it had been designed. It made a weekly journey to the baker's van; buns and softies went into it, but the loaves my mother carried in a clean pillow-case slung over her shoulder, as all Glen housewives did.

In winter the cairt became a sleigh, the horse was shod with sharps, and if we failed to hear the jingling bells on the harness, the baker blew a shrill whistle to herald his arrival. There were long periods when even the sleigh could not negotiate the deep drifts, and home-baking was the order of the day . . . not merely scones but soda bread, using Borwick's baking powder, and a sweet loaf with Cakeoma, a forerunner of the cake-mixes of today.

The Manse was a good five miles from Ballater, and often appeared to be farther, but everybody 'travelled' in those days and long before we acquired bicycles we were seasoned travellers. From the age of eight I travelled the Glen road every Saturday, except in winter, for a music-lesson, my mother having grounded me well.

My teacher was a benevolent Yorkshireman who was organist at the Parish Church. My lesson was followed by a look round the shops. They were comparatively small. Two were, by their own designation, 'Draper, Grocer and General Merchant'. This meant that, as you entered, drapery was on the right, groceries on the left, ironmongery on the floor and in the back shop, and upstairs was the millinery department where hats were made and trimmed. There were no ready-trimmed hats nor any ready-made dresses. There were two chemists' shops, known as 'the druggists', two jewellers, doing a good trade in silver-mounted horn and cairngorms, two bakers, a fishmonger-fruiterer, a news-agent, a fishing-tackle maker, a taxi-dermist fully occupied in mounting stags' horns and foxes' heads, and a barber, but no hairdresser for ladies who were expected to dress their own hair with the aid of curl-papers, wire curlers, and steel curling-tongs. There were more shops in Ballater, it was said, than any place in the country outside London, with the distinction of displaying a gilded crest which proclaimed that they had the honour of supplying goods to the Queen, 'By Royal Command'. There were also four churches, two public halls, named the 'Victoria' and 'Albert' respectively, and several hotels.

Shop-doors had bells which jangled when the door was opened. The white-aproned grocer, the Provost in person, would hurry from the back-shop, beaming and ready to fill blue paper-bags with tea or barley, rice or sugar, tapping them on the counter to make the contents settle, while the customer sat comfortably on a bentwood chair by the counter. Those were the days of leisurely shopping, without crowding, or the vestige of a queue.

Ballater was normally a place of quiet roads lined with substantial stone-built houses, each standing in its own grounds, with flower-garden in front and vegetable-garden in the rear. Older houses were pleasantly secluded over-looking the river. The residents spoke of going 'down the village for the messages', that is, shopping for essentials. In the season it became a popular resort, packed with visitors who returned every year when it was fashionable to take a house for several months, basking in the reflected glory of Balmoral. The hotels were full; residents let their villas and retired for the summer to a cottage in the back-garden. There were rooms with attendance, and all the big houses in the neighbourhood were rented for the season to wealthy people who brought their own domestic staff, and were gratified to move in the aura of high society. Tradesmen made the most of the season. 'Is it for yourself or your visitors?', enquired the coal-merchant when taking an order . . . the answer made a difference to the price.

Housewives who met when out for their messages had much to discuss. They all knew each other's business, the rent they were charging, and their opinion of their visitors. While the grocer deftly scooped their orders from bins behind the counter into paper-bags, briskly conversing all the while, they compared notes on the state in which their tenants had left their houses, denouncing alike those who left them in such a condition they were fair scunnert, and those who left everything swept and garnished, with no left-overs in the kitchen or a usable waterproof-coat in the lobby.

All through the summer months at the Manse there was a steady procession of relatives and friends from the south, who stayed for a fortnight or longer. Their visits had an enlivening effect upon my parents, and conversation at table sparkled with discussions on current events, politics and politicians, music, local legends, and the latest clash from Balmoral. On the long light nights we bairns lay in bed unable to sleep, hearing the grown-up voices and laughter downstairs, and wondering, with Robert Louis Stevenson, why we had to go to bed by day. All the bed-rooms being occupied, my father had a shakedown on the study floor and my mother had one in the morning-room. Guests made their own beds, shelled peas, and picked fruit when required. It took our little maid all her time to scrape potatoes for such a large family and assist my mother with her numerous tasks. Our maids were invariably fresh from school, filling in time at £5 or £6 for the half-year, till they were old enough to have 'a farm place t'gang til'. Lads and lasses who were fee'd on farms got the day off on term day, but had no regular holidays. At the Manse, however, local girls were allowed home any evening and every Sunday, and were frequently taken on our family holiday to help with us children.

Going for the milk was a monotonous errand which nobody liked, and in the absence of volunteers, there were times when my mother had herself to go to Tamnafeidh, half a mile away, to fetch milk at tuppence a pint in her large tin pail. On her return she would make one of her celebrated milk puddings, with cinnamon or pink sugar sprinkled on top and served with a dish of fresh raspberries and clotted cream in little brown pots.

Ellie and I, with our cousins, who had all been out of earshot when the milk had to be fetched, were generally at hand when it was time to sound the brass gong, swinging on its stand in the lobby. With its knobbed stick we were ready to beat it all round the garden, if necessary, to gather in from their favourite haunts the guests, among whom, from time to time, were various uncles.

There was Uncle Jim, who had a fine baritone voice which was a great asset to the praise in our small church when he came to stay.

There was Old Uncle, for whom we used to carry a folding-chair and set it in the spot he selected, where, in his old Panama hat, he sat on a clover-scented bank enjoying the sunshine, and wreathed about with a haze of tobacco-smoke.

Uncle Tom was our favourite—always full of fun and ready to join in our games. One summer, after our first experience of lunching out, we were never tired of playing at 'resterongs', and he delighted my sister by escorting her to the summer-house every afternoon, and ordering 'wasp-bike biscuits and Mazawattee tea', tactfully correcting my spelling when I, in a borrowed cap and apron, presented a card with a 'stake' pie on the menu.

Uncle George was unpredictable. He was an eccentric, with a full, dark moustache, a quick temper, and a curious idea of fun. One afternoon he tied the nursemaid to her chair in the garden, so that she was unable to get on with her knitting while keeping an eye on us at play. My mother, returning, was not amused. He acted as locum for my father on one of his vacations, and on Sunday morning demanded a carriage to take him to church. As no such conveyance was available, and my mother at her wits' end, he was eventually persuaded to walk by the riverside path as we all had to do. He put the Manse in such a state of tension that it was only dispelled when, at the end of his visit, the hire from Ballater took him to the station.

Uncle William was one of those restless beings who fail
to settle and prosper. He held many charges but never
stayed in one parish for long. In retrospect I see him as a
mild, prim, fussy little man, who wore on all occasions a
clerical frock-coat and soup-plate hat. He affected indoors
somewhat mincing steps, but actually could walk great
distances, possibly from necessity. He always arrived
unannounced and stayed for long periods, and was invited
to occupy the pulpit on one or two Sundays. Unlike his
brother, George, he did not complain of the distance between the Manse and the church. Once he walked all the
way from Laurencekirk, over the Cairn o' Mount, arriving
at the Manse at a late hour in a state of exhaustion. On
another occasion he travelled over the Lecht from Tomintoul, where he had been preaching for a few weeks, and
stayed for well over two months, when an embarrassed
hostess felt impelled to suggest that it was perhaps time he
rejoined his wife, who was, meantime, living with her
aunts in Cullercoats.

My sister and I learned early to lay the table, to wipe
crockery and stack it in the press, to polish silver, and to
make knives bright by rubbing them briskly on a board
sprinkled with gritty bath-brick which certainly removed
the stains but scratched the steel. One of our tasks was to
fetch, from a spot near the briggie, silver sand which was
used to scour the kitchen table. With carpet-beaters of
bamboo we made a game of beating carpets and rugs
spread out on the clean, sweet-smelling grass. We helped
to hold sheets and table-linen in place while they moved
slowly through the wringer-rollers.

We had no regular pocket-money; we were expected to
do what was required of us without thought of payment,
and were given pennies when there was opportunity and
an object on which to spend them. My mother repeatedly
quoted the saying, 'Take care of the pence and the pounds
will take care of themselves', which meant less than

nothing to us with four pennies rattling about in a money-box and showing no sign of growing into pounds.

We were encouraged to buy fruit instead of sweets, though there was a marvellous selection of sweets that could, in fact, be obtained for a penny . . . a thick stick of liquorice or six mint balls; two sticks of striped rock or a wee bag of mixed sweets. We were sometimes given chocolate creams and chocolate drops in pretty boxes. Plain drops cost threepence a quarter, and those coated with tiny balls of sugar were a trifle dearer. Tuppence was the price of Fry's chocolate cream bars marked in four sections; the same delicious sweetmeat is still available, but it is many years since I saw their advertisement showing the expressive face of a boy in a sailor suit eating chocolate in stages which began with anticipation and ended in blissful realization. There was a penny cake of plain chocolate, marked in four sections, two of which showed the impression of a cocoa-bean and the other two a Fry's shield. These medallion cakes were first made in 1885 and were sold at a penny up to 1916 when the price was increased to three ha'pence!

Scotch Mixtures consisted of small hard white sweets . . . some round, some oval; the curly-murlies had a clove embedded in each, there were discs of pink sugar, and an occasional sugar-almond. Cupid's Whispers were smooth, scented rounds of sugar in pastel colours, inscribed in coloured lettering, 'I love you', 'You are my Sweetheart', and similar sentiments. Conversation lozenges were in different shapes, bright colours and distinctive flavours. Their object was the same as the Whispers . . . to provide backward swains with an excuse to convey a word to the beloved. The lozenges were not so refined as the others, nor were the messages . . . 'How are your poor feet?' was a sample, but the sweets were long-lasting if allowed to lie on the tongue, dissolving slowly while the flavoured juices trickled down an appreciative throat. Butterscotch was sometimes bestowed on us; Uncle George brought us Turkish Delight, smothered in fine powdery sugar, in

drums of thin pale wood embellished with Eastern calli-
graphy; and when we ventured into the wider world we
tasted the delights of Forfar rock, Harrogate toffee, barley
sugar, and jujubes. When my father went to the General
Assembly he brought us Edinburgh rock, and from Aberdeen
Easter Eggs of decorated sugar, chocolate mice, and sugar
pigs with curly tails. One wonderful summer Mr Forder, a
shooting tenant, came back to the Shiel for salmon-fishing,
and gave us a huge tin of most delectable toffee in slabs
which had to be broken with a hammer. Splinters flew,
but we retrieved every one.

Looking back on those childhood years I realize more and
more how essentially happy was our lot. The practice of
rigid economy did no harm in its bearing on our later and
more abundant years. We were brought up in the simple
creed that we must give freely to others whatever we could
spare, but nothing must ever be wasted. Our parents' one
ambition was to give us a good education, and only by
constant economizing over the years were they able to save
enough to send us to boarding-school. No grants, bursaries,
or exhibitions were available to ease the burden, nor did we,
their daughters, realize what personal sacrifices they were
making, or show any proper awareness and appreciation.
We took it all for granted; that, and their little unremem-
bered acts of kindness and of love I shall ever regret.

# CHAPTER SEVEN

# EARLY SCHOOLDAYS

Oft in the stilly night
Ere slumber's chain hath bound me
Fond memory brings the light
Of other days around me.
                              Thomas Moore

James Drawbell, recalling the happiest days of his life, says he remembers playing Scotch Horses on the way to school. In the Glen it was strictly for the lassies, a method of progression reminiscent of a country dance. Two girls skipped along side by side with their crossed hands joined. At the end of each couplet they changed places without breaking the hand-clasp, singing as they went, 'Twa Scotch horses gaun awa' t'Fife, Comin' back on Monday wi' an aul' wife'. As we danced along it helped to shorten the road. It was significant that never were we Scotch Horses on the homeward journey.

The path from the Manse to church and school wound its way through a wood which in spring was carpeted with wind-flowers which we called anemones; then it twisted and twined for half a mile or so till it left the riverside and became a road little better than a cart-track. In summer our footsteps threw up a trail of dust behind us; on wet days the ruts became rivulets.

When I first trod this path schoolwards at the age of five, my father accompanied me all the way and collected me in the afternoon. Next day I had to go alone, and within sound of the big boys shouting in the playground, I turned and fled, running for dear life every step of the way home only to be escorted back later. Having no brothers to tease or tame me, it took me some time to overcome an unreasoning fear of noisy loons. There was no bullying at that little school, only a normal amount of hair-pulling and tammy-snatching.

My mother was aware that it was common then for children, even those from good homes, to have nits in their long hair, so she warned me from the start not to allow anyone to wear my hat. It would seem that trying on hats has been a favourite pastime among girls of all ages since headgear was first invented. It was sheer bad luck that the first little girl who wanted to try on my hat was the teacher's own child. She repeated to her mother my reason for declining, and my mother had some awkward explaining to do. Ailments such as ringworm and lice were common enough in elementary schools until medical inspection of schools put an end to most of the cases. I recall only one case of ringworm; a boarded-out child brought it from Glasgow, but fortunately did not spread the infection.

Our school was designated a public school, as opposed to the type of private schools which existed before the state began to take responsibility for education. It was stone-built, surrounded by a low wall enclosing two playgrounds which were separated by a wall too high to climb. It was a bare barn of a place; its unhygienic conditions would not be tolerated now. It was dusty, it was stuffy, it was cold. In winter we were permitted to group ourselves round the fire, but as soon as we withdrew to make room for others we shivered again. The teacher must herself have tended

[101]

the fire, chopping wood, carrying coal, and removing ashes, for no help was provided. The unplaned floorboards were scrubbed only after a social gathering, by a woman engaged for the purpose and paid half-a-crown for her trouble.

Girls entered by one door through a porch with pegs for outdoor clothing; boys entered by a similar porch from their own side of the wall. That was the extent of their segregation.

The windows were placed high in the walls, presumably to discourage wandering attention on the part of the scholars. They were never opened, even in the height of summer. The walls were distempered that sickly green shade that is supposed to be kind to the eyes. Scholars sat in pairs on narrow deal benches facing scarred tops hardly worthy of the name of desks, as they sloped but slightly and had no lids, merely a shallow underspace in which to keep a couple of books. The fixed seats were clamped to a cast-iron support. At 'socials' it took strong men to move the desks to make room for dancing.

The building contained two rooms, the main one known as the School, in which we were taught; the smaller one, called the Classroom, used only for storing equipment, handicraft materials, paraffin-lamps, and the big boiling-urn.

All grades were taught by a single teacher, who somehow contrived to keep every child occupied. Each group stood in turn in a semi-circle round the teacher's chair and answered questions. Whoever answered quickly and correctly moved to the top of the class and remained there till displaced by somebody quicker off the mark.

The teacher used no desk, but a large table stood in the middle of the room and was called the big desk. It had a hinged top which, when raised, disclosed a recess in which were stored out-of-date textbooks, old copybooks, a set of Indian Clubs, and . . . the tawse.

My first teacher had heavy family responsibilities, and I believe it was her perpetually worried state that led to her harsh treatment of the scholars. She used the tawse freely and unkindly, reducing even the biggest boys to tears as she lashed repeatedly round their bare legs and feet. (In summer all the loons went barefoot but at other times wore, like their fathers, strong boots shod with steel.)

Once, in her successor's time, the loons stole the tawse, cut it to ribbons and threw the bits in the Gairn. 'Whatten a row ye'll get! mocked the queyns. The jaunty reply 'A'm no' caring'!' maybe hid a fear of the consequences, but among the queyns there were no clypes. That teacher used the tawse so seldom that I doubt if she missed it; she made no reference to its loss, which was a decided anti-climax, and took all joy from the exploit. She was indeed very different from a teacher in a neighbouring parish, of whom a former pupil remarked, 'She wis the best wheeper o'bottoms that iver I saw!'

The Three R's . . . Reading, 'Riting and 'Rithmetic, were hammered home by repetition and practice. They were the foundation of our education and we were plunged into all three without delay. After learning to identify the letters of the alphabet we proceeded to master three-letter words descriptive of the crude drawing on each page of our Primer, a small brown paperback. It contained no coloured pictures. On the first page was a drawing of a brindled cat seated on a recognizable mat . . . the original 'cat on the mat' now quoted in derision of an antiquated method of teaching; but it was a straightforward method, and by the repetition of letters and words in a concerted chant, we did learn to read, and quickly, too. The Primer convoyed us from our ABCs up the thorny paths of knowledge through various 'Readers', which contained ballads and chapters of history and travel, until each was supposed to be turned out, The Compleat Scholar, in Standard VI at the ripe age of fourteen.

We had pleasant reading-books in Cassell's 'Eyes and no Eyes' series, designed to interest children in country life. They awakened interest in nature study and gave new values to much we had hitherto taken for granted. From

Nelson's 'Royal Osborne Readers', and similar textbooks, we received instruction in geography and history; these largely consisted of feats of memory . . . the names of continents and countries, the population of cities, long lists of exports and imports, strings of dates of battles and sieges, the reigning years of monarchs, and Acts of Parliament up to the time of Queen Victoria's accession to the throne, and the repeal of the Corn Laws.

Our classwork was done on slates with slate-pencils that, when new, were an attractive grey colour, wrapped halfway in harlequin paper. The colour wore off with usage and so did the paper, leaving the functional dark-blue pencil squeaking its way across the slate. In theory, sums or writing were rubbed out with a wet rag; in practice, a saliva-moistened grubby handkerchief came handier. The loons scorned such refinements and found that a drop or two of spit and a rub with the sleeve of a well-worn jacket did the job most thoroughly . . . thus a surreptitious game of noughts and crosses was soon obliterated. At times a slate would clatter to the floor; half the slates in the school were cracked. A new slate was a proud possession. Girls inked their names across the top of the wooden frame; boys carved theirs with pen-knives.

Arithmetic was taught from textbooks containing set sums in addition, subtraction, and long-division. We had to be fluent in reciting the multiplication tables, and in due course were promoted to problems concerning the filling of baths from taps A and B, and the length of time it would take a man and a boy to mow a field of hay.

Under our breath we muttered

> Multiplication is vexation,
> Division's just as bad,
> The Rule of Three perplexes me
> And Practice drives me mad.

After learning to write on slates we were promoted to copybooks, pen and ink. First, between two parallel lines like railway lines, we had to make row upon row of pothooks, carefully formed as shown at the top of the page. In later books, between narrower lines, with fine upstrokes and broad downstrokes, dipping the pen in the inkwell sunk in the desk, we faithfully copied 'Honesty is the best Policy', 'A stitch in time saves nine' and other copybook maxims. By this system we learned to write really well, in spite of inky fingers and occasional blots. Lead pencils were issued for drawing-lessons, which entailed the copying of an object outlined on the opposite page. No crayons, coloured pencils, or water-colours were used in the school, nor did the teacher use coloured chalk on the blackboard.

On the back cover of our copybooks were set out multi-plication tables, tables of avoirdupois weights, cubic measures, troy weight and other features, all of which had to be learned.

We recited in mechanical fashion

> Thirty days hath September,
> April, June and November,
> All the rest have thirty-one
> Excepting February alone
> Which has but twenty-eight days clear,
> And twenty-nine in each Leap Year.

Books of every kind were handed down till their contents were outdated, and the arrival of a new issue was an event. As soon as we laid hands on a new book we laid claim to it by inscribing on the fly-leaf the owner's name and address, extending it to Aberdeenshire, Scotland, Great Britain, Europe, The World, adding a gloomy verse which is known to date back to the year 1736 . . .

> When I am dead and in my grave
> And all my bones are rotten,
> This little book will tell my name
> When I am quite forgotten.

At times a doggerel verse was substituted, on these lines . . .

Willie Thomson is my name,
And Scotland is my nation;
Fenzie is my dwelling-place
And Ballater my station.

Time marches on, but not where children are concerned; I am told they scribble much the same versification in textbooks today.

We learned a vast amount of poetry by heart, but it had little of the charm of that enjoyed by children in modern schools. Not for us Wordsworth's delicate lines on daffodils; instead we were introduced to the lachrymose child who regularly ate her supper in the churchyard. We learned of Hohenlinden with Iser rolling rapidly at the end of every verse, and a poem in which Tennyson told in twenty-two verses how Lord Ronal brought a lily-white doe to give his cousin, Lady Clare. The grandeur of *The Lays of Ancient Rome* was not brought to our notice; instead, melancholy ballads like *Casabianca*, *The Wreck of the Hesperus*, *The Burial of Sir John Moore*, and Southey's grim tale of the bloody battle of Blenheim, in which we reiterated in sing-song fashion at the end of every stanza, 'It was a famous victor-ee'.

But the saddest of all, to my mind, was one I rediscovered recently in a book dated 1874, and have since found in *The Family Book of Best-Loved Poems*. Written by Henry Glassford Bell, it depicts in a series of vivid word-pictures, scenes in the life of Mary, Queen of Scots, and her weary years of captivity, ending on the scaffold.

'Curfew shall not ring tonight' was another dramatic poem in our Reader, illustrated by a drawing of a young woman clinging desperately to the clapper of an enormous bell while it swung dangerously to and fro.

It says much for the thoroughness of our teaching that after seventy years I can still repeat stanzas from *The Lady of the Lake*, Polonius' advice to Laertes, and the rousing song of the Western Men that maintains that should Trelawny die, twenty thousand Cornish men will know the reason why.

Shiny old maps hung on the school walls, lowered by a pole when required. We gathered round to learn the mountain ranges, the source and course of every river and its tributaries, the situation of islands, lochs and promontories, towns and their industries, urban districts and their produce . . . wherever the pointer paused, the answer had to be forthcoming. The map of the world showed an immense area of pink. There was no British Commonwealth in those days; Empire was the word and it had a proud and satisfying sound. Maps were splashed with red to show the extent of that Empire. The red splashes had faded on our school map, but there was nothing faded about the Empire.

We had a weekly singing-lesson, learning by ear, for there was no piano, such songs as 'Jock O' Hazeldean' and Tannahill's 'Bonnie Wood o' Craigielea'. A modulator was unfurled and draped over the blackboard and we intoned the scales of the tonic sol-fa from low doh to high doh and down again.

By folding small squares of glazed coloured paper into triangles, rhomboids, and octagons and pasting them in a book, we were expected to become familiar with geometrical figures.

Girls were also required to prepare samples of darning, hemming, and patching on squares of white cotton and red flannel, mounting them in a book for inspection.

We were taught a simple form of the ancient craft of basketry, soaking the cane in water to make it pliable. Our baskets were somewhat fragile, but we were dab-hands at making tea-pot stands.

We sewed the simplest of samplers, nothing so ambitious as the admirable achievements of our great-grandmothers, and spent hours weaving strips of coloured paper to make silly little mats and baskets; we also learned fretwork, patchwork, and clay-modelling.

'Dear Aunt', wrote a little girl dutifully on her birthday, 'Thank you for the pincushion you sent me. I have always wanted a pincushion, but not very much.'

Remembering the pincushions of my childhood I can echo her guileless candour; walnut shells stuffed with velvet, pads filled with sawdust and covered with crochet-work, silk bags of emery powder, and an elaborate cushion presented to my mother, so encrusted with beads and embroidery that pins could not penetrate. There was one I was obliged to make at school from the cone of a Norway spruce. It was trimmed with strands of narrow ribbon attached with rows of pins and gathered into a loop for hanging, but pins rusted, ribbon faded, and another useless article was soon discarded.

Senior girls had lessons in domestic economy, reading from a textbook; senior boys had what they called 'agrie', a weekly lesson from a book on the principles of agriculture, and the fertilization of land, which technically was far removed from their experience of life close to the land culti-vated by their fathers using the methods of their forebears.

The conversation of bairns in the Glen, like that of their parents, was mainly of soos and coos. Wee Georgie Rettie, piping up in a lull in the hum of a class at recitation, was heard to announce, 'We've got a sooie wi' a tail as lang's that', demonstrating its length to his desk-mate, with hands wide apart like a boastful angler and the big fish that got away.

School attendance was fairly good. Some bairns had to walk several miles to school by devious by-roads from distant Sleach and Morven, and though they soon got hardened to the long tramp the Coutts laddies often tru'd the school, spending fine days on the hill. In winter, moorland tracks were impassable. There was a certain amount of absentee-ism when loons couldna win because their help was required in the fields wi' the neeps, or howkin' tatties, or at the moss castin' peats.

Six weeks school holidays in August and September allowed for earning a pound or two at the grouse-driving, and full participation in the hairst. There were no children's allowances then, no grants for Further Education. All the boys who left Glen Gairn School were obliged to find work on farms in neighbouring parishes; when they were old enough, many emigrated. So did the girls after serving some years in domestic service in private houses, farm-kitchens, in the laundry at Balmoral, or in hotel still-rooms in distant towns.

On the other hand, many of those who did not emigrate carved very satisfactory niches for themselves in the nursing profession, and there were lads who rose to responsible posts in the police force.

We had no homework nor were we bothered with weekly tests or end-of-term examinations. Once a year one of Her Majesty's Inspectors of Schools paid an unheralded visit, examined our copybooks, tested our mental arithmetic, heard us read, and was duly impressed by the array of articles in elementary handicrafts which the teacher displayed in the classroom. It was the latter, I believe, which obtained satisfactory reports for the school, for she was not a certificated teacher and her methods were her own. She lived a very solitary life, encouraging no callers and making few friends. She was a tiny woman, and moody. One glance at her morning face as she minced her way across the playground and through the assembled girls in the porch, told us what the forecast for the day would be . . . if stormy, she was apt to let fly at any face within reach of her hand, accompanying the slap with an intimidating scowl. On such a morning she would neglect to call the roll, and it caused her acute embarrassment that on one such day the Inspector walked in and wanted to know the reason for the omission.

Normally, only the children who lived near the school

[109]

went home at the midday break; the rest brought their 'pieces' . . . loaf bread saturated with syrup, treacle, or jam. A jeely 'piece' washed down with milk was soon consumed, leaving plenty of time for play, and maybe a trip to the shoppie at Rinloan, where Mrs Davidson stocked, among other things, liquorice sticks and peppermint rock. She would twist a paper poke, shaping it like a forcing-bag, and was always willing to sell a bairn as little as a ha'penny-worth of pan drops or bull's eyes. She also stocked a barrel of syrup and one of black treacle. When a child brought a tin pail to school and was seen to disappear with it in the dinner-hour, there was little need for others to shout, 'Far ye gaun the noo?' The inevitable reply was 'A'm gaun t'Rinloan for traycle t' tak' hame'.

Queen Victoria knew Rinloan, which was once an inn. In her *Journal* she described an expedition in September 1859, when her party set off from Balmoral one morning. They drove to Corndavon at the head of Glen Gairn, mounted ponies and rode along the shore of Loch Builg, up to Inchrory where they saw 'the fine broad water of the Avon flowing down from the mountains'. After a picnic meal they remounted and came down on the far side of the Broon Coo, and landed at Dalnadamph. They rode along the old military road at the foot of the hill on which stands Corgarff Castle, with Cockbrig on their left. By devious ways they reached and crossed the Glas-Choille, and descended to Gairnshiel. At Rinloan, where the ponies were to have a rest and a good feed, the carriages were waiting. Darkness had then fallen, so they drove slowly over the Stranyarroch, which was, in a royal understatement, 'not a good road and steep in parts', arriving home at 8 o'clock well pleased with themselves. They had covered thirty-five miles of hilly country, pony-trekking for nearly twenty 'o'er heather tracks wi' heaven in their wiles'.

The sight of a blacksmith working at his craft has attracted bairns since time began. Donald Grant was a crofter-blacksmith with a smiddy near the school. When, in our dinner-hour, we heard a tinka-tinka-tink coming from the small thatched building across the green, we ran to watch Donald at his anvil, blinking as our eyes became accustomed to gloom, for the interior was lit only by the glow of the furnace. We never wearied of the clang of the hammer on the anvil, of the great roar of the huge brass-studded leather bellows with long handles laboriously pumped by hand, and of watching the sparks fly to all corners as Donald unerringly brought down the hammer on the piece of dripping white metal. Long after he ceased to act as blacksmith and horses had to be shod at Fit o' Gairn, we haunted the derelict building and played on the smiddy green. Nearby were the Poolocks, shallow pools in very marshy ground which froze over in winter and became our favourite playground. We made slides as smooth as glass, and a string of scholars would skim across in quick succession, run round the pool and back again to 'keep the pottie boiling', an unwitting corruption of 'the pot a-boiling'. When the bell rang for afternoon lessons we ran back, peching, to thaw our hands at the blazing fire enclosed by its big black fireguard, tholing without fuss the pain that dirled the fingers that had lost all feeling and came painfully to life.

One winter we took the wooden forms which were used at socials, from the disused stable in the church grounds where they were stored, and used them, upturned, as toboggans on the steep field behind the school. Six or eight of us to a form, holding fast to each other and to the supports, careered madly down the slope. It was rare fun, and we had damaged several supports in this way before the exuberant game was discovered and firmly stopped.

Except in winter, when the well was frozen, an uncovered pail of water and a tin mug stood on the window-sill of each porch for communal drinking purposes. Scholars took it in turn to fetch water from the well across the moor at some distance from the school. Willing feet carried us there. It was a chance to linger on the moor, to bury our noses in the thymy short grass, and to suck the white, juicy end of a certain grass that came out of a green socket, carefully avoiding the stem that was embellished with Cuckoo Spittle. We picked the sweet-scented marsh orchis, and the lamb's tongue plantains which we called carrel doddies. Willing hands carried the pails, but we set them down from time to time to indulge in a game we played with the object of knocking off the heads of our opponent's carrel doddies. There was quaking grass growing on the moor and cotton grass with tufts of silky white fleece which resembles the cotton-tails of rabbits. Sooner or later we had to get back to school, leaving our trophies in the porch.

When a hand shot up for 'Please for leave', it was to a sheltered angle in the school wall that we went: only dire necessity drove us to the placie at the far end of the playground, which had no ventilation, not even conventional star-shaped cut-outs in the door. There was a sneck but no bolt on the door of the odoriferous cabin. There was a primitive fixed seat consisting of a large hole in the middle of a planed plank, under which stood a galvanised bucket, which some unfortunate Unknown had to remove from a pit outside when it became obvious that his services were urgently required. The boys also had a privy on their side of the wall. There were no facilities for hand-washing.

On certain days we did drill indoors, a dust-raising, deafening performance in our sturdy boots; we spent hours inexpertly swinging Indian Clubs, but had no organized outdoor activities. We had, however, a wide variety of seasonal playground games . . . there were special seasons for skipping-ropes and bows and arrows, for catapults, and jews' harps (derived from jaws' harps) which the loons called their tromps. The hoop, the kite, and marbles are among the most ancient of toys, and my generation had its own version of them all.

The Glen loons played bools in the spring, outside the concrete playground so that a hole could be made in soft earth with the heel of a tackety boot. They did not encourage queyns to join in, but tolerated us as spectators. We gathered round to watch them span the ground with grubby paws, then flick the bool between the knuckles of a bent thumb and curved forefinger suddenly straightening the thumb. A taw was the bool actually used by the player from his stance six feet away, to knock out those of his opponents. There were triumphant yells at every good shot. The bools, ten a penny, were nearly all of baked clay, glazed brown or sand-colour; there were a few treasured glass ones with streaks of bright colours through them. Bools were known by different names . . . commonies, alleys, stonies, and glessies. Plain ones could be had from lemonade bottles which were sealed with a green glass marble, and unstoppered by pushing the stopper down. Break the neck of an empty bottle, and you got a green glessie for naethin'! The alleys were the most valuable, reserved for use as taws. The *Boys' Modern Playmate*, published in 1890, devotes seven pages to the correct method of holding marbles and the variety of games which may be played with them, but, looking back, it seems to me the rules of the game played by the Glen loons were freely adapted from those of bowls, billiards and curling.

Bows and arrows were home-made. A supple sapling made the bow, trimmed and bent, with a piece of fine twine attached to each end. Arrows were straight, short hazel sticks pointed by the diligent use of a pocket-knife. Slings and catapults were easily contrived from string and bits of leather, forked sticks, and india-rubber. Kites were made of newspaper and two birch saplings tied together, balanced by a few twisted screws of paper tied on the long tail. Nobody owned a real ball of string, but knotted innumerable collected pieces till the necessary length was achieved and the clew was an imposing size. We went to the top of a steep field on a windy day and, amazing to relate, our kites actually flew.

A skipping-rope with wooden handles was kept for home use. At school a length of tracer-rope was preferred, but soon frayed by constant friction. Hairy binder-twine, though easy to come by, had not the right weight or substance; a crisis was averted when somebody's mother donated a piece of clothes-line.

'Salt, mustard, vinegar, pepper' . . . hundreds of thousands of children have, through the ages, blithely skipped to the old chant. Two girls ca'd the rope, the others, in a steady stream ran in, skipped the agreed number of times, and ran out at the other end. To trip was to be out. The last girl in had to skip on the spot at a great rate till she, too, tripped, was caused to trip, or gave up for want of puff. We skipped through in rapid succession to keep the pottie boiling; other games were complex and required much practice to make performance perfect. 'French ropes', for example, called for skilful manipulation of two ropes.

A game in which loons and queyns freely joined was tig, dell, free, an adaptation of hide and seek, and much more exciting. We played it all over the surrounding fields and moors, chasing the rabbits from hillocks dotted with their holes, but the dell itself was within the school gate. IT (or HIT) covered his or her eyes while counting to a hundred, facing the wall. By then all the players were well-hidden, and IT had to go far afield to seek them. If one crept out un-noticed and raced back to the dell, 'tig, dell, free' was the jubilant cry. The first to be caught had to be IT, or could cry a barley, which is a plea for immunity.

Before the start of play, of course, there had to be some counting out. Lined up against a wall, a leader pointed a finger at each of us while reciting a rhyme, till all but one were eliminated. The last one had to be HIT. There are countless counting out rhymes. Not for us the common 'Eeny, Meeny, Miney, Mo'; we liked our own version of

the rhyme that Marjorie Fleming* taught Sir Walter
Scott . . .

Wonery, twoery, tickery, seven,
Alaby, crackaby, ten and eleven:
Ping, Pang, musky-dan,
Tweedilum, toodle-um, twenty-wan. You-are-OOT.

or, for a quick change, we rattled off

Inky, finky, figgery fell,
Ell, dell, dominell,
Arky, parky, tarry rope,
Am, tam, Toosy Jock. You-are-OOT!

but for a real time-saver there was nothing to beat

Eetle, Ottle, Black bottle,
Eetle, Ottle, OOT!

Many of the rhymes we repeated when the spirit moved us
have been handed down from one generation to another,
for example . . .

Queen Queen Caroline
Washed her hair in turpentine,
Turpentine made it shine
Queen Queen Caroline.

and

I'll tell Mamma when I get home,
The boys won't let the girls alone;
They pull my hair and break my comb,
And I'll tell Mamma when I get home.

The comb referred to was probably the flexible semi-circle
called a crop-comb, which held the hair in position off the

* Marjorie Fleming, the little friend of Sir Walter Scott, died four days
after her eighth birthday. She has been called 'the youngest Immortal in
the World of Literature', and wrote amazing little poems for one of such
tender years. Her original headstone is let into the back of the modern
pedestal, the white marble cross to be seen in Abbotshall Churchyard,
Kirkcaldy.

face. The ends were sometimes joined by elastic which slipped behind the hair at the nape of the neck and left it hanging freely down the back. An Alice band is the modern substitute.

There was, of course, a season for stotting balls in the playground, our piping notes keeping time with the bouncing ball; and we had a large number of singing games handed on by an endless chain of children down the ages, and said to be derived from customs of great antiquity. There were some in which, without knowing it, we were probably joining in a pagan ritual in honour of the Goddess of spring; when we sang

> Here we come gathering Nuts in May
> On a cold and frosty morning,

we were unaware that we might be enacting a marriage by capture, nor did we query the inference that nuts could be gathered in May; even the assumption that it should be sung 'Nuts and May' or 'Knots of May', hardly explains that cold and frosty morning; but more feasible is the interpretation of the rhyme as a chain of events in the seasons of the year . . . spring with Mayflowers, autumn with ripe nuts, winter with cold and frosty mornings.

Another game with its origin in marriage-customs we sang in a moving circle

> Here we go round the Jingo Ring
> About the Merry-ma-tanzie.

Right through the sunny summer days we Dropped the Handkerchief, sitting in a ring on the grass. Two girls were involved at a time . . . she who dawdled outside the ring singing,

> I sent a letter to my Love
> And on the way I dropped it,
> I dree, I dree, I dropped it,
> Somebody has picked it up
> And put it in her pocket.

and she, behind whose back the handkerchief was eventually dropped, had to rise and give chase before the sanctuary of the vacant place was reached.

'Water, Water, Wallflowers', and 'Poor Nelly is a-weeping' were played in a slow-moving ring while one girl knelt in a weeping attitude, in the centre. Most of our singing games seemed to be founded on love, marriage, and death; for example, Nelly was a-weeping for a sweetheart. To her and to 'Sally Waters' we sang

> Now you are married
> We wish you joy,
> First a girl and then a boy.

She who had to go Round and Round the Village had at last to stand and face her lover; the wallflowers complained that they were all maidens and they must all die . . . even the farmer in the dell wanted a wife. There was one game which might have been gloomy had we not sung it so light-heartedly; it went on . . . and on . . . and on, about a sadly-overworked Jenny. It began

> We've come to see poor Jenny,
> And how's she today?

The answer    She's up the stairs washing
> And you can't see her today.

A succession of duties such as ironing and baking kept her in the background, till at last she was said to be 'up the stairs dying, and you can't see her today'. Finally, 'she's up the stairs dead' but that was not the end. The next problem was 'What shall we wear at the funeral?'

> White is for weddings and that will not do
> Blue is for sailors and that will not do,

nor will red, which is for soldiers, but 'black is for mourning, and so that will do'.

'London Bridge is falling down', with its well-known

procedure, has its grim origin in human sacrifices, but our version had no reference to a gay lady or a chopper to chop off her head; we imprisoned each girl in turn, gave her a choice of sides and ended the game with a tug-of-war.

We also played 'Looby Loo', with its right hand in, left foot out, routine, on which the hilarious 'Hokey Cokey' is based.

In guessing games it was usual to recite, with hands behind the back,

> Nievie, nievie, nick-nack,
> Which hand will ye tak'?
> Tak' the richt or tak' the wrang,
> I'll beguile ye if I can.

When the teacher's attention was elsewhere we indulged in a bit of finger-play, whispering

> This is the Pope,
> This is the People,
> This is the Church,
> And this is the Steeple.

When school skailed at three o'clock we scholars dispersed, tearing home in winter, but in summer lingering on the road, trailing our coats, swinging our satchels, yelling and singing for no reason but the joy of being free for the rest of the day. A generous member of the Coats family of Paisley endowed remote schools with small libraries in a glass-fronted case, and gave every school-child in Scotland a satchel.

The standard greeting from folks on the road was 'Weel, did ye get yer licks the day?' Sometimes they called it a leatherin', skelps or wheeps.

On the first of April we had to be careful of Hunt the Gowk, traps which playful grown-ups set for the unwary. The word gowk is derived from the old Norse word gaukr, meaning simpleton; only simpletons could possibly be taken in by the practical joke which made him the unsuspecting bearer of a note that he was made to carry from one house to another under the impression that it was an urgent message, whereas the letter contained the lines

> This is the First of Aprile
> Send the gowk anither mile,

and on to another destination he would be sent till some kind soul took pity on him. Long before our day, such a leg-pull kept a village in a state of merriment for a week.

Nothing like it was prepared for us, but a few harmless jokes were valid up to midday.

In spring we watched the lambs at play in the fields, leaping and frisking and buffeting each other with their knobby foreheads. Sometimes a silly lamb, calling plaintively, would run to a yowe who would move on eating steadily, ignoring him while he tried to nuzzle her. Puzzled, he would stand bleating till at last he recognized his true mother and ran to her; soon, with furiously wagging tail and firmly planted legs, he drank, till she gave him a little push and sent him off to play.

There were days when we would meet a farmer leading a bulling cow bellowing its head off; on rare occasions we met a stallion led by a long rope by his attendant groom who looked very insignificant beside that mighty strength and beauty, chestnut coat, and big feathery feet.

We climbed gates and wire fences as a matter of course. At a dyke there would be a stile . . . two shaky steps up and two down. We noticed that women lifted their skirts above the ankle to negotiate a stile, and that inspired a favourite ploy for the queyns. We would tie our coats by the sleeves round our middles to make trailing skirts to lift ostentatiously with one hand, and minced along holding over our heads giant stalks of cow-parsley which grew in umbrella-shapes taller than ourselves. We called them Ladies' Lace and pretended that the big clusters of white flowers were the lace on our parasols.

Butterflies fluttered about the fields, and when we caught one clinging, folded, to a flower, we gently stroked the velvet wings and let it open and flutter away. We chased but could never catch the iridescent dragonflies that on transparent wings darted through the woods, soaring up to the tree-tops in pursuit of insect prey, feeding on the wing.

Overhead, swallows performed their amazing aerobatics and pied wagtails rocked back and forth insecurely on the boulders by the water's edge; away in the distance we might hear the bark of a collie rounding up the kye.

Like country bairns everywhere, we made endless daisy-chains and necklaces of rose-hips, blew dandelion clocks, chewed the leaves of sorrel, sipped nectar from honeysuckle spurs and white clover, and tested each other with butter-cups under the chin, relieved to see the faint golden reflection that proved we did indeed like butter. We plaited green rashes into little baskets, made dolls' umbrellas from the fragile Scottish bluebells, and from the brittle stems of bracken cut the tiny facsimile of an oak tree. There was a profusion of wild flowers in spring and summer . . . anemones and cowslips in the woods, kingcups and forget-me-nots by the burns, pansies fluttering in short grass, creamy meadow-sweet, the yellow potentilla, prickly thistles by the roadside, and the purple knapweed which we thought resembled artists' brushes. Spring brought dangling catkins to the Manse Brae; in autumn we gathered nuts from those same hazels, cracking them on a stone and devouring the kernels on the spot.

There were in the Tamnafeidh fields a mixed lot of cows, black, brown, white, and combinations of these colours, that grazed knee-deep in buttercups and daisies, switching their tails in the heat of a summer's day with stoical indifference to the world around them. The Blue Cow was different, not only on account of her blue-grey hide but of her temperament. She was aggressively unbovine and would glare and come after us with pounding hooves, and, having scattered and scared us out of our perspiring skins, would suddenly resume her quiet grazing as if buttercups would not melt in her mouth.

When fodder was scarce, the old hand-chopper hidden away in the barn, would be brought into use. I remember the old turnip-cutters with scythe-like blades attached by an iron ring at one end to a wooden stand. Chopped turnips were carried to the fields and laid in shallow troughs for the sheep; so were hard, brown locust beans, which we sampled. Their very name and strange appearance created mystery. The flat pods, full of juicy pulp containing sugar and gum, imported from Palestine, were thought to have sustained John the Baptist in the wilderness.

Bird life abounded in the Glen in spring when the wild, wistful cry of the whaup was the typical voice of the moors, and the softer notes of the dipper made music by the river. Oyster-catchers, redshanks, and peeweets were every-where; skylarks had returned and the cooing of cushat doos could be heard in the trees. Peeweets, when they first arrived, were excitedly brimming over with the joys of spring, twisting, diving, falling in erratic aerobatics, but later they wheeled overhead when we crossed the fields, making wild swoops with a perpetual wailing cry

> Pee-weet! Pee-weet!
> Dinna rob my nest an' gar me greet!

In early May came the cuckoos and the corncrakes. Corn-crakes were numerous then, shy birds skulking in long grass, rarely showing themselves except at haytime. We often heard their harsh, grating cry, ache-ache-ing right through the night.

In May, cuckoos were calling from first light, flitting silently from tree to tree to resume their calling as soon as they were settled. The cock cuckoo is a dullish blue-grey colour. It is he who keeps up the musical but monotonous call. It lasts for a few weeks only, then he begins to stutter, and in no time, it seems, he is preparing to leave. No longer is the air filled with his call ringing from dawn to dusk.

| In April | come he will, |
| In May | he sings all day, |
| In June | he changes tune, |
| In July | prepares to fly, |
| In August | go he must. |

In autumn, grouse were calling 'Go back! Go back! Go back!' among the heather and crowberries, and the buzzard, at home 'twix Gairn and Dee, could sometimes be seen swooping and soaring and gliding like an eagle, though he is a much smaller bird.

Nobody went hatless in those days, even the loons wore bunnets, tweed affairs with broken peaks and the lining hanging out, the result of much kicking around. To go out-of-doors without a hat was, we were warned, 'just asking for a dose of the cold'.

As small children, Ellie and I wore in summer white muslin sun-bonnets, gathered and flounced and edged with lace. Later, our straw hats, as often as not, hung down our backs, caught by the elastic chin-strap. Once I possessed a stocking-cap of soft, knitted silk, called a cowl. It was striped in many colours, tapering to a pointed top that hung over loosely and ended in a tassel. I wore it twice. The Glen bairns thought it was a daft-like hat: tammies were the thing! Like the ladies in *Cranford*, our dress was independent of fashion, and, like them, it did not matter how we were dressed at home where everybody knew us. My clothes were often made down from dresses hoarded from my mother's trousseau, and Ellie's were mine handed down.

In winter we went to school warmly clad in woollen cloaks which fastened at the neck with a large hook and eye. There was no other fastening, so we put our woolly-mittened hands through slits in the sides and hugged the

cloak about us. On our heads we wore pink woollen
fascinators with bobbles, a cosy adaptation of the wisps of
billowing chiffon with which society ladies framed their
fascinating features. We carried round for the greater part
of the year a burden of clothing. First, a pair of long, neck-
high combinations, or a knitted vest called a semmet. Next
a flannelette chemise. Knickers were not then elasticated
but buttoned on to a bodice. Then came two petticoats, one
of which was flannel, and a dress. Over this we wore a little
jacket, forerunner of the cardigan, and a white calico pinny
with frills and epaulettes of Swiss embroidery. On our cross-
country tramps heather never scratched our legs for we
wore long black stockings held up by loops and tapes. My
mother knitted these in 'rig and fur' till we learned to knit
our own. She also knitted her own stockings, and my
father's socks, and re-footed them when necessary, and
unravelled part-worn knitted garments. She re-knitted this
wool and sewed together long strips to make blankets.
Indoors we wore soft felt slippers; out-of-doors black boots
with laces which were threaded through eyelet holes all
the way up; the ends were then passed twice round the
top of the boot and tied in front.

Boots were bought from Finlay Coutts, who had a shop
in a cul-de-sac near the Railway Bridge in Ballater. He
was known as the Soutar, the old Scots name for shoemaker.
Ellie and I liked to sit in the little shop which smelled
pleasantly of new leather, its shelves packed with shoe-boxes
from floor to ceiling, while my mother and Old Finlay,
white-bearded and patriarchal, gravely considered the merits
of various qualities of shoe-leather. The boots and shoes
were all made on the premises. Behind a partition worked
Young Finlay who must have been nearing fifty—a shy,
silent man bent over his last, the fragrance of leather,
varnish, and resin all around him. Lacing boots for adults
and children were quite plain, with perhaps a little fancy
stitching on the toe-cap.

Bootlaces had metal tags on the ends which we called

points. When points became detached through usage, we had to moisten the ends 'twixt finger and thumb to make a point fine enough to go through the brass eyelets. As soon as our new boots were brought home my father placed them on his cast-iron stand which had three iron feet of different sizes, to take the boots of men, women, and children, on which he fitted our boots while he hammered in curved studs in strategic places to take the first strain of hard wear. They were called Blakey's Steel Protectors.

Boot polish was not then available as a liquid or cream. Blacking came in the form of a semi-solid sausage; an inch or two was cut off and pounded to a paste in a saucer with a little water. This was applied with a brush, and when dry rubbed with another brush till the leather shone. My father cleaned all the family footwear. He brushed with vigour, making a hissing noise similar to that approved in the grooming of horses. He was of the opinion that a little spit enhanced the final polish, a custom dating back to his boyhood when it was very common, hence the expression 'spit 'n polish.'

Boarded-out children in the parish were provided with good boots and warm clothing by the Glasgow Poor Law Authority. The girls were issued with head-shawls of shepherd's plaid, which they discarded as soon as possible, demanding tammies to be 'like thae country yins'. They talked incessantly of a way of life that was strange to us. They spoke of the Poor's Hoose and the polis, of tenement-life and closes, and street-games of which we had never heard. They used a skipping couplet:

> I like sugar, I like tea,
> I like sitting on a black man's knee.

Their Glasgow accent sounded droll in our ears, as our way of speaking did in theirs. They soon stopped saying, 'Ah'll tell the teacher, so ah wull', for that was clyping. They learned to say 'I will nut' and 'I will sut', and to swear solemnly 'as shair's death'.

Among them was Katie, who at ten had the face of an old woman, and a frame that spoke of rickets and mal-nutrition; and Jamie, who was described as just a wee sharger, but, years later, proved to have courage in his under-sized body, enlisting in the Bantams of a Glasgow Regiment and marching off to war; and there was Maggie, who arrived with ringworm, and wore on her shaven head a close-fitting cap indoors and out. The Glen folk were kindly foster-parents and all the children thrived. When their school-days were over some of them were content to find employment on neighbouring farms and returned to the Glen from time to time; some married and never left the district; others speedily found their way back to Glasgow and were never heard of again.

We had few formal treats, and these we enjoyed in anticipa-tion and long after they were a thing of the past. Such an event was Bostock and Wombell's Menagerie, which pitched its tents one summer on a grassy strip on the bank of the Dee near Ballater. Several of us travelled there one sunny afternoon, and, having paid threepence each for admission, wandered round the cages to gape at the pathetic wild animals . . . only the elephants were free, and they were paraded round the big marquee giving rides to a few venturesome bairns. Small boys who lacked the money for admission peered under the tent-flaps till chased away by irate showmen. The show was on a very modest scale but we thought it well worth the money! In high spirits we chased each other round the outside of the big grey tents, jinking under taut guy ropes before setting off for home.

We often heard of the wonders of the cinematograph, forerunner of moving pictures, but never attended such an entertainment; but I do remember one enchanted evening when a magic lantern show was given in the school by a professional showman, who recited for our benefit the substance of the stories pictured on the crudely-painted lantern-slides. Audible waves of wonder rippled over his audience as he told the short and simple annals of the poor city children whose way of life we dimly understood, whose plight seemed unreal. There was the Little Flower Girl underneath the gaslight's glitter, pleading 'Won't you buy my pretty flowers?' There were ragged crossing-sweepers, and street urchins who warmed their blue hands at burning braziers, and clamoured for hot baked potatoes from a barrow. Most pitiable of all was the Little Match Girl, lovely and unloved, standing in the bitter cold, glimpsing through a lighted window a group of fortunate children making merry at a Christmas party, while she was forced to strike her matches one by one in a pitiful effort to keep warm. Alas! she was found next morning, lying frozen in the snow, her last match gone.

Communal social life was largely regulated by the moon, and as the school was the only meeting-place, events were planned to take place on Friday when the school-week was over, and to coincide, if possible, with the full moon. The school Christmas treat was always held in November before the first snow-fall. Donations were collected and a useful present bought for each child, such as a muffler, handkerchiefs, warm gloves, or a tammy. Names were attached and the gifts hung, unwrapped, on the tree.

As children were seldom out after dark, the night of the Christmas tree ranked as high adventure. However dull the day might be, we assured each other, 'It'll be fine the night!' and it always was.

Skipping restlessly round our parents, quivering with excitement, Ellie and I at last stepped out on the mile-long road which we were about to tread for the third time that day, and which took on a glamour unknown in daylight hours. Giant trees loomed up in the woods, the river had a new voice, every little sound was magnified and our eyes gradually grew accustomed to the different densities of darkness. We developed a kind of night-sight and, with my father leading the way with a lantern in which a candle flickered inadequately, we knew no fear.

As we neared the school we saw approaching from every direction, down the well-worn tracks which connected farm to farm, the lights of stable-lanterns converging on the school; the music of the pipes came to meet us, Jamie Smith having a blaw in the playground, and at last we all trooped in. The school was ablaze with light, we thought; there were at least half a dozen oil-lamps hanging on the walls. The huge pine tree, its tip nearly touching the ceiling, stood in a corner hung with colourful presents, but without tinsel or glass baubles. From it wafted the fresh, invigorating scent of the pinewoods. Speculation on the future ownership of the gifts helped to pass the waiting-time, for everybody arrived much too early. The proceedings began with a Con—sert in which every child took part. A temporary stage had been erected on trestles with a solid pair of steps at one end. A middle-aged gallant gave a helping hand to the girls; the boys left the platform with a flying leap which was part of the fun.

From the age of six, my mother taught me a new song every year to sing at the concert. The first was a charming little song very suitable for a small child to sing in a quavering treble.

> Tiny little snowflakes in the air so high,
> Are you little angels floating in the sky?
> Robed so white and spotless, chaste and pure as love,
> Are you little creatures from the world above?
>
> Whirling on the pavement, dancing in the street,
> Melting in the faces of the ones you meet;
> Loading all the housetops, painting all the trees;
> Cunning little snowflakes, little, busy bees!

She later taught me 'Robin Redbreast', A Child's Song, by W. Allingham, the music by Claribel. The refrain runs

[127]

Robin, robin redbreast, O Robin dear,
Robin, singing sweetly in the falling of the year.

I also learned 'Cuddle Doon', written by Alexander
Anderson, known as 'Surfaceman', a little-known poet then
living in Kirkconnel. He died in 1909. In later years I
learned 'Ho-Ro, my nut-brown maiden' (and privately
thought Ho-Ro an odd name for a girl), 'The Lass of
Richmond Hill', and 'Killarney'. Then I went off to
boarding-school where solo performances were fortunately
not expected of any but girls who had special singing-lessons
from the visiting master.

The first part of the Christmas tree programme ended with
the distribution of gifts, and tea dispensed from an urn
boiled at a nearby cottage, and fetched by fathers in the
audience. Mugs were handed out, and pokes whose contents
never varied . . . a 'soft biscuit' which resembled a morning-
roll with an umbilicus, a bap encrusted with sugar crystals,
a cookie and a cake. The latter could be one of three . . . a
sponge-cake with a paper bandage round it, which gave it
its name of a 'sair heidie', a triangle of shortbread called
a petticoat tail (from *petit gatel*), or a queen cake (or Prince
of Wales cake) containing a currant or two. Men carried
round the big tin tea-pots, so heavy that two hands were
needed to lift them, and poured strong tea into out-held
mugs, which had then to be balanced on the sloping desks.
It was a miracle that under such cramped conditions nobody
was scalded. When all had finished and the loons had pelted
each other with half-eaten buns, they blew up the empty
pokes and burst them with gratifying bangs. Juggies were
collected, litter gathered up, and the concert resumed.
Nobody paid more than a shilling for the entertainment,
including tea. Children were charged half-price. What
followed was well worth an extra shilling. The schoolroom
had now to be cleared. Desks were carried outside, the
platform removed, and the floor swept and prepared for
dancing.

A dance arranged without a concert was designated a ba-all. I was never present at a Shepherds' Ball, which was organized by a self-appointed comma-tee, but I heard of the coming spree from the maids at the Manse, who talked of this and the new blouses in which they would blossom forth, for weeks before and after the event.

The name was probably a survival of the custom of an earlier day when there were bigger flocks and plenty of shepherds to celebrate the end of a successful year with the sheep, but, by the time of which I am writing, Farmers' Ball or Ploughmen's Ball, would have been equally appropriate . . . anything for an excuse for a ball. Young men and rosy fair maidens with not-so-quiet eyes attended from miles around, and it followed the pattern of the dances which were part of all social gatherings, except that, being free-and-easy frolics, they took place in barns as often as in the school.

When people had to make their own amusements, a social meeting, or soirée, was a welcome get-together when the busy season was over and folks were prepared to enjoy an evening's relaxation. A soirée (swarrey or sor-ee) comprised a concert mainly of local talent, augmented by contributions from guest-artistes who came from Ballater in a hired 'machine'. They used the classroom as their retiring-room, being ushered in with ceremony and vociferous welcoming cries when their items were announced from the Chair. All performers sang unaccompanied. My mother was happy to teach many a young woman who had never before sung in public, to be an acceptable soloist. She favoured the Auld Scotch Sangs . . . 'I'm owre young tae mairry yet' was a great success, so was 'Logie o' Buchan', and 'Willie's gane tae Melville Castle' . . . the last-named sung by the Torran girls. I can see them yet, with the necks of their new green blouses reaching to their ears, buttressed by whalebone stiffeners, and their hair, in the current fashion, piled on the top of the head and adorned with fancy combs. There were solos, duets, and fiddling, but the star was Charlie Mackenzie, who invariably did a comic turn. Wearing a lum hat and a tattered coat, he carried a shilleleh with which he menaced his audience, thumping the platform, grimacing and mouthing strange sounds while the women and children squealed, and the lads at the back whistled encouragement. He maintained his speech was the Gaelic. Off stage, Charlie was the courtly gentleman who assisted lady singers on and off the platform. David Rogie was another star turn, acclaimed at every soirée for his rendering of 'The Tinkers' Waddin'', with its lively refrain,

> Drum-a-doo-a-doo-a-day,
> Drum-a-doo-a-daddin' o,
> Drum-a-doo-a-doo-a-day,
> Hurrah, the tinkers' waddin' o'.

A favourite duet was 'The Crooked Bawbee' and another was 'Huntingtower', both on the theme of the long-lost lover returning to claim his bride.

At the conclusion of every item there was much tramping of feet and loud cries of 'CORE'.

Tea was served, as always, from the big tea-pots into large earthenware mugs, with the inevitable bag of buns, and when this was over the floor was prepared for dancing by making the boards slippery with shredded candlewax.

Women and girls sat self-consciously on forms placed along one wall; men and boys in unaccustomed collars and neck-ties and Sunday suits ranged themselves on the opposite side of the room, facing the girls in their finery. There were no 'home perms' in those days, no wigs or hair-pieces, but every female-body, from the oldest to the youngest, had freshly-washed hair wonderfully crimped and curled with the aid of rags and curling-tongs.

The fiddles tuned up, the smoky wall-lamps were forgotten as the Master of Ceremonies made his opening announcement . . . 'Gentlemen, take your partners for a Highland Schottische!' At once there was a sound like a stampede of cattle on a Western ranch; skidding across the intervening space, each man made a dash to secure the partner he had marked when looking the girls over. He crooked his arm, offered it to her with a bow and mumbled 'May-I-have-pleshur-of-this-dance?' At once, she took it and they joined the Grand March, conversing politely as they moved round the room. When there were enough couples in the parade the signal was given for the dance to begin, and when it ended the lady was escorted back to her seat, her partner bowed low and left her. Soon the dance was in full swing, the piper with one foot thrust forward tapping in time with his music, and the toes of seated folk tapping in appreciation. There were reels, waltzes, quadrilles, and lancers, when the men delighted in whirling their partners off their feet. There were 'The Flowers o' Edinburgh', 'Petronella,' 'The Triumph', and 'Rory o' More', besides the Circassian Circle and the Waltz-Country-Dance, a restful slow dance for four to the tune of 'Come o'er the stream, Charlie'. There was gaiety and friendly chaff. The strident music, provided in turn by fiddles, bagpipes, melodeons, and mouth-organs, the odour of sweat and paraffin, the smoke from many pipes of Bogie Roll, the stamping of heavy boots that made dust rise from cracks in the floor-boards, the clapping in the lancers and the hooching in the reels . . . all contributed to an atmosphere of abandonment and enjoyment; even the elderly birled on the floor, the old men hooching as loud as any, while all laughed and twirled to Kafoozalum, Cawdor Fair and Tullochgorum.

Fizzy lemonade in green glass bottles, and ginger ale in stone bottles were available, and conversation lozenges. Jock could buy his Jenny a tuppenny poke of sweeties that cost sixpence a pound. From time to time it would be announced that Miss J. or Mr B. would 'favour the company with a song'. A lass would produce the sang-book she had in readiness, or a farm-lad would consent to render a bothy ballad. Sitting on the end of the big desk, with arms folded and feet swinging in the true tradition of the corn-kisters

[131]

(who drummed their heels on the corn-kist in time to the music) the lad would sing in a nasal, indifferent tone, quite unlike his usual robust voice, one of the songs of the land . . . of ploughing matches, of feeing markets, harvesting, courting, and all the other occupations that made up the life of the countryside. One I remember well was the ballad of Johnny Raw, a guileless loon up from the country for a day in town, who was left literally holding the baby. All joined in the jeering refrain, 'And I wish ma Granny saw ye'. We had a different version at school which said:

> Johnny Raw shot a craw
> Took it hame tae his Ma-maw,
> His Ma-maw ate it aw
> An' left the banes for Johnny Raw.

The ballads which the farm-lads sang are now well known, having been collected, published and publicized, but when I was a child they were handed down by word of mouth from one ploughman to another, and were lengthy and uninhibited in sentiment.

Everybody at the dance was on their best behaviour, at least until midnight, when the Manse party, having joined in heartily said 'Good Night' all round and went home by the light of the fully-risen moon. I would not say that our presence had cramped the style of any of the young men, but it was whispered that after we departed the atmosphere became somewhat rowdy. Wilted collars were removed and dancing continued into the wee sma' 'oors. We had not seen any whisky-bottles but it was suspected that some were circulating among the men in the darkness of the play-ground. Their conduct became wilder as the night wore on; we heard rumours of bare-knuckled fights which took place to decide who should convoy a popular lass to her home.

At four o'clock, when dawn was breaking, after singing 'Auld Lang Syne', the revellers went home, changed into their working clothes, and went straight to their work in byre or stable. Yokin' time was 6.30, and men and horses had to be fed before that. Balls were not so frequent that they could not afford, once in a while, to lose a night's sleep. This seems a good opportunity to emphasize the plain fact that Auld Lang Syne is sung for the sake of days long since gone . . . since, since . . . not zince, and to implore sociable Sassenachs to refrain from pronouncing the words in a way that causes Scots to shudder . . . 'Old Lang Zyne'.

The Stirling Opera Company was the first amateur company to produce Gilbert and Sullivan operas. They produced *H.M.S. Pinafore* in 1880, and *Patience* and *Trial by Jury* in the following years. My mother, at the age of seventeen took the leading soprano parts and, as proved by her waistbelt of nautical blue and gold, which I treasure, achieved a 17-inch waist for her début as 'The Lass who Loved a Sailor'. A photograph shows her as 'Patience', a milkmaid in frilly muslin with a skirt that in those days must have appeared very short indeed. It was natural, therefore, that Little Ellie and I were nurtured on the score and libretto of many of Gilbert and Sullivan's operas. We were also made familiar with *Messiah*, *Elijah*, Stainer's *Crucifixion*, and operettas by Balfe and of Hamish McCunn, a young man of my mother's own generation who made a great success at the age of eighteen with a fine overture, 'Land of the Mountain and the Flood', and 'Bonny Kilmeny', a lovely setting of Hogg's poem.

From her well-worn copy of *The Northern Psalter*, new in 1872, we learned many fine tunes, including 'Crimond', which was not then well known. It was Sir Hugh Roberton and the Glasgow Orpheus Choir who brought it international fame.

My mother could not live without music and attended practices of the Ballater Choral Society. Even in the depth of winter she seldom missed a week, wading through deep snow, wearing (a daring innovation) a pair of my father's trousers, doing the double journey on foot and staying in the village overnight.

At the end of the season a Grand Concert was held when choral pieces were performed, and professional soloists were engaged.

At the first concert I attended, seated with my father in the body of the hall, two sisters were the special singers. Liberty gowns which fell straight from a yoke of lace were then in fashion, and the Ritchie Sisters were arrayed in flowing 'tea-gowns' of pink satin. I thought them very grand. Belle, the dark contralto, wore a posy of violets with floating purple velvet ribbons; Nellie, the fair-haired soprano, wore a corsage of roses and pink ribbon-streamers. On another occasion, Mary Garden, an Aberdonian with a Lowland name, graciously came to sing. She had had a Cinderella-like rise to fame and there was great excitement prior to her arrival. She was escorted with great gallantry by the President of the Society, and had a wonderful reception. She was a statuesque figure in a superbly simple white gown. Seventy years later I was to hear Maggie Teyte say, 'To me, Mary Garden was the real prima donna', implying, I believe, that she was regal and temperamental, but known to be kind and helpful to young singers. She sang at receptions held in stately homes in Edwardian days, and at the height of her career was regarded in America as the greatest opera singer in the world. She never married and when she died in January 1967, at the age of ninety-two, there were very few of her old friends left to mourn her.

One year, when Cowan's *Rose Maiden* had been the Society's winter study, my mother was invited to sing the soprano solo, 'Bloom on, my roses'. She also sang, at various concerts my father's favourites, 'Apperley Mill', 'The Old Countree', 'The Holy City' and 'The Lost Chord'.

I remember her book of Moody and Sankey Hymns from which she played her favourites. She had heard the evangelists sing in Glasgow, and had often sung their hymns at Baker Street Mission Hall in Stirling, where the audience consisted of poorly-clad people who did not care to attend church on that account, but were made welcome at 'The Mission' and raised lusty voices in the stirring hymns, such as 'Pull for the Shore, Sailor', and 'Hold the Fort'. My mother possessed a book called *The Thistle*, a miscellany of Scottish songs 'with notes critical and historical', compiled by Colin Brown and James Merrylees, whose names deserve to be remembered, for theirs was a fine achievement.

*The Songs of the North* was another collection, from which we learned 'Maiden of Morven' and 'The Skye Boat Song'.

'What will a child learn sooner than a song?' asks Pope. My mother had the same idea. She held a little singing-class at the Manse every Saturday afternoon, which all the children in the Glen attended, primarily to practise hymns to swell the praise on Sundays. This class became an institution. Progressing from hymn-singing, it undertook a cantata called 'Christiana', based on *The Pilgrim's Progress* with my father giving the connective readings.

Year after year my mother trained a succession of boys and girls, encouraging them to sing solos at the little concert she gave in her drawing-room at the end of the session, inviting all the mothers to come to hear their offspring perform, afterwards providing tea and cake. With the aid of a modulator on which she taught the sol-fa system, a lined blackboard on which she drew the notes of bass and treble clefs, and with a small tuning instrument which sounded the keynote at the turn of a screw, she made certain that every child understood the elementary rules of music.

She taught us a wide range of songs including 'The Bonnie Banks o' Loch Lomond', but only in later life did I understand that the high road and the low road are not highland tracks but highways of the spirit. The words of the song refer to two Jacobite soldiers imprisoned in Carlisle Castle after the '45. Eventually one was pardoned, the

other sentenced to be hanged on the Gallows Hill at Harraby. His true love walked all the way from Lennoxtown,
beneath the Campsie Fells, to plead for his life. She arrived
too late but was permitted to stay by his side to comfort
him at the end. The words attributed to the doomed man
are intended to convey that his fellow-prisoner would take
the high road to liberty, while he took the low road to the
gallows, but his spirit would be in Scotland where he and
his true love were ever wont t'gae.

From one of our young maids I learned snatches of songs,
such as 'After the Ball is over', 'The Tin Gee-Gee', 'The
rich man rides by in his carri-age and pair', and a nameless
ballad about a maiden whose lover 'has ta'en her by her
lily-white hand, and by her waist sae sma' ', and then he
took his little pen-knife and cut her lily-white throat. Not
long ago a friend assured me that the words are from an
ancient ballad beginning, 'Fair Rosianne has tae the green-
wood gane'. He recited six or more verses, one of which
began,

> He has ta'en her by her snaw-white hand
> And by her waist sae sma',
> And he has ta'en his will o' her
> Afore she got awa'.

He was

> Lord Alvin's ae only son,
> Newly returned frae the sea.

And she, distraught, cries

> If ye be Lord Alvin's ae only son,
> Then what's tae become o' me,
> For I am Lord Alvin's ae dochter
> An' he never had anither ane but me.

# CHAPTER EIGHT

# THE SABBATH DAY

To walk together to the kirk
With a goodly company,
To walk together to the kirk
And all together pray.
          Samuel Taylor Coleridge

No one in the Glen indulged in a long lie on Sunday; the keeper had his dogs, the crofter his cow, the farmer his beasts, and all had to be fed; in the Manse it was the busiest day of the week.

We walked the familiar lang Scots mile, setting out soon after 9 o'clock for Sunday School followed by Divine Service arranged at midday to allow the farming community to attend to essential tasks, leaving time for even the most distant families to make their way to church.

My father taught the senior scholars, my mother the younger children. From her we learned 'The Lord's Prayer', 'The Apostles' Creed', and the Order of the Books of the Bible so that, in church, we could find our own places in the Lessons, and follow them verse by verse. She taught us the New Testament Story and gave us each a text to

[137]

memorize for the following Sunday. 'Texts' were pictures purchased in sheet-form and cut into inch-squares. Each square bore a text from the Bible and a coloured picture. Older scholars learned whole verses from the Bible, and were given unpalatable doses of The Shorter Catechism, which was intended to be theology explained by question and answer in simple language. The language was far from simple, and was away above our heads. To the first, easiest and briefest question in the thin booklet with beige covers, 'What is Man's chief end?' the answer was given without drawing breath, 'Man's-chief-end-is-to-glorify-God-an-tenjoy'm-f'rever'. Some questions were short, but the answers were long, and a severe test of memory. Mr Munro, a friend of my father, when staying at the Manse, had a dismal habit of making a schoolboy fellow-guest squirm at the breakfast table by posing in a stern voice questions from the Catechism, such as, 'George, what is Effectual Calling?', the answer, if he knew it, being totally incomprehensible to the lad.

I have always had a fellow-feeling for the bairns in that chuckle-inducing play about Scottish life less than a century ago, 'Bunty pulls the Strings', which Graham Moffat created round the Parish Church of Baldernock, in Dunbartonshire. One scene shows the blinds still drawn in the living-room in the afternoon, because it is the Sabbath. The bairns are caught peeping at the wee birds in their nest in the tree just outside the window, when they ought to be learning their Shorter Catechism. Rebuked by his outraged Papa, Rab protests, 'But I don't *unnerstand* it, Faither!' and receives the stern reply, 'Ye're no' *expeckit* tae unnerstand it . . . LEARN it!'

Before and after the Sunday School lesson we sang a hymn selected from favourites, such as Andrew Young's 'There is a happy land', 'Jesus loves me,' 'Golden harps are sounding,' 'There's a Friend for little children,' and one which has recently been adversely criticized by a minister,

[138]

> Around the Throne of God in Heaven
> Thousands of children stand,
> Singing 'Glory, Glory, Glory'.

With great gusto we sang,

> Onward, Christian so-o-o-oljers,
> One in charit—tee.

On frosty Sundays our breath mounted visibly with our voices.

Fortunately we did *not* have to learn any of Dr Isaac Watts' 'Divine Songs for the use of Children', which include Solemn Thoughts of God and Death, Thoughts on Heaven and Hell, and one Against Pride in Clothes, which begins,

> Why should our garments, made to hide
> Our parents' shame, provoke our pride?
> The art of dress did ne'er begin
> Till Eve, our mother, learned to sin.

and continues,

> How proud we are, how fond to show
> Our clothes, and call them rich and new,
> When the poor sheep and silkworms wore
> That very clothing long before.
>
> The tulip and the butterfly
> Appear in gayer coats than I;
> Let me be drest fine as I will,
> Flies, worms and flowers excel me still.

But the best known is about love between brothers and sisters.

> Whatever brawls disturb the street,
> There should be peace at home,
> Where sisters dwell and brothers meet
> Quarrels should never come.

[139]

Birds in their little nests agree,
And 'tis a shameful sight
When children of one family
Fall out and chide and fight.

Hard names at first, and threatening words
That are but noisy breath,
May grow to clubs and naked swords,
To murder and to death.

From an early age I had to play the American organ to accompany the Sunday School praise, which involved practising at home a new hymn every week, till my repertoire was fairly extensive, and included, 'There is a green hill far away'. It vexes me that to this day we sing 'without a city wall' when 'outside' would scan as well and convey the meaning more clearly, eliminating confusion in child-minds. Personally, I accepted the statement that, apparently, the city had no wall; nor was I troubled by that notorious Child She-Bear, but, before I could read, I believed that Willie Owen was His servant's name.

Unless there was a real blizzard we never missed the Sunday trek to church; that anyone under the Manse roof should even *think* of staying at home that day would have been as unnatural as not eating or sleeping. There are still a few who will remember the simple services in that quiet little church, and the sincerity that shone on the face of the pastor. His kind eyes had that calm look of inner peace which comes to men who have held communion with and have lived for years among the hills from whence has come their aid.

My first day at a church service must have seemed interminable to a child of three . . . I recall that I was lifted on to the seat in the Manse pew at the back of the church, and joined heartily in the singing, loudly la-la-ing throughout the hymns, and continuing a little longer than the congregation. Little Ellie was barely three when she was taken to church. I remember her snuggling in to her Mama's bosie and going cosily to sleep.

Children's contributions of the offertory were apt to be ha'pennies, sometimes called maiks or bawbees, old friends that came down in the world as the years went by, and are now pushed into oblivion. I remember one wee girl, who, at church for the first time with her grannie, Mrs Spence, was very bored, and half-way through the service, in an audible treble, piped 'Gie them their maik and let's awa' hame'.

The organ sat on a small stage directly under the pulpit. I was only ten when, in my mother's absence at the funeral of her uncle in Birkenhead, I was called upon to play it in church. I had always liked to experiment with the stops, as I had seen organists do in town churches. There were only four essential stops, but I made full use of the lot. Pulling and pushing lent variety to the performance from my point of view. I doubt if it made much impression on the congregation.

In a country parish the minister becomes the pastor of the place, not solely of the congregation; he gets to know every individual, is welcome in every home, whether the occupants are church-goers or not . . . so it was with my father. He was the father of his flock, not a being apart, and was judged not merely as a preacher but as a good neighbour and a conscientious visitor, especially of the sick and aged. Nothing vexed him more than to hear that someone had been ailing and he had not been informed. Once when this happened, my mother remonstrated with the wife of the sick man. 'He should ken withoot bein' telt', was the curt reply.

He devoted a great deal of time and thought to the preparation of his sermons . . . no last-minute homilies for him! Every one was carefully revised and written out in longhand with, at the top of the front page, the date and place where the sermon was delivered. He was on friendly terms with colleagues over a wide area, and was often invited to an exchange of pulpits. In his time, he preached in most churches in the Presbytery and further afield. He was a stickler for punctuality and, at times, when bicycling against wind and rain, would arrive perspiring, but never actually late, because he always set out in ample time. He must have given of his best, for he was invariably invited back.

Though overfond of introducing quotations from the classics and the lives of great men like John Stuart Mill and Livingstone, he did bring a variety of studied subjects into his sermons; unlike a Donside minister of an earlier day who, it was alleged, preached on The Widow's Cruse in every pulpit he occupied.

> An' through the Cabrach an' Strathdon
> He fairly ca'd the weeda on;
> Up through Forbes an' Tullynessle
> 'Twas aye the weeda an' her vessel.

On weekdays Glen farmers wore corduroy breeks supported by galluses. No collars were worn on the heavy cotton striped shirts, a brass-topped collar-stud glittered in the front of the neckband, and in winter a cravat was added for warmth. They might show a light stubble of beard, but never on Sundays. On Saturday night every man shaved in preparation for the Sabbath, when they donned their Sunday blacks. Most of them turned out to church in tail-coats, and hats of a type rarely seen nowadays, except in pictures of John Bull. The younger men wore cloth caps and home-spun suits with waistcoats, and preserved a more-or-less respectful silence while their seniors discussed stock and crops, all sitting under the trees in the church grounds till the bell stopped ringing, when they trooped in just as the minister emerged from the vestry and paced up the aisle.

The pitch-pine pulpit was placed midway between two tall narrow windows at the west end of the church. The minister ascended a short flight of stairs, entered the pulpit by a door and faced the congregation with his back to the

windows. On either side of the pulpit was a horse-box type
of pew, with a door and fixed benches round a table; there
was a similar one at the back of the church for the minister's
family and friends; the remainder of the pews were benches
set in rows on either side of a central aisle.

Womenfolk took their seats after a brief chat at the door,
long before the minister entered. The older women wore
black bonnets tied under the chin, adorned with jet and
knots of ribbon, similar to those worn by Queen Victoria in
her declining years. Like her, too, they wore short black
capes, or fitted dolmans, braided, beaded, and edged with
frilling or fringe, according to the means and taste of the
wearer. Under the dolmans were high-necked, close-fitting
bodices hooked down the front, the hooks concealed by folds
of satin. Their black skirts were edged with brush-braid
where they swept the ground. Every douce body wore black
kid gloves and carried a very white folded handkerchief, and
a sprig of appleringie tucked into the broad elastic band
which encircled her Bible. She had a few pan-drops for the
sermon in her pooch, which was a deepish pocket inserted in
a side seam of her skirt. In summer, she would pick at the
church-gate, a sprig of eglantine, that sweet briar which is
scented in wood, leaf and bloom or, perhaps, one of the
fragrant Scotch roses growing nearby.

In the summer months, the gentry from the Shiel, as the
tenants of the shooting-lodge were called, augmented the
congregation.

The Crewdson family from Alderley Edge, who had the
tenancy for many years, attended regularly and filled
several pews, including those occupied by the coachman and
his family, and half a dozen members of the domestic staff.
Attendance at church was taken for granted in that household, and Mr Crewdson, from his corner seat facing the
door, cast an observant eye over the pews to note how many
members of the staff were in their places. He and his
family of sons and daughters and grandchildren in procession, were preceded into church by Mrs Crewdson, a

majestic figure like a ship in full sail, her voluminous skirts trailing with the frou-frou of silk upon silk, as she made her stately way up the aisle. Her elegant bonnet with osprey feathers and her dolman elaborately embroidered with beads and bugles enhanced her air of a grand duchess.

The Metrical Psalms were sung with real fervour to well-loved tunes, such as 'Stroudwater', 'Palestrina' and 'Coleshill'. The Hundredth Psalm was, of course, sung to the 'Old Hundredth', and always will be, I trust, by one generation of worshippers after another. 'O send Thy light forth' is forever related to Invocation, and 'Ye gates, lift up your heads' to St George's, Edinburgh.

Beloved in Scots kirks for generations, paraphrases like 'O God of Bethel', and 'I'm not ashamed to own my Lord' have now been included in *The Church Hymnary*. Oft-sung hymns were 'My faith looks up to Thee', and 'Rock of Ages', besides a great many that are universally sung at the present day.

In pronouncing the Benediction my father raised both arms from his sides and the wide sleeves of his gown were spread like wings. He said a prolonged 'A-a-amen', though many ministers favoured the softer 'Ay-men'. In 'The Lord's Prayer' he prayed, 'Forgive us our trespasses' though, to this day, 'debts' is more familiarly used in Scotland.

The Sacrament of The Lord's Supper was celebrated once a year, on the third Sunday in July. There was a Service of Preparation on the preceding Thursday, called the Fast Day, when tokens were issued to those who intended to take Communion. The Fast Day was religiously observed, not as a day of actual fasting, but comparable to the Sabbath Day when no unnecessary work was done. On the Saturday prior to Communion, a woman was paid three shillings to spring-clean the church and from the Manse we carried to the church the Communion Plate, which consisted of two pewter goblets and two plates, one for the cubes of bread cut in readiness and wrapped in a napkin, the other for the offertory which only on Communion Sunday was taken at the door.

We spread long strips of white damask on the flat bookboards on the left of the aisle and secured them with tapes; on the right were sloping bookboards on which no cloths were spread. Non-communicants sat there. The Communion Wine, which cost 2s 4d a bottle, was decanted into the goblets and covered, ready for the elders to carry to the communicants. The bread and wine were dispensed by the minister at a white-clothed table set below the pulpit. During the solemn service in a packed church, for every able communicant attended, bees buzzed at the sunny windows and the scent of roses wafted in at the open door. The service lasted for an hour and a half. Afterwards the Kirk Session revised the Communion Roll; then, while my father carried the Sacrament to aged people in the vicinity, we helped my mother to remove the cloths and put the tokens back in their box. Tokens were then in use in hundreds of kirks in Scotland. They were a warrant of character for admittance to the Sacrament, and were collected by the elders at the church door prior to the Service. Inevitably, some were not handed in, and as they were not given to all and sundry, the possession of a token indicated a measure of respectability. The Glen token was a disc of lead cut into a rectangular shape with a chisel, and roughly indented with a punch. It bore the letters MK, signifying 'Ye Thrie Parochines of Glen Muick, Tullich and Glen Gairn', which came under the charge of one minister in the early part of the seventeenth century. Tokens were gradually superseded by printed cards.

In winter an ugly black cast-iron stove stood upright in the middle of the aisle and was fed with coal, which then cost 1s 3d a bag. It sat there in unsightly state, with a tall pipe that went straight up through a hole in the ceiling and gave out reluctant heat and a peculiar smell, which mingled with the sanctified odour of old Bibles and hymn books and the coconut matting which was laid the entire length of the aisle. When my father was ordained, the collection was taken in a wooden ladle, a plain, painted deal box, with a ledge on which a coin could be placed if change was required, and a long handle which reached along the pew. This was replaced by a red plush bag mounted on oak, with short handles, made by my grandfather. It was in regular use for seventy-three years. Within living memory, the custom of expecting change had not quite died out. I heard a true story of an elder at the plate in a south country kirk, who was annoyed by a member of the congregation habitually seeking change and contributing only a penny. 'O, ay, I can gie ye change', he said, one Sunday morning, 'but we canna stand here Sabbath efter Sabbath giein' change wi'oot a bit o' profit; there's yer penny . . . the ither eleeven can lie in the plate tae pey for past business.'

Squeaky shoes are a thing of the past, and the saying that boots that squeak have not yet been paid for has long been obsolete; but I remember when men's Sunday boots had a persistent squeak, very noticeable when the elders were taking up the collection. Lavinia Derwent puts it, in the words of a child,

> An' jings, when it's time for auld Rab tae come roon,
> Wi' the plate in his haun' an' a squeak in his shoon,
> He rattles the siller for a' fowk tae see,
> An' I'm gey sweirt tae pairt wi' my Sawbath bawbee.

There were no Rabs rattlin' the siller among the Glen elders; I remember them all as sincere and reverent, with a natural dignity.

My father always wore a dog-collar and black clothes, which he ordered by post from Vanheems and Wheeler, London specialists in clerical garb. He cycled in a short jacket, but on all other occasions wore a long coat, and detachable, starched cuffs with links. On high days and holidays he added a clerical vest of ribbed silk.

Winter after winter he turned out in a heavy, dark blue

Inverness cape inherited from my grandfather. With this over his black clothing, strong boots, and spats for extra warmth, woollen gloves and a balaclava helmet under his soup-plate hat, he faced the elements. Although there were days when his legs were rain-drenched to the knees before he had travelled very far, he never missed a Sunday.

When, owing to snowstorms, only two or three were gathered together, he held a service in the vestry, Donald Grant acting as precentor and leading the praise in 'I waited for the Lord my God' to 'Ballerma', his favourite psalm tune. On one or two occasions no service could be held because the minister alone turned up. Wallowing in snow up to his 'oxters', it must have been disheartening to find nobody at church when he got there, but on days when the surface was beaten down and frozen over, the going was easier.

In summer, when pulpits were exchanged, he often preached in Glenbuchat, on Donside. The kirk there is a little gem and well preserved, though no longer in use as a church. In my father's time the Glenbuchat minister's name was Spark. When he first preached in the Glen, old John Fleming, who was a sermon-taster and critic, and had a pawky wit, was heard to remark, 'Thon meenister may be a spark, but oors is a lowe'. This indirect tribute to my father's preaching did not mean that John was ever satisfied with his sermons. In his opinion 'the meenister is aye owre hopefu'; he should gie's mair hell-fire an' brimstone', but this was foreign to my father's teaching. His theme was ever the Love of God.

In days long before he entered the ministry it had been a well-known practice among preachers of the old Calvinistic school to thunder and rage in the pulpit, loud in the denunciation of SIN, and eloquent in the promise of hell-fire for sinners. To the delight of many an old body who sat entranced by the performance they would 'ding the dust oot o' the poopit cushions'. One such minister, by his continual thumping, scattered his notes and lost the thread

[147]

of his discourse. Searching and fumbling, he kept repeating 'And fifthly, my brethren . . . fifthly . . .' till a cailleach in a pew immediately below the pulpit handed up a sheet of paper, audibly remarking, 'I doot I hae yer fifthly, meenister!'

My father knew of an old woman who had a harassing life and told her minister she enjoyed coming to church because only on Sundays had she 'sic a saft seat an' sae little t'think aboot'. Such a one was Maggie, who was 'on the parish', and worked on a Glen farm for her keep and a trifle to keep her in sweeties. All day and every day she carried pails of water from the Gairn, and toiled and moiled in the woods, felling birches and hauling them back to the farm. There, in the stick-yard, she hacked and sawed, and never did one see her take a rest. My father said compassionately that she was the epitome of the Biblical hewer of wood and drawer of water. Church was her only relaxation. She attended regularly, and daundered by the waterside till we would overtake her, greeting us with a cheerful grin and pleased to have our company on the remainder of her journey to her cheerless home. Toothless and scanty of locks, she appeared to be well on in the sixties, but she cannot have been more than forty then, for, more than fifty years later, she died at the age of ninety-four.

The epitaph of a tired woman who died in 1744 may here be appropriate:

Here lies a poor woman who always was tired,
She lived in a house where help was not hired;
Her last words on earth were, Dear friends, I am going
Where washing ain't done, nor sweeping, nor sewing,
But everything there is exact to my wishes,
For where they don't eat there's no washing of dishes;
I'll be where loud anthems will always be ringing,
But, having no voice, I'll be clear of the singing;
Don't mourn for me now, don't mourn for me never,
I'm going to do nothing for ever and ever.

On the way home, on a springtime Sunday, my father delighted to watch the swift flight of the oyster-catchers and to hear their shrill whistle. It was a sign that winter had gone when they appeared, having moved from the sea-coast gradually up-river from the Dee to the Gairn, and so to the upper reaches of both rivers. They arrived in March and stayed with us till June. My father would point out how they were not easily seen when perched on a wet boulder in the Gairn, their plumage seemed to blend into the background of dark stone and foaming white water, but it was boldly black and white when they were on the wing.

On an average Sunday it was nearly two o'clock when we arrived home, hungry as hawks; in winter we were content with a tea-dinner of bread and butter with tinned mince or tinned tripe heated over a hastily-revived fire. Both were very appetizing fare. We had to eat in haste for very soon boys and girls appeared at the door and were taken up to the study for my father's Bible Class.

In summer, my mother gave our house-party jugs of lemonade, made with Eiffel Tower crystals, biscuits and cake, before we all set out for church, and on our return, our visitors declaring themselves ravenous from their unaccustomed two-mile walk, we sat down to summer Sunday lunch of cold roast sirloin of beef (what the butcher once tenderly described as 'a bonnie wee roastie') with new potatoes and peas from the garden, 'Fruit Puddine' with jelly, tinned fruit and, perhaps, a melon.

As children, we had none of the deprivations of a Calvinistic Sunday. We were not forbidden to read, or to look at picture-books, but we could not play any of our usual games or sing a secular song. We could, however, 'play at churches', using the organ-stool as our pulpit, and an enormous bound volume of the Minutes of Proceedings of long-forgotten General Assemblies as our pulpit-bible. When we were very small, after lunch my father would say to us, 'Be good, now,

and Mama will sing to you', then, sitting by the fire in the
nursery with us at her knee, she sang the hymns she had
loved as a child, 'Sweet hour of prayer', 'In the sweet by-
and-by', and our special favourite,

> When Mothers of Salem their children brought to Jesus
> The stern disciples drove them back and bade them
>   depart,
> But Jesus saw them ere they fled, and sweetly smiled
>   and kindly said
> 'Suffer little children to come unto Me.'

It was part of our Sunday ritual, unchanged throughout our
early childhood. Later, regardless of weather, we went for a
family walk, always by the same path, the road to Balno,
where old blackthorns lined the bank, their lifeless branches
shrouded with greyish-white lichen. There were days when
spring rain in icy blobs stippled the water-splash at the gate,
and roadside cow-parsley was blanched with scudding rain.
When the long-stemmed cowslips appeared on the Manse
brae, and anemones with rain-fresh scent in the woods, we
could not resist picking a few though they wilted before
we reached home. The colourless juniper bushes turned
grey-green, with green berries like capers which turned to
blue with a fine bloom on them. My father and mother
walked arm-in-arm, my father in great good humour
swinging his staff and decapitating tansy-heads.

Sometimes we visited the ruined chapel and forgotten
burial-ground in the heart of the birkwood, the last resting-
place of the Macgregors who owned the lands of Dalfad
in the seventeenth and eighteenth centuries. My father
endeavoured to keep clear the inscriptions on the grave-
stones which time and the elements have now completely
obliterated. He used to point out the headstone on the grave
of the priest which was the only one within the ruins, and
told all our visitors how, at one time or another, there
were Macgregors in Delnabo, Recharcharie, Torran, Dalfad
and Inverenzie, fairly small lairdships which gradually

passed into the hands of bigger and richer landowners. The Macgregors were Highlanders to the core; the most famous was Calum Og who added Ballater to his lands in Glen Gairn but did not keep it long.

On our Sunday walks we took great pleasure in the company of animals . . . a baby rabbit hopping across our path, a wary hedgehog which curled itself into a spiky ball when my father gently touched it with the tip of his staff, a bird swaying on a branch, all added interest to our stroll. The Froggie's Pool was an unfailing source of attraction. In spring when they congregated there for spawn-laying purposes it was alive with the creatures. Little Ellie took some in her hands, fondling them as she did all wild things, murmuring, 'Bonnie wee froggies'. We sat on the bank and watched the croaking mass at their antics, and were amused when some appeared to be carrying others on their backs. 'Are they playing leap-frog?' I asked, innocently, but got no answer. Our parents did not believe in giving nature-lessons of that kind. A very small trickle of water flowed into the pool and kept it full. In a few weeks it was chock-full of frog-spawn and still the continuous croaking, and then one Sunday we found all the frogs had gone. So we transferred our attention to the frogs' eggs; later the pool was alive with tadpoles and we watched them grow into bonnie wee froggies.

Ellie and I were taught to be obedient in the true Victorian way of life; we were not encouraged to ask questions or to think things out for ourselves. 'Wait till you're older, *then* you'll understand', said my mother in reply to any awkward question, so we grew up ignorant of the basic facts of life, though at the age of seven I had acquired some very confused ideas from fragments of un-printable songs sung, when gathering sticks, by a servant lass from the clachan of Piperhole.

Every day at the Manse began and ended with family prayers, which was called 'The Reading'. My father read a portion of Scripture, waling it, like the Cottar, with judicious care, then we knelt at our chairs while he prayed aloud for blessings, guidance, and forgiveness. My mother did not kneel; she sat in the low crimson-buttoned chair which had been her mother's nursing-chair, and bowed her head without disturbing the baby in her arms. As the child grew, she still remained seated, with her knees slightly apart and in due course Little Ellie knelt, her face buried in the well thus created in my mother's ample lap. When we were older my father persuaded us to read alternate verses, and ultimately to read the whole of the chosen chapter.

Every morning we knelt at our bedside to recite, 'The morning bright with rosy light has waked me up from sleep', and prayed 'Bless Papa, Mama, Sister and all my friends'. At bedtime again we knelt and repeated

> This night when I lie down to sleep
> I pray the Lord my soul to keep,
> If I should die before I wake
> I pray the Lord my soul to take.

with a plea for further blessings on family and friends. For years I added a silent prayer, 'Lord, let me not die this night'; I did not want to die before I waked, for there were many things I still hoped to do.

To this nightly expectation of death, borne out by continual reading of Victorian children's books in which, on the last page, a good child expired very gently of an unnamed malady, must be attributed my state of being excessively prone to a sense of sin. We heard a good deal about Hell, the Wicked Place, the kingdom of Satan, who waited round the corner to ensnare us. 'Satan finds some mischief still for idle hands to do', quoted my mother, who could not tolerate the sight of us doing nothing, and immediately devised some occupation for our idle hands. She taught us the hymn 'Yield not to temptation for yielding is sin', and exhorted us to say, 'Get thee behind me, Satan', when tempted to be naughty. I firmly believed that when we merited a scolding it had been Satan's work.

Friends perpetually wondered aloud why my father never took up fishing when the Gairn wimpled so invitingly within earshot, and the burns were full of speckled trout, but he only smiled.

His chief interest lay in the spiritual well-being of his people, in observing all the duties of a parish minister, and in preaching the Gospel as he believed it. He found all he needed in his parish, his garden, and the world of books.

All his life he was profoundly interested in education, eager to impart to the youth of the parish book-learning and book-keeping, which he considered would be useful to them in after life. He lent from his overflowing shelves to old and young, the classics, books on travel, history, and the lives of the famous, and held informal classes in his study, his own interpretation of Further Education. What an old woman once said of Samuel Rutherford Crockett might also have been said of my father, 'He affen comes into ma hoose, sits doon aside me an' cracks awa', speirin' hoo I'm gettin' on, an' askin' gin I've read the books he lent me. He's no' ane o' the kind that's aye spoutin' aboot religion bit he aye lives up tae it.'

He was Chairman of the School Board which had been formed on the passing of the Education Act of 1872, and noted the progress of every scholar. His interest in each member of every family in his flock was almost patriarchal; he followed their careers when they grew up and left home. On a train journey he would point out to secretly-amused fellow-travellers Sandy's signal box, Watty's farm and the place where Jock used to work. Some emigrated to harvest wheat in Saskatchewan, Manitoba, and British Columbia, and to set up lonely homesteads on the free undeveloped land offered to immigrants by the Canadian Government. My father obtained for them quantities of free literature and discussed with them their prospects before they took the great step. He entered in his log-book the date of their leaving home and the name of the ship on which they sailed. The maps in his atlas were heavily marked with indelible dots, each spot being associated with an individual, and referred to as Mary Mackenzie's village, Jamie Ritchie's town, or Johnny Kilgour's place. He kept a record of all their movements by close contact with their Glen relations, valued their personal letters and welcomed them to the Manse when, after long years, they came home on a visit. They remained unalterably his boys and girls. They gave inexhaustible material for his unfinished book on 'The Scot Abroad'. It was his favourite topic for leisure hours on which he read widely and was constantly bringing his information up to date; though he had no thoughts on publishing he gave many lectures on the subject. He found a kindred spirit in William V. Jackson, a Glasgow jeweller twenty years his senior, who wrote:

> The Scot abroad, though seas divide
> Still wafts his thoughts to home;
> Not spreading leagues nor rolling tide
> Can bind the exile's heart to hide,
> To rest and yet to roam.
>
> His pride is to be Scotland's bairn,
> Tho' banished from her breast,
> Tho' of her soil, hill, strath and glen
> She spared no foothold's space,
> She breathed the birthright of her men,
> And bade his brave heart win again
> The battle of his race.

It was of such men that my father wrote and spoke, taking the title of his lecture from that poem.

As a boy he had enjoyed *The Boy's Own Paper*, and for light reading had a liking for magazines and short stories such as the tales of old salts by W. W. Jacobs, that harbour-master who never went to sea. He had the first number of

*The Strand Magazine* in 1891, which contained the reproduction of a sketch done by Queen Victoria five years before,
published with the Queen's permission. Early numbers of
*The Strand* had on the cover a picture of that famous
thoroughfare, and an old-fashioned gas-lamp. Other periodi-
cals which came to the Manse were *The Leisure Hour*,
*T.P's Weekly*, *The Windsor Magazine*, and *The Quiver*.
My parents read *The British Weekly* all their lives and had a
high regard for its distinguished Editor, William Robertson
Nichol.

In 1898 they were among the readers of *Pearson's
Magazine* who were revelling in Cutcliffe Hyne's series of
stories of 'The Adventures of Captain Kettle', and I can
remember the cocky little captain with his pointed beard,
his aggressive chin, and cap at an angle. I recall, too, the
orange covers of the magazine and the Cover Girls, pretty in
their be-feathered hats, looking coy on a swing, showing an
inch or two of lace petticoat.

For many years, from 1899 onwards, my father had given
to him, at the end of every shooting-season, by Mr Forder, a
tenant of the Shiel, piles of *The Badminton Magazine*. It
cost a shilling and was printed on paper of excellent quality.
Some of the articles were of general interest but, on the
whole, being a sporting magazine, it did not greatly appeal
to my father who knew nothing of the technicalities of
sport. Advertisements in some of those old copies make
amusing reading and present a certain picture of the times.
There was 'Glen Livet' whisky at forty-five shillings per
dozen bottles, 'soft and mellow, carrying the wild rough
scent of the Highland breeze'; and at thirty-seven shillings
per dozen, 'Islay' whisky, 'with its peculiar peaty flavour
acquired by drying malt in a kiln heated by peat-fire'. There
was also a cheaper whisky called 'Lowland Malt', at 2s 9d
per bottle. Advertised too, was cream for use in shaving
without water, conjuring up a picture of my father wielding
a brush in a lather of yellow soap, scraping his face with a
steel cut-throat razor, his chin projecting stiffly.

[155]

Burberry suits with testimonials to their efficiency in the wet season of 1896 would hold no interest for him, nor would Horse Powders for Pedigree Hunters, but he probably found diverting the published views of General Gordon, Lord Lytton, and Bishop Hall on the condition of the human stomach, and their personal tributes to 'Eno's Fruit Salt, Nature's Own Remedy'.

Paperbacks are nothing new. Mrs Henry Wood wrote over fifty novels and my mother possessed a dozen or more in a paperback edition called *Macmillan's Sixpenny Series*, published in 1902.

She also had *John Halifax, Gentleman*, written by a lady who married her publisher and became well known as Mrs Craik. This was one of three hundred sixpenny paperbacks published by Routledge in 1896. She was a great lover of Scott's novels and made witty reference to her best-loved characters, one of whom was Baillie Nicol Jarvie. She often made use of his sayings, quoting 'a' the blessings o' the saut market', 'I'm fair forfochen', and advising us to 'keep a calm sough'. My father read and re-read his beloved classics, appearing to find mental refreshment in pages which he knew almost by heart. Stacked by his study chair, near his *Red Letter Testament* and *The Holy Bible* were Cruden's *Concordance*, Cassell's *Dictionary*, and other works of reference. He always bought the latest edition of *Pears' Cyclopaedia*, which had the flags of the Empire and the flags of foreign countries, in colour, on the inside covers. It was crammed with information on miscellaneous subjects, potted biographies, maps galore, and all for a shilling. He was never content till he had traced an unfamiliar place on the map, or found the meaning of a new word. He encouraged the habit of 'let's look it up' to help our pronunciation and general knowledge, and in the *Dictionary of Phrase and Fable*, *Familiar Quotations*, and *The Book of Days* I learned a great many words that gave me a quaint vocabulary. I have no recollection of the magic moment when I realized I could read. 'Without ready-made entertainment, children in my day were obliged to turn to the perusal of fairy-tales, romance, and history for the stimulus of the imagination which broadens the mind and widens the horizon', wrote Lady Mary Wortley Montagu, who professed to have largely educated herself by being turned loose in a well-stocked library. She continued, 'A child will not want new fashions, nor regret the loss of expensive diversions or variety of company if she can be amused by an author.'

Over a hundred years later how true I found her words!

Several times a year we had a visit from the colporteur, a venerable old man who wore a wide-brimmed felt hat and a black cloak lined with scarlet which nearly swept the ground. His successor wore breeches, more practical attire for tramping the by-ways selling books and tracts, from the box covered in black American cloth which he carried on his back. Everybody in the Glen read a great deal in the winter evenings, and everywhere he was hospitably received. From him my father bought books for birthdays and Christmas, Sunday School prizes, the 'Line upon Line' and 'Peep of Day' series, and a Victorian tear-maker called *A Peep behind the Scenes*. From time to time we had from the black box *The Prize*, a readable little paper produced by the publishers of *Chatterbox* which survived it by many years. We read *Gulliver's Travels*, *Robinson Crusoe*, and *The Pilgrim's Progress* in W. T. Stead's 'Books for the Bairns' in pink paper covers, costing a penny or tuppence. Out of the box, also, came *Eric, or Little by Little,* by Dean Farrar, *Jessica's First Prayer* by Hesba Stretton, *The Lamp-lighter* by Maria Cummins, as well as *Little Folks*, *Little Dots*, and *The Child's Pictorial*, also *Christie's Old Organ*, and the stories of Juliana Horatia Ewing, which would appeal to children still were it possible to obtain copies of *Jackanapes* and *A Flat Iron for a Farthing*. We appreciated book-gifts and thus acquired *Black Beauty*, *Aesop's Fables* and *Rab and his friends*. I cannot remember when I first met *Alice* but the drawings were by Tenniel, and I pored for many an

[157]

hour over *Uncle Tom's Cabin*, being haunted by the picture of the intrepid Eliza negotiating the ice. My mother did not like to see me continually with my nose in a book except in the evening when the day's work might be said to be done; she did her own reading then. Her spare time, as a girl, had been spent on needlework, and she considered that reading was a waste of time when one could be doing a useful job about the house. My father had no such ideas and from an early age I was allowed free range over the books in his study. My reading was mixed and, to a great extent, unsupervised . . . not always a wise policy, but in my case it answered pretty well; I read everything I fancied, and nothing I ever regretted. There were bound volumes of *Chambers' Journal*, *Good Words*, and *Blackwood's Magazine*, a complete edition of the works of Dickens, all Scott's novels, and a great many biographies. I read *The Mill on the Floss*, *Silas Marner* and *Adam Bede*. Off the shelves I picked Ralph Connor's *Sky Pilot*, and the works of Silas and Joseph Hocking.

I was, by inclination, a solitary child, dreamy and introspective. 'To be solitary without loneliness' says James Drawbell, 'is one of the gifts of childhood.' Andrew Lang craved only 'a houseful of books and a garden of flowers'. I was fortunate . . . I had both. I carried a book wherever I went, preferably to the farthest corner of the garden, out of sight and sound of all but the birds. 'Always read, read, reading!' my mother would exclaim in exasperated tones when at last I came forth from my retreat and dreams of palaces and perilous seas and faery lands forlorn. Indoors I was much given to browsing, lying prone on the study floor in uncritical contentment; I even took a book to the bathroom, remaining there in blissful seclusion till my mother called me to 'come down from the library'. She possibly resented my self-sufficiency, and my 'creeping away', as she called it, to be alone. Little Ellie's need of her every hour of the day was something she understood and cherished. I sometimes wonder how much my parents guessed of the world of fantasy in which I spent my days, of my imaginary adventures in woods and fields, of the flights of fancy that made a living thing of the old elm by the garden wall that creaked and groaned and almost spoke to me when the wind attacked its leafless branches. I never passed it without a friendly glance, believing it liked to be noticed.

# CHAPTER NINE

# GLEN FOLK

He sees the blue smoke skyward curl'd
From many a lowly glen hearth-stone,
Each with a pleasure and a pain,
A pathos and romance its own,
Each little house a world.

J. Stevenson

Seventy years ago I had from the pen of an old man, John
Reid, some recollections of his boyhood, and quote from his
letter:

I remember the old priest well, the Rev. Lachlan
Macintosh. He used to come down from Ardoch to
Balno, where I was born, to fish in the Gairn.
Many a piece of black sugar I got from him. He was
born at Braemar, and educated at Valladolid in
Old Castile in Spain. When he was there the Duke
of Wellington passed through and offered com-
missions to any of the students who would join the
British Army. This offer proved too strong for
young Lachlan who changed the College uniform
for that of George III. Afterwards he returned to

Valladolid, and was ultimately ordained priest in the
Mission of Glen Gairn, Corgarff, and Balmoral. It
was his custom, once a month, to walk the long
distance to one of his stations, accompanied by a
crowd of Glen Gairn folk, reciting the rosary as
they went. An old parishioner was telling of this
one day to someone unacquainted with the district,
who remarked what a beautiful custom it was.
'Aweel, sir', said the old man 'wi a' the lads an'
lassies larkin' ahint, it wis whiles a gey roch rosary.'
Lachlan laboured in the Glen for 64 years, always
enjoyed good health, and was in his 93rd year when
he died. He left behind at the Auld Hoose at Ardoch
his two sisters, one aged 96, the other 91. After
his death, the coffin was taken to the chapel at
Clashanruich where it lay for a day or two, during
which time many strange visions and lights were
seen prowling round the chapel. He is buried in the
kirkyard at Fit o' Gairn. Clashanruich means 'the
hollow at the foot of the hill' . . . in this case,
Maamie. Superstition was rife among the Glen folk
at that time. I remember John Davidson of Balno,
a very decent man but full of superstition, set off
one day to the Braes o' Cromar. When passing Lary
in the early morning he met a man called Ally
Ritchie, who lived at Candacraig, and was said to
be an 'unlucky foot'. There was no way to avoid
him, so after wishing him 'good morning', John
went on to the burn saying to himself, 'I'll come
nae speed o' my errand the day'. There was no
bridge and, when crossing the stepping-stones, John
slipped and fell on his back, crying 'Sorrow tak' ye,
Ally Ritchie', and turned back and went home.

Next morning he went over Morven to the Braes
for fear he should meet Ally again.

I remember when sixty scholars attended the
school in a house at the Laggan, kept by a woman

named Meg Cattanach who was Lewie o' the
Laggan's step-mother. There was a cock-fight held
in the school every year. The scholars, accompanied
by their parents, brought the cocks, and all the
birds that were killed in the battle were claimed
by Meg.

I remember, too, when a hundred Glen Gairn
men would turn out to a funeral; and oh! the
marriages! There were no invitation-cards; the bride
bade her people by word of mouth and the bridegroom did the same. The wedding presents consisted
of eatables and drinkables. There were many little
farm-towns and crofts with illicit stills from which
whisky was smuggled on ponies to Braemar and
beyond. There was generally a special broust made
for a marriage, up one or other of the glens.
The fun began on the booking night; that was the
Saturday before the proclamation of the banns;
then there was the 'washing' of the bridegroom's
feet with soot from the chimney on the night
before the marriage. On the wedding day there was
piping, fiddling, and dancing, and the firing of guns
and pistols like a regular Waterloo.

It was then the custom in Scotland (and possibly in
Cumberland) to have at a funeral a black hearse with glass
sides drawn by black horses beautifully groomed, with coats
shining like satin, long tails, and on their heads nodding
plumes. There was no such custom in the Glen, but I saw
such a funeral equipage in Edinburgh, and there were
funeral horses stabled at Harraby Farm in Carlisle, some
six or seven years after the end of the First World War.
When the Harraby horses were not required at funerals
they were employed on other duties, one of which was taking
His Majesty's Royal Mail to, and fetching it from, the Irish
Mail Train, known to all as Paddy, as it rushed at full speed
at midnight through Carlisle on its way to Stranraer.

Funerals in my childhood were sombre occasions; every household seemed to share the grief of the bereaved. Invitations were delivered verbally by the eldest son, or nearest relative, who formally called at every house. On the day of the funeral the minister held a short service in the house, attended by immediate relations and friends, before the coffin was 'lifted'. In fine weather the black coffin was placed on chairs outside the door, then all the neighbours were able to gather round for the service. Every man who was able attended as a natural act of courtesy. On leaving the house the coffin had sometimes to be man-handled across ditches, over dykes, and along unmade roads before the road itself was reached. There stood the simple hearse, the mourners formed up behind it, and the cortège moved off to the kirkyard of St Mungo at Fit o' Gairn. There was great reverence and dignity about a funeral procession in years gone by. A stranger meeting one would stand, bare-headed, till it passed. Women did not take part in the procession or attend the graveside ceremony; they stayed at home.

When snow lay thick upon the ground there was no question of a hearse. From afar we often watched the straggling, black procession wending its toilsome way over the Glas-choille to Corgarff, or down the road to Fit o' Gairn. At such times the coffin was placed on a horse-sleigh, and if that could not be managed, it was carried all the way by the younger men who bore it in turns. At intervals an older man assuming charge of the party would call out, 'Ither fower', and four fresh men would step forward to relieve the tired bearers. So it went on, mile after mile. At the graveside, silence was observed, apart from a whispered word of direction regarding the allocation of the cords, a deeply appreciated honour. Weather-beaten faces showed no emotion beyond quiet, serious attention. It was a melancholy fact that all-too-frequently one funeral led to another. Old men caught a chill and were themselves carried off in a lamentably short time. My father used to suggest that they kept their hats on at the graveside, but they never

[163]

would, but stood with their scanty locks stirring in the chill air. After the brief interment service the eldest son, or a family friend, formally thanked the mourners for their attendance. In those bygone days every man appeared in decent black, with a lum or pot hat, but war shortages and clothing coupons changed all that, even the conventional black armband is now seldom seen. Motor-hearses and cars make the funeral journey less of an ordeal, but the old, unhurried approach to God's Acre seemed more reverent.

When she heard that someone had slippit awa', my mother used to go at once to offer comfort to the bereaved, for under her dignified and somewhat aloof manner she had a heart full of infinite sympathy and understanding.

She made a wreath of flowers from the garden to place on the coffin whenever she had the opportunity, arranging the lilies and other flowers in their season, round a circle of wire, with moss and greenery as a base. For a baby's funeral she made a little posy of snowdrops, cowslips, or violets on a background of ivy leaves. Her simple tribute was often the only one.

In the spring of 1902, I recall watching with her and other women, the burial of Young Brackley, Sir Allan Mackenzie's son and heir, from a distant spot in the wooded grounds high above the family burial-ground. He was an officer in the Guards who had died in South Africa and had been brought home. His funeral drew a crowd of quiet watchers, unseen in the wood. The gun-carriage rumbled over the uneven ground, there were muffled drums, and pipers played 'The Flowers o' the Forest'. His horse, with his boots reversed in the stirrups, followed the gun-carriage bearing his coffin under the Union Jack, with his helmet, sword, and badges upon it, and a company of soldiers moved as one with steady footfall. Six riflemen stood on either side of the grave and fired a volley into the air, after the flag was drawn away and the coffin lowered into the grave, and a lone trumpeter sounded 'The Last Post'. It all made a deep

impression on us in that crowd of silent sympathizers. My
parents felt it deeply for only a few months previously they
had been guests at a banquet and ball at Brackley, given in
honour of the young laird on the eve of his departure for
South Africa and had noted with gentle amusement his
boyish teasing of his mother, who laughingly flicked him
with her fan.

My father was intensely interested in the history of the
Glen, its associations with clan warfare and its connections
with freebooters and smugglers. He knew the names of all
the larachs from a study of the Ordnance Survey map; the
story of their former inhabitants he learned from elderly
parishioners who had heard it from their fathers; like many
in the lean agricultural eighties, some had gone to America
to seek security, if not a fortune. He was baffled by persistent
speculation regarding a family which had lived on the
barren moors beyond the Stranyarroch, and had departed in
haste without disclosing their destination or plans for the
future. Their neighbours, lacking evidence, simply jaloused
that they had, on the peat-moss, unearthed a hoard of gold,
possibly the hidden treasure of a duinewasal in the '45, and
had left for foreign parts.

There are many Flemings in Scotland, their name stem-
ming from the Flemish weavers and small farmers who fled
from the Low Countries when they were persecuted for
their religious beliefs. In very early times they settled in
Aberdeenshire, and their descendants found their way to the
Highlands where their skill in making arms was in demand.
Many men have written about the Flemish refugees and
their influence on Britain. From one, Arnold Fleming, I
quote: 'They improved our kail-yaird, taught us how to cook
vegetables, and generally raised our standard of living.
They were more than expert weavers and artisans; they
were intelligent people, ahead of their times in acknow-
ledging the value of education.'

There were humbler Flemish families in Glen Gairn,

Strathdon, and farther north, as may be gathered from a study of lists of Jacobite prisoners of the '45.

The Flemings of Auchentoul in Glen Gairn got their lands from the Earl of Mar after the Battle of Harlaw. Peter Fleming of Auchentoul, who survived the carnage of Culloden, was one of the few to escape with his life, for after the battle the wounded were butchered by order of the Duke of Cumberland. When the English soldiers approached Peter, lying wounded on the field, he feigned death while they removed his boots; afterwards he crawled to the safety of a cottage near-by. Eventually he returned to the Glen bringing with him as his bride the girl who had nursed him back to health.

John Fleming was the last of the Flemings in the Glen, short and broad-shouldered, with whiskers outlining his cheeks, the last of the local worthies, and immensely proud of his Flemish ancestry.

He cultivated by the sweat of his brow the stony slopes of his croft at the Shenval, ploughing with horse and stot in double harness. The land was poor and he must often have felt dowie and frustrated, but he was not one to grumble.

One disastrous day the stot choked on a piece of turnip and died. This was a severe loss, slightly offset by John's one and only entry into the butchering trade. A dead stot was worth money and could not be wasted. Word was sent round the Glen that fresh meat was for sale. Assisted by his nephew, Allan, John cut up the carcase, and all the guidwives flocked to buy. I remember the occasion well; it was my first experience of standing in a queue. There was strong competition among the customers, for fresh beef was hard to come by at the best of times. John rationed the meat as he thought fit. My mother wanted half the beast's head to make the brawn that in Scotland is called 'potted heid'. John had other ideas. 'Tell her she's no' t'hae't', he told his helpers. He could afford to be autocratic, and had it in mind for another buyer. His sister, Babbie, who kept house for him and her son, worked hard on the croft, as all country women had to do. From dawn till dusk they toiled . . . milking cows, feeding calves, pigs, and poultry, baking, cooking, washing, and cleaning with only primitive aids; they lived and died in harness.

Old Mrs Ritchie of the Torran, who wore on weekdays a mutch and black knitted capelet pinned across her bosom, finished all her housework and milked the cows the night before she died. I shall always remember her calm, indomitable figure, coping in her late seventies with the milking and the calves and moving slowly back to the house with her pails, then setting to and turning out a batch of oatcakes for her men-folks' supper. It was she who lost a daughter very tragically on the afternoon of 6 January 1902. May had gone to Kirkstyle to collect her repaired shoes from the baker's van which had brought them from Ballater. They were her best sheen and she wanted to wear them on Sunday, or she might not have ventured out, for there was a high wind and all the burns were in spate. Incredibly, she was swept away in the Torran burn which normally was little more than a narrow ditch. It was thought that she must have slipped on the plank which spanned the burn. William Duguid of Tamnafeidh passing by saw her body tossed over the waterfall into the Gairn and ran to the bank hoping to reach it, but it was borne swiftly away in the swollen river.

There is none so leaden-footed as the reluctant bearer of bad news; William, dragging his shocked footsteps homewards, met my father who with him carried the news to the Torran, and then to Balno to set in motion the dragging of the river. My father described to my mother the terrible sensation of dead weight in his limbs as like trying to run in a nightmare and making little progress. The river was dragged daily for many miles; every man and boy turned out to work in relays in the search.

Every Sunday we sang special hymns and the bereaved were remembered in prayers from the pulpit. It was feared that May's body had been swept out to sea. It was not

M                    [167]

recovered till over three weeks later, a local man had a dream that it would be found on an islet at Cambus o' May . . . and it was.

I must have seen many farmers sowing oats by hand, dipping first one then the other, into the canvas creel slung round his neck and shoulders, but it is Willie Ritchie, May's brother, who I remember best. The steady, methodical stride up and down, the rhythmic swing of the arms, in and out in a sweeping movement till the whole field was covered, was fascinating to watch.

Old William, his father, a canny old man who smoked a black pipe with a silver lid on the bowl, had no liking for the singing of Amen at the close of hymn-singing, which my father had introduced. He used to vie with William Mackenzie of Belnaan in seeing who could sit down the faster. They occupied opposite pews across the aisle and kept a watchful eye on each other. When the last word of the last line of a hymn was being sung there were to be heard simultaneous resounding thuds, which indicated to all present that once again the two Williams had made it a draw.

'Proochey moo', from the French *Approchez-moi* was, I believe, the familiar call to cows at evening milking time in many parts of Scotland, and 'Treesh, treesh' in others, but the auld wife o' Torran called 'Trose, Trose!' till the cows with swaying udders heavy with milk, came slowly in response to her call, which is of Gaelic origin.

If we children were within earshot of the lowing of the kye in the late afternoon we lost no time in making our way to the byre and, leaning over the half-door, watched while strong hands pulled smoothly at the teats. The milking was invariably done by the womenfolk. Mrs Ritchie sat on a creepie, her head tucked into a warm flank, while the milk purred and foamed into the pail with a soothing noise. We helped to carry the full pails to the milk-hoose and were given a drink of milk warm from the cow. Everything in the milk-hoose had its place . . . the cogies and creepies, the big brown crocks that held cream, the milk-sieve of fine mesh, and beside it the skimmer which was a tin saucer full of holes which let the milk run through but would 'kep' the cream. There were egg-baskets, wide-mouthed crocks full of eggs pickled in water-glass, crocks for salt-butter, a buttermilk pail, and a sowans bowie. In every milk-hoose the upright churn stood on the floor. A certain knack had to be acquired before cream could be beaten into butter; the churn-stick had to be plunged steadily up and down, a slight twist being given at the same time till at long last a satisfying plop-plopping told that butter had formed. The stick was withdrawn with the churn-lid, and a pailful of water thrown over the butter to wash off surplus milk. The butter was placed in a large wooden bowl, turned and kneaded and carefully pressed by hand for, if any moisture was left in, the butter would not keep. Salt was added and more kneading done till all the minute air-bubbles had disappeared and the butter was satin-smooth. It was then weighed into pounds, slapped into shape by rectangular pieces of wood ridged on one side, which left a criss-cross pattern on the surface. Butter sold for about a shilling a pound.

In late summer, or early autumn, while milk was still plentiful, butter was put down for the winter months. Extra salt was mixed in, and the butter stored in brown crocks with a thick layer of salt on top. Cheese was also made, with milk fresh from the cow with rennet added, the curd separated from the whey and put in the great stone press, an important piece of equipment built into the wall of the farmhouse, or set outside the milk-hoose door. It had an immense screw at the top by which the heavy stone press was raised and lowered and pressure regulated. Crowdie was made with sweet milk curd and butter well blended, with plenty of carvies added, and pressed into a small bowl. When turned out it was very tasty, eaten with bread and butter.

Mrs Ritchie used to speak of her schooldays, and describe how the old dominie at Dalphuil not only caned the loons but 'garred the queyns turn roon an' lift their cots' before they, too, got the cane. I remember Dalphuil's old walled garden on a sunny day, the peony roses, the huge scarlet poppies, and many other old-fashioned flowers. There were a few hives of bees in the garden and a couple of cows in the byre. There was generally a honeycomb on the tea-table, a pat of fresh butter and boiled eggs in a china dish in the shape of a white clockin' hen with a red comb. It was there I first tasted beastie cheese, made with the first milk after a calving, boiled to a thick consistency, somewhat resembling new-made cheese, with the flavour of rich egg-custard.

Dalphuil means 'the field of the pool', a probable reference to a well-known salmon-pool in the Gairn a few yards from the cottage. It is the oldest building in the Glen, considerably older than the church nearby, which was built in 1800. Up to about the time of the Disruption in 1843, the minister was also the schoolmaster and lived and taught in Dalphuil, which, for long was known locally as the Old Schoolhouse.

The schoolroom was the kitchen with its cobbled floor and open fireplace in which a peat-fire burned brightly, maintained by contributions which every child was expected to bring daily. Small boys, weary of carrying a peat every day across the moors, were known, on occasion, to lift one from the dominie's own stack in passing, and, a moment later, to appear, the picture of innocence, on his doorstep with their offering.

After the Disruption, the schoolmaster was James Coutts who continued to live at Dalphuil after his retirement, which coincided with the building of a school and schoolhouse beside the church, in 1879. His son, William, a graduate of Aberdeen University, became Assistant Professor of Humanity there, and later, classical master at George Watson's College for Boys, in Edinburgh. In 1898 he published *The Works of Horace translated into English Prose*, which was used, for a time, as a textbook in the College.

Dalphuil was last occupied in 1930, and subsequently fell

into disuse, till, in 1938, Queen Elizabeth the Queen Mother, acquired the tumbledown cottage and had it restored as a picnic house for the little princesses. It is still a happy place for children and a royal retreat.

On 15 May one year, cuckoos were shouting away in the distance, and there was no other sound at all as I walked to school through the Manse wood with fear in my heart, and I never shall forget the day. Word had been circulated that a lunatic had escaped from an Aberdeen asylum and was being sought in the Glen. He had been seen early that morning not far from the Manse. Cold and hungry after a night on the hills, he had called at Ardoch and had been given milk and oatcakes which he ate standing. When a burly forester entered the kitchen the silent, restless man, taking him for a keeper, fled to the fields. All that day he was at large while our imagination regarding madmen ran riot, but in late afternoon he was found near Delnabo. We saw him being escorted back to where he had to go, not, alas! to where he felt he belonged . . . a tired, frightened little man whose brief taste of freedom was over. Mercifully, in the care of the mentally-sick, the words lunatic, asylum, and keeper are no longer used by thinking people.

There were in the Glen, as elsewhere, a few mentally-disturbed people who were called daft in a good-natured, sympathetic way. There was one simple-minded soul distinguished by the name of Graavats. A graavat is a cravat or muffler, and he wore in winter's cold and summer's heat a collection of these, all at the same time. At Loinahaun there was Sandy, who had periodic fits of melancholia and had to go away for spells of medical treatment. There were two eccentric sisters who each occupied one end of their but-an'-ben for years without exchanging a single word.

There was Willie who lived with his sister who was a recluse. His three brothers were always away with sheep and Willie would have fared ill had he not been given odd jobs like shawin' neeps at Balno, where he got ample food and a neighbourly welcome from the widowed Mrs Farquharson, whose sole help on the farm was Jock Kilgour. Willie, 'peer stock', had a muddled mind, stumbling speech, a shuffling gait, and a radiant smile. I can see him now, ambling along, dribbling in his beard, always beaming. His unchanging greeting to us children was 'Peer thing', which from him was a term of affection. Nothing gave him greater pleasure than a present of Bogie Roll from which he cut fragments, worked them round in the palm of his hand, and packed them into the bowl of his short clay pipe.

Harking back to John Reid's reminiscences, there were Ritchies still at Candacraig when I was a child. Malcolm Ritchie, a bit of a dandy, fifty years before Stanley Holloway ever thought of Little Albert, used to carry to church on Sunday a stick with a horse's head handle. Lewie o' the Laggan was then an old man, with his son, Charlie, working the farm (with the help of his son, Young Lewie) and his two daughters nearby. Laggan means 'a small hollow', an exact description of the situation of the cottage where lived the Mackenzie sisters, well known and respected characters. Maggie had seen something of the world of stately homes, and had witnessed the whirl of the London Season in Victorian days when she was a nursemaid in the employ of the Baroness Herries, whose little girl, mother of the present Duke of Norfolk, was her cherished charge. She talked of Miss Gwen, and life with the Herries family, and the house-parties of great ladies and fine gentlemen, to the end of her days. When her sister died Mary lived alone. One marvels how cailleachs and bodachs existed before the days of pensions. Too old to work, too proud to beg or to ask for Parish Relief, they lived frugally. Their welfare was the constant concern of large-hearted neighbours. The Old Age Pensions Act of 1908 gave needy folk five shillings a week. In the Glen they were actually able to live on this sum, supplemented by the hospitality of neighbours and occasional gifts from private benefactors at Christmas which my father was empowered to disburse. It was touching to see how gratefully they received the odd half-crown.

My father went regularly to Ballater to collect pensions for the aged and housebound, and for Charlie Timmer, who was neither, but being unable to read or write, could only 'make his mark'.

Mary Mackenzie fared well enough with milk and butter from the farm, and eggs from her own bonnie chuckies; besides, she was adept at taking, with a cleek of her own making, salmon from a pool in the burn which flowed within a few yards of her door. She saw no harm in this practice and had been known to offer a piece of salmon to William Ross, the gamekeeper at Candacraig. He, good man, would not have dreamed of reporting her activities.

She was by no means the only Glen body who knew how to take a salmon without rod, line, or permission. The Daldownie shepherd once showed us his home-made cleek, and we heard of a certain day when Douglas of Torbeg with a fish dangling from his right hand, was entering his house sideways because only one half of the door stood open. He happened to glance up at the road as he stepped inside, and with great presence of mind waved a cheery, left-handed greeting to the water-bailiff who chanced to come along at that inopportune moment. Jock Kilgour and other young men were not averse to 'borrowing' paraffin from the Manse, omitting to explain that they required it to make flares for poaching salmon in Pool Mary, a secluded, teeming pool in the Gairn below Lary.

The Mackenzies were followed at Inverenzie by the Shaws . . . he a staunch elder of the church—she a hospitable soul with a gentle manner and a wonderful way of coddling eggs. Their son, Robert, became one of the leading heavies in the country, competing with conspicuous success at all the important Highland Games. Their daughter, Margaret, became mistress of Balno, which means 'the new ferm-toun'.

Over the water from Balno, beside the Milton Burn, stood

the cottage where lived James Cameron with his wife and bairns, very conscious of his status as road-mender in the Glen. The stretch of road for which he was responsible was narrow, with numerous corners and hair-pin bends. From early spring till winter put an end to roadwork, James assiduously spread patches of broken road-metal here and there to fill up the worst of the holes. There was no road-roller on that stretch. It was assumed that passing traffic would in due course crush the metal into the road. Passing traffic, such as it was, contrived to avoid the rough patches, and it was left to the elements to do the work of a steam-roller. It was a solitary occupation, but James would not have changed with any man.

> Altho' he was poor, did not want to be richer,
> For all such vain wishes in him were prevented
> By a fortunate habit of being contented.

A stranger to the district, on foot, meeting James once casually observed, 'You won't see many people on this road', 'O ay', said James, 'there was a man yesterday and there's yersel' the day'.

He wore to church a tail-coat and black felt hat, and was prepared to hold lengthy discussions with my father on the way home. As he punctiliously read the *Aberdeen Free Press*, his head held a store of subjects for comment and argumentation, and in this stimulating way the meandering mile was soon covered.

Midway between Torbeg, 'the big hill', and Rinloan, 'The point of the meadow', still stands the cottage, Stranlea, locally pronounced Stran-lye. It faces Geallaig, 'the white mountain', with its back turned to Maamie, 'the little round hill'. The name was translated for me by William Ross who had the Gaelic, as Stron-liath (with the -th silent) meaning 'the grey nose', or, alternatively, Strath-liath, 'The valley of the grey river' . . . the latter being more appropriate.

For Meggie Bremner and her mole-catcher husband, who lived at Stranlea in my childhood, time had little meaning.

One day Old Bremner saw Douglas of Torbeg at work on his land and reproached him for 'plooin' on the Sabbath'. It was, in fact, Monday. He and Meggie had lost a day in sleep. He used to carry a bunch of knobbly iron traps and a half-moon spade, walking daily over a stretch of ground setting his traps with cunning. The following day he went over the same ground digging out the furry little animals that lay dead in the traps. While he was alive there was certainly no work for the itinerant mole-catchers who were employed farther south. There were, however, other types of Gaun-aboot-Bodies. Some would pay for the privilege of camping on a farmer's land, or for sheltering in his barn, by making horn spoons for him and his family. They made a spoon by softening a ram's horn in hot water, and moulding it with their hands. The small ones were called cutties and were intended for children's use.

There was Besom Jamie who came round regularly with besoms for sale, and slept in hospitable barns. To see him at his work it looked easy, but it was not a case of taking a bunch of birch twigs, tying them with string and putting a stick through the middle. He made birch brooms for outdoor use in the garden or round the steading, and there was a real knack in the way he tied his bundles of twigs together. He made besoms and pot-rinsers from heather, with birch-wood handles. The besoms were excellent for stone floors, and were very durable. The pot-rinsers outlasted many a manufactured article.

Charlie Timmer, whose real name was Wood, was another regular caller . . . in summer he called every week peddling bootlaces and matches, acquiring pokes of tea and sugar, and his tinny filled with freshly-made tea. He did odd jobs on farms, sleeping in shed or barn. When, as school-children in a gang, we teased him by shouting 'Timmer', he would feign anger and, shaking his fist, pretend to chase us.

Besom Jamie died, full of years, in the Aberdeen 'Poor's Hoose', and Charlie Timmer died of exposure on the Donside hills.

When the present century was in its infancy there were a great many tinks on the roads. Some set up primitive shelters called bender-tents, and while the men made pegs and other things for sale, and did a bit of poaching, the women tramped the Glen from end to end, stepping out at a steady pace; invariably, one had a shawl round her shoulders and tucked firmly under her left oxter, with a baby securely resting in the ample folds. Calling at every homestead, they proffered, in a typical whine, pirns and preens, combs and other small articles, as well as cans and pans.

My father visited all the tent-dwellers, especially if he saw children among them. Once he saw a couple with a baby camping by the Gairn near the briggie. He offered to baptize the baby and arranged to do this at the Manse. When asked about his marriage certificate, the man replied, 'O sir, we wis never mairret'. In due course the marriage ceremony was performed, the bride suitably decked out by my mother, then the baby was baptized, and the little family returned to their tent, carrying, among other things, a cloutie dumpling in lieu of a cake, with instructions to reheat it in their three-legged pot. This hung on a tripod outside their tent, and under it would soon be crackling a cheery fire of juniper and cowes.

While they continued to camp there, the man occupied himself in making sculls, the name given to a cradle-shaped basket with oval rim and rounded base; willows were inter-woven to make the body, and, for the rim, pliable strips of rowan or hazel. They had a ready sale in the neighbourhood. Farmers sought them for their potato-crop; my mother used hers for logs.

Not all our regular callers were tramps. Some were well-to-do. There was, for example, Mackie the Pig Man (pig meaning crockery), who went on his rounds in a pony-cart. He not only sold crockery, but gave it away in exchange for rags, rabbit and hare-skins which he examined very closely. A good skin was worth threepence; if it had been damaged he cut the price. He paid for them with a plate or a pudding-basin.

May Leys of Sleach was the last woman in the Glen to practise the homely arts of spinning and dyeing. There were two kinds of spinning-wheel . . . the small one at which she sat and operated it with a treadle, and the big wheel, with a diameter of three feet or more, at which she stood, gave it a tirl with her foot, and spun it with her hand. Spinning was skilled work calling for sureness and swiftness of eye and hand lest the yarn should vary in thickness and be either too fine or too coarse. The next process was that of twisting the single thread into three- or four-ply yarn. Before dyeing it had to be made into hanks because bobbins were too tightly packed to allow the dye to penetrate.

When May retired to Ballater she was often called upon to demonstrate to people interested in the preservation of rural crafts her skill in spinning wool off the sheep's back through all its stages, as she had done all her life at Sleach. She was pleased to display hanks of her own worsted, and to explain her methods of obtaining dyes from the flowers of broom and the poisonous ragwort, from bracken-buds, and the roots of cow-parsley and yellow bedstraw. She spoke of crotal, the dark grey lichen which she scraped off stones on the hillside, and gave a warm brown colour. Dockens, she said, made a beautiful black. Her dye-pots were enormous cauldrons. She had an unlimited quantity of rain-water, which is kinder to wool and produces purer colour than hard water. It was at Sleach that I first tasted rowan jelly, cranberry, and averin jam. May and her sisters, as children, every autumn were sent out to strip red berries from the rowan-trees, to take a clothes basket to fill with cranberries and averins from the highest slopes of the hills beyond their remote dwelling in the shadow of the Broon Coo, trudging home in late evening with their burden of berries after an exhilarating day on the hills. May had large capable hands, the stature of a man, and threw her head back to enjoy the heartiest laugh that I have ever heard. When we sometimes stayed with her in Ballater she would put a 'pig' in the bed and prepare a dish of sowans for supper. She liked a hand at whist, and would blandly enquire when the game was well-started, 'Fit's trumphs?'

Her speech was full of old Scots expressions. Doubtful ventures were 'nae mows'; she sounded the 'k' in knees and knot, and made free with diminutives. Wee wifies and lambies were terms of affection, a mannie was a slightly disparaging term, a moosikie was a very small moosie. 'Gweed be here!' was her reaction to surprising news.

To express disgust she grimaced and exclaimed 'Feech! Feech!' or 'Fooey! Fooey!' Speaking of her childhood she would tell us how some of the cailleachs made birk wine, to which I found a reference in a book published in 1832. 'Piercing the bark of the trees, they extract the sap of the birks, and by a curious process ferment the same and make wine of it, which is very pleasant to taste, and thought by some to be little inferior to wine of Champagne and other outlandish countries.' More explicit is Mrs Dalgairn who, in 1829, wrote 'about the end of March, or later if spring is backward, bore a hole in a tree and put in a faucet. It will run for two or three days without hurting the tree, then put in a pin to stop it. Next year you may draw as much from the same hole.' Her ingredients comprised sugar, almonds, raisins, and crude tartar. The cask had to remain bunged up for five months before the wine could be bottled.

May Leys knew all about heather ale, a popular home brew in olden times, which was made in August or September when heather was at its best. They filled a large pan with the purple flowers, covered them with water and boiled them for an hour. This was strained into a large wash-tub, and ginger, hops, and golden syrup were added. Again the mixture was boiled and strained, and yeast was added when the mixture cooled. The liquid after a few days was gently poured off, leaving the barm at the bottom of the tub.

Every farmhouse and cottage had its kailyaird, and there, too, were the gooseberry and currant 'busses'. Gooseberries were grossets. An expression borrowed from *The Fortunes of Nigel* commending a project, was, 'Fowk will jump at it like a cock at a grosset'. Oatcake was called cake or bread, baker's bread being loaf-bread. Thick bannocks were cooked on a brander, eased off with a flat implement and gently, because so friable, propped against the outer row of glowing peats to get their final toasting, the embers being constantly collected with long tongs to keep the fire at the right heat. I possess a relic of old Scots crofting life in the shape of a timmer caup . . . a plain wooden bowl of generous size finished with a metal band after the style of a cask. From such a caup bothy lads ate their brose with a horn spoon. They were of the opinion that it had a better flavour if the caup was first heated at the fire. All it got when empty was a rinse, the spoon being wiped and hidden in its own particular crack in the bothy wall, so that ownership was readily established. An old ploughman was known to give a halflin this canny advice . . . 'Steer the brose wi' the end o' the speen, syne dicht it on yer breeks an' sup up. Fan ye've feenished dinna wash the caup. Mebbe ye kin gie't a bit wash ilka sax month fan ye be't tae be fee'd til anither fermer.'

Farming folk toasted friends and neighbours with the words

A weel-stockit girnal an' a horn speen,
An' aye a tattie fan the tither's deen.

Cottagers fattened a pig for Michaelmas and cured their own bacon and hams which hung in butter-muslin bags from hooks in the kitchen rafters. In a farmhouse kitchen there was no room for anything but essentials . . . the box-bed, the press, the girnal, the hinged table folded against the wall behind the settle and brought down when required, and the chiming nock on the wall. The family ate at a scrubbed deal table. There were plain wooden chairs, creepies for the littlins, and one cushioned armchair for the gudeman. . . . The dresser had pride of place with its cupboards and drawers and scoured top, on which stood a rack filled with willow plates. From the ceiling, richly

[179]

tinted with the peat-reek of generations, hung the brass berry-pan, the cast-iron girdle and frying-pan. On either side of the wide hearth was a neuk with ample room for a stool. Sometimes the gudeman preferred to sit there in the chimney lug, the gudewife in her place on the other side, and there they would sit through the lang forenicht. The blacksmith-made sway was bolted to the inside of the lug and, crane-like, could be swung forward. It had a chain of stout links and varied lengths of crooks. On these the kettle and goblets hung. A paraffin lamp was usually suspended by a chain from the ceiling. The parlour was known as the Room, with bright linoleum on the floor, and a scattering of cloutie rugs to give it a couthie look, but a fire was laid in the grate only on special occasions like weddings and christenings. There was a saying that if you were invited to 'gae but', into the Room, courtesy was being shown, but if you were told to 'come ben the hoose', into the kitchen, you were being treated as a friend of the family. I can, therefore, modestly affirm that wherever we Manse folk went we were received as family friends for we seldom saw the Room. Few windows were made to open, but doors stood wide open except in the most inclement of weather. Neighbours faced with a closed door were not expected to knock and wait, but to lift the sneck and walk in sure of their welcome. One old body, Meggie Mitchell of Candacraig, who had taken to her bed early in life, and was waited on hand and foot by Annie, her devoted daughter, lay for a lifetime in the box-bed in the kitchen of her cottage. The small window did not open and most of the light which penetrated its tiny panes was excluded by an array of flourishing geraniums in pots on the wide sill. The air that reached her curtained alcove came through the open door. She lived to be a centenarian. Her bed-goon and frilled mutch, carefully goffered by Annie, were spotlessly white, and she had the fine, clear, transparent skin of one who never had to face the elements. She had never seen a railway-train, but she saw one of the early motor-cars, whose proud owner, the Laird, brought it close

to her window, so that, propped up in bed, she could behold
the phenomenon. In her latter years she was nearly blind,
and would peer up at us as we approached to enquire after
her health, and her reply never varied . . . 'Prett—y well,
thank you'. When she died, her daughter was already an
old woman. She had dedicated her whole life to the care of
her helpless mother and when deprived of her reason for
living swiftly declined in health of mind and body, and died
soon after.

Diligence, compassion, bravery in tribulation, goodwill
and Christian charity were predominant attributes of the
Glen folk, but it would be wrong to convey the impression
that all were warm-hearted, honest and devout; there were
some who stand out in my memory because they lacked
these qualities.

There was one mother who had the unpleasant habit of
ducking her children in the ice-cold water-barrel as punish-
ment for a misdemeanour. Another woman was so devoid of
maternal affection that if her son was late in coming in from
the fields for his midday meal he got none. He possessed no
watch, and tried to learn the time by peering in at the
window to see the clock, but when his mother discovered
this she hung a towel over the face of the clock and
continued to deprive the youth of his dinner. No wonder he
left home.

As a child I saw a man tie a dog's muzzle with string and
hang a log by rope from its neck to prevent it from jumping
fences; I saw him beat it with a spanner and send it limping
away, whimpering, head down with the weight of the log,
and in deep dejection.

There was a farmer who, long after other farms were
fenced, made his sons act as herds; bare-foot and underclad,
they stood out in the wind and rain till neighbours said their
blood was 'gealed'. They were 'sair hadden doon', cowed and
broken young men.

I remember a man, bluff and hearty in appearance, of
whom it was said, 'Fan he wins hame, he hings up his

fiddle ahint the door'. He had no fiddle. The saying meant that he kept his genial manner for ootbye, and was a tyrant under his own roof. It was rumoured that when his frail wife lay dying, he sat on the side of the box-bed, excluding light and air, puffing thick tobacco smoke in the poor woman's face. Like all country folk, neighbours turned out to give a hand at all crucial times in the farming year ('that's fit neebors are for') pre-eminently those connected with sheep. I can think of only one who was not a good neighbour . . . the farmer at Blairglass who, in the early years of this century, herded on to his own land any sheep which strayed over their natural boundaries, and obliterated their owner's mark, substituting his own. In course of time he was arrested, tried, and received a long sentence. In an earlier day he would have been hanged.

Glen folk were, for the most part, very healthy, but when there was a case of illness it sometimes happened that, on account of having to pay for medical attention, they sought it too late. This was the case when a girl of thirteen at Rinloan contracted diphtheria. When the doctor at last was sent for he summoned the ambulance, which, stationed at Aboyne, took four hours to arrive; meanwhile the child had died.

Consumption was another dreaded disease, not uncommon, in spite of the fine air. Young girls were said to have 'gone into a decline', or death was vaguely attributed to 'inflammation'.

A patient sufferer was Mrs Hay of Ardoch, who was immobilized for many years with arthritis in all her joints. When we visited her she would beg me to play her a 'spring' or two. Her chair would be wheeled through to the Room and there, on her old upright piano, I worked my way through a book of reels and strathspeys, from 'The Deil amang the tailors' to 'The Muckin' o' Geordie's Byre'. She would nod her head in time with the music, for she could not beat time with her painfully-twisted hands, nor tap her crippled feet. She attributed her disabilities to years of constant exposure to severe winter conditions when she was a girl. She spoke of wading through much deep snow, and though she always had a warm sark she had no drawers. She recalled how her bedraggled cots swished against her bare legs till they lost all feeling.

Women in the Glen did not work in the fields, as a rule, except at turnip-singling, haytime, and the hairst. The gudewife at Blairglass was, I recall, out in the turnip-fields a few days after her baby was born. She worked at the neeps all day, with the baby lying well-happit up at the end of a drill. As she worked from one drill to the next she transferred the sleeping infant to another sheltered spot . . . and a fine little red-haired loon he grew up to be!

# CHAPTER TEN

# THE FARMING YEAR

To everything there is a season, and a time
To every purpose under the heaven;
A time to plant and a time to pluck up that which
  is planted;
A time to cast away stones, and a time to gather
  stones together.

*Book of Ecclesiastes*

In the Glen, life assumed a rhythm dominated by the seasons which were clearly marked by the lengthening and shortening of the days; summer went out with the first autumn gales; winter was one long snowstorm after another. Each season brought its own work and its own way of life.

Sunrise being late in December, not till about ten o'clock were the hills flushed with a rosy glow but, long before that hour, beasts had to be fed and byres mucked out. Men stumbled round in the dark by the wavering light of stable-lanterns, using hessian sacks to protect them from the weather . . . one worn as an apron, another slung round the shoulders, and a third draped over the head.

There was a considerable period during the winter when

[184]

little could be done on the farms. The darkest mornings were round about Christmas-time and winter clamped down on farm life for a couple of months.

It was a fine sight to see from the Manse windows a herd of red deer trek across the white waste of Geallaig, with a noble stag in the rear. At the slightest sound of danger he appeared to move forward and lead the herd, with the hinds following, strung out in a long line. Only when desperate for food were they to be seen on the lower reaches in daytime. It was generally at night that they, and the mountain hares in their winter garb, came down from the corries where they normally grazed, driven by hunger to raid parks and turnip-fields.

My father was constantly absorbed in the weather, particularly as it affected the farmers' crops. He kept careful notes on rainfall, frost, and snowfall, and compared conditions with those prevailing at the same period in previous years. He quoted Dr Alexander Buchan, the Scots meteorologist who deduced from his scientific examinations of the temperature in Scotland that there are six spells during the year when the weather is colder than normal. In early February my father would remind us that 'this is one of Buchan's cold spells'.

> He loved all changes that the seasons bring;
> Enough for him the homely natural joys;
> The wayside flower, the heath-clad mountain rift,
> The foamy woodland, were his favoured choice.
> Each year with grateful heart he hailed the gift,
> The princely gift of Spring.*

After the thaw, the floods, and the driving rain, at long last the sun would shine on a still morning, with the first celandines out on the braes and all the birds singing. Soon the Glen would be alive with the piping of oyster-catchers, and the long-drawn-out lonely cry of the whaups.

All winter the cattle were chained in the byre, but when

* John Buchan wrote these lines about his own father, a country minister.

spring came they were let out to grass and raced round the fields with their tails high; the queys, known as coys, the young heifers, kicking their heels in excitement at their freedom. At first they were brought in early in case they should overeat, but through time they were brought in only for twice-daily milking and were turned out again to grass.

The birk-woods were wrapped in a haze of new green, their tops flushed with the purple bloom that comes to many trees at the first stirring of the sap; the ploughlands were drying out and farm work could begin. A hard-working farmer once told my father that he calculated that in order to plough a single acre in a nine-inch furrow he had to walk eleven miles; sometimes he ploughed an acre and a half in a day, say, a matter of sixteen miles . . . not straight-forward walking, mark you, but staggering along uneven ground, guiding the plough and controlling a pair of horses. It was particularly heavy work at the turning at the end of every furrow. The old ways were slow ways, but there was a sense of well-being and deep satisfaction in working with horses and farming by old-established methods which are in danger of being lost in this age of mechanization. A ploughman of the old school said not long ago, 'For rale gweed plooin' gie me horse every time; there's skill in wark wi' horse, bit tractors . . . fegs! Onybody kin drive thae things!' Notwithstanding the old man's prejudices, I am bound to admit that ploughing in the Glen in the old days was not the admirable operation it is now. On some crofts there were many windings around boulders, crooked ridges which had to be left unploughed, and consequently few straight furrows.

To plough a straight furrow had some meaning at the ploughing-matches, which were great occasions, intended partly for neighbours to give mutual aid, and partly to indulge in friendly rivalry. Owners of teams were proud to parade their horses decked with ribbon in their manes, with straw and ribbon plaited into their tails which had been allowed to grow long, shining brasses on their foreheads and harness, their haunches gleaming like satin. Every piece of harness was polished; ploughs were freshly painted and shone like new. The points on which the ploughing was judged were straightness, neatness, and evenness, so matches were held on level fields. The judges were brought in from another district; their decision was final, and not always appreciated.

> The judges cam' frae far an' near
> Tae pit them richt they had nae fear,
> Bit some wad say their sicht wis peer
> That day amang the ploomen.

I recall the hoeing matches, too, in the turnip-fields in June, speed and neatness being the qualifications for a prize. There was one farmer who had level fields but was notorious for getting behind with his work. He was a splendid organizer of an annual ploughing match and a hoeing match on his land, for any farmer on whose land a match was held got his turnips singled in record time at no cost to himself, merely the time involved in publicizing the affair, and in begging prizes from Ballater tradesmen.

Sometimes a tattie-bogle made of a crude, upright stick and crossbar, clothed in a tattered coat and decrepit hat, was placed in a field of turnips or newly-sown grain, supposedly to scare away marauding birds. It was doubtful if they accomplished much; crows are not easily deceived.

There are now a host of machines for cleaning and cultivating the land that had not been dreamed of in my young days. The only implements at that time were the plough, harrows, the turnip-sowing machine, the stone-roller, the scythe for cutting hay and corn alike, and the big rake that was pulled through the fields to gather hay and straw. Wooden hand-rakes took the hay clear off the ground; it was then tossed and turned and forked by a long-hafted, two-pronged fork into coles, like upturned Christmas puddings. I have read that, in their anxiety to make dry hay, some crofters ended by making ideal bedding and little else. They had such a dread of cole-ing the hay before it was sufficiently won, that to hasten the winning they tossed the stuff about till practically all the substance was out of it. It has been known for horses to eat the straw with which they were bedded rather than the hay in their manger because it was dry and fushionless.

After dotting the fields for weeks the coles were placed, one by one, on a low trailer and dragged by a horse to the stack-yard, or to a corner of the field to be built into a loaf-shaped stack called a soo. This was laid on a foundation of brushwood and built high in the middle at first, so that the hay would slope downward from the centre all round, and so keep rain from soaking and rotting it. Instead of back-breaking work with a scythe there came the days when a man could sit comfortably on a reaping-machine and be drawn round the field by horses. Today all is done speedily and efficiently by tractor.

After the advent of the horse-reaper the scythe was not immediately scrapped, but was used to prepare a road for the reaper round a field of oats or hay, and the hand-hook was retained for attacking nettles and tares.

In every farmyard there was a grindstone in the shape of a wheel, turned by hand, but a man using a scythe invariably carried a whetstone in his hip-pocket, and frequent honing was a well-known sound in the fields.

It was Dr Johnson, I believe, who remarked that one green field is much like another, but he knew nothing of the drudgery of farm-work . . . 'aye somethin' tae see til' . . .

> Kye tae milk an' neeps tae pu',
> Muck tae spread, an' parks tae ploo,

besides sowing oats and watching anxiously for the breer, the first green shoots to appear. They also grew bere which is not unlike barley. Bere-meal was used in the making of home-brewed ale, and some of the older folk enjoyed a bere-meal scone eaten hot from the girdle. Dr Johnson had never suffered the heartbreak of seeing a haycrop ruined by rain, hailstones dashing growing corn to the ground, or heavy rain laying a crop when it was nearly ready to cut.

The steading of most of the small farms was a comfortable huddle of outbuildings, the ferm-toun, comprising the byre, the stable, the cart-shed, the barn, surrounding the midden high and yellow with dung and wet straw. There was a feeling that the reek of wet dung piled on a cart and dropped in forked heaps on to ploughed fields was the very breath of the spirit of farming.

In spite of the saying,

To talk o' the weather's the folly o' men
For when rain's on the hill there'll be sun in the glen,

farmers continued to look at the early morning sky and give a fairly accurate forecast of the weather. A whirl of high-feathered cloud could mean wind; too much sunshine in the early hours with low, tight-packed clouds on the horizon were liable to end in dull weather by midday.

When the distant hills seemed to be clearer and nearer, then rain was sure to be coming, and morning mist was often followed by a warm, pleasant day. There was a pawky tendency to understatement. In expressive phrase, a smirr described the soft smudge that drifted over the hills and provoked a cheerful prophecy, 'I doot it's ganna rain'; a misty morning on Maamie was a wee thingie hazy, a real drizzle was a Scotch mist. If rain began to fall, they said, 'It'll mebbe be a shoo'er later on', and a drenching shower might elicit the laconic remark that it was saft, fair dingin' on, or even a rale coorse day. I doubt if much credence was given to the saying that

A red sky at night is the shepherds' delight;
A red sky in the morning is the shepherds' warning.

but they were undoubtedly knowledgeable regarding weather signs.

[189]

Ever since the Psalmist sang, 'Thy rod and Thy staff they comfort me', staffs, crooks, and cromachs have been the support and comfort of the traivellin' man, be he shepherd, farmer, keeper, or weary pedestrian on a lonely road. My father always referred to his staff and found it a comforting companion on the long miles he travelled round his parish. Shepherds' crooks had many uses. The staff was three or four feet long, made of hazel gathered in the woods in autumn and left lying about for a year or two till properly seasoned. The crook on the handle was made from a sheep's horn softened and shaped by boiling, and bent into shape while pliable. The long staff was used to plunge into snow-drifts to locate a buried sheep, the crook to help to free one from entanglement in briers and bushes, or for the man to lean on when weary of tramping through deep heather. It was also a good weapon against destructive invaders during the lambing season, such as foxes and carrion crows.

Apart from the small farms, most of the acreage of the Glen consisted of hill-pasture for the hardy blackface sheep. There were families, like the Andersons, Macdonalds, and Murisons, who provided successive shepherds for flocks pastured on hills rented to owners who lived in other districts, but most of the flocks belonged to the farmers who had grazing rights on the hills adjoining their land. Shepherds went south with their flocks before winter came, and returned in spring for the lambing; but small farmers could not afford to do this, so the care of sheep was often associated with hazardous winter work. When storms came they had to go out in blizzards when they could hardly see a hand in front of their face; many times in a night they would go out with a lantern to inspect the huddled yowes and see that all was well.

Came the spring, and in a single day they might be dazzled with sunshine and half-blinded by stinging rain and hail. The old men called them lamb-storms. They swept across the hills when the early lambs were taking their first weak strides, making the pathetic creatures wish they had never been born. Lambing-time called for constant vigilance and attention, and often a feeble, motherless lamb shared the warmth of the kitchen, bottle-fed, wrapped in an old shawl in the ingle-neuk. The sheep were rounded up . . . 'gaithered' was the word used . . . at lambing, clipping and dipping, and the familiar call could be heard, 'Come in ahint, min!' to an over-eager young dog, one of the friendly collies that stood on their hind-legs at any farmhouse door, and put front paws on our shoulders, with tails wagging furiously. Older dogs were watchful and aloof to all but their master and the job in hand.

Clipping in summer was done by hand, a laborious undertaking requiring great skill so that the surface was left in even ridges. Experienced clippers with their shears twinkling in and out the wool could clip a docile sheep in a matter of minutes, but a few awkward yowes could slow down the number clipped in a day.

The yowes were then driven back to the hills where they remained till the severe weather arrived; but, prior to this was the dipping which was supposed to free them from parasites. They awaited their turn in a primitive pen of planks and hurdles adjacent to a burn which had been diverted to fill a concrete tank. A benevolent policeman looked on as the law demanded, and neighbours turned out to give a hand, restraining a struggling sheep while it was dipped in the solution of sheep-dip and encouraging it to flounder out at the other end of the four-foot tank, when it ran off, shaking itself and loudly protesting at the indignity it had suffered.

As Gilbert White explained in *The Natural History of Selborne*, there is always a distressing sound of bleating and crying after the ewes are shorn, for they do not seem to recognize each other. The lambs do not recognize their mothers, not so much because of their changed appearance but by the lack of their own familiar smell which has been removed with the fleece. Lambs do not like the smell of sheep-dip, so the same thing happens after the dipping.

A year with the sheep ended with the autumn lamb sales. We used to see on an early morning the shepherd from Daldownie travelling slowly down the road across the water behind his flock, with a couple of collies frisking round to keep them on the road. There were no double-decker motor-lorries in those days to transport them swiftly to their destination. They had to be walked, but not over-tired, every mile of the way.

Shepherds are silent folk not much given to talking about their job. Instead of speaking they would, in passing, merely give one a friendly nod with an upwards sidelong twist, a typical gesture very difficult to describe. With country folk, to pass a fellow-traveller on the road on foot or bicycle without recognition would be thought the height of bad manners; always there must be a civil word of greeting, even a nod, or that peculiar twist of the head.

About the middle of the eighteenth century crofters began to realize that scattering lime on their land wonderfully increased their crops, and limestone was at their very doors. In the vicinity of farms in the Glen may still be seen kilns which were in use up to the middle of last century and possibly later. Traces of the old roadways the carts had to take may be seen, to bring the limestone for burning from the nearest available source, and the large open doorway at the front where the fire was fed, using mainly peat from nearby mosses. Primitive methods were no longer necessary when modern limeworks could supply the needs of a wide area.

The Glen road today has a steady stream of traffic moving at top speed over its excellent surface, but in my childhood a solitary farm-cart was an object of interest. The iron-rimmed wheels revolving noisily on the rutted road and the slow clopping of hooves were audible long before the cart came into view and after it had passed from sight. By that time most observers had made a shrewd guess at the identity of the driver seated on the side of the cart, reins loosely held for the horse knew every zig and zag of the way. Farm folk wasted no time on speculation; they fetched the 'gless' and at once identified horse, cart and owner, and guessed the object of his journey.

'Man, A telt ye it wis Geordie Rose gaun doon the road. The cairt's teem, A doot he'll be awa' doon for a bit ile-cake for the beasts.' 'Dod, ay, mebbe ye're richt.'

The gamekeeper at Morven assured us that, with the aid of his glass, he could spy a white hare on the summit of the hill in winter. He missed no movement on the surrounding hills at any time, of sheep, hare, visiting neighbour or infrequent stranger. He and other keepers, when hares were plentiful and much prized for food, used to organize hare-hunts, and invite every available man who could handle a gun. There might on occasion be twenty-five guns, and a bag at the end of the day of 150 hares, every man staggering home with a load on his back of half a dozen hares or more, a dead weight, but pleasant to share this much-appreciated addition to the larder in cottage, farm-house and Manse.

For the tweed-hatted, knickerbockered gamekeeper, life was strenuous all the year round. In spring his face was clouded with anxiety when heavy rain and spreading floods threatened to ruin the breeding-season of game-birds. Later in the year he had to keep a sharp look-out for poachers.

Every keeper I ever knew had a wonderful constitution and a vigorous nature, exulting in the bracing hill air, revelling in his chosen occupation; trudging knee-deep in heather, allowing for the wind, noting the light, keeping down vermin, in daily observation of all branches of wild life. Muir-burning in spring to get rid of old rank heather was done in systematic patches for the sake of the young grouse who cannot struggle through dense growth. It was heavy work for the keeper and his helpers, straining to keep the fire within the selected stretch for, once out of control, it might spread for miles, and beating it out was an exhausting business. From a distance the burned patches gave a curious chessboard appearance, and in the following spring the mass of bloom on the young shoots was vivid in colour.

The first heather to bloom was the crimson bell-heather, but when autumn came, the moors were richly purple with ling, and the sound of shots echoed over the landscape, sending grouse toppling out of a blue sky, to be retrieved by the gun-dogs from the keeper's kennels and brought to the feet of the marksmen.

The latter were known as the guns and those at Gairnshiel, as I remember them, had a decided look of a gathering of variously-built editions of Sherlock Holmes, enveloped in immense ulsters of a style and material familiar to all readers of early illustrated productions of Conan Doyle's masterpiece, and since copied, more or less accurately, on television. Breeches and Norfolk jackets, and thick-knit stockings were weightier than anything worn nowadays, and must have felt like chain-mail when rain-soaked; peaty soil clung to the hand-made, well-oiled boots built like battleships, with soles encrusted with enormous tackets. At a grouse-drive the guns stayed in the butts with loaders, and beaters drove the birds in the approved direction. Because of the way the butts were sited, the hill was no place for the foolhardy; only by continual alertness and strict adherence to discipline were shooting accidents avoided. Any gun who followed a bird beyond the line of safety was a source of constant worry to the keeper. It was every gun's ambition and expectation to bring grouse down right and left when they swerved in hundred-miles-an-hour pace over a wind-swept ridge. The joys were not confined to those who carried a gun; ladies who were not 'out with the guns' joined them for lunch, and stayed to watch the well-trained labradors at work on the sun-dappled moors. At Gairnshiel the game-larder was outside the kitchen-door.

It was made of metal gauze. In it the game-birds were left hanging by their necks for perhaps a week, and were then considered fit to prepare for the table. In that primitive larder, long before deep-freeze methods were practised, the game actually kept for months.

In the grouse-driving season, men who could be spared from farm work were glad to earn money as loaders, gillies and beaters. All the boys were engaged as beaters at five shillings a day (and bring your own flag), their mothers depending on their earning enough to get new suits and winter boots. They took a 'piece' to the hill and were 'gey hungert and trauchled' when they got home at the end of the day. When it was a royal shoot, lunch was provided, men getting in addition a bottle of beer apiece.

The small farmer, also, took his sheltie to the hill to bring down the game in panniers, which were covered baskets shaped to lie on the pony's sides, but I remember, long before Land Rovers were designed, a car with caterpillar wheels, built for Alexander Keillor of Morven, crawled over the hills on that estate, bringing down the day's bag, thus outmoding the panniered-pony.

In his youth King Edward VII had been tireless on the hills, but when he came to the throne he was close on sixty and had become stout. In spite of this, he liked to be out on the hills and moors, seated on a pony with his Inverness cape wrapped about him. When he used to shoot over Geallaig a sturdy pony was provided to carry him up the quarry road to the Royal Butt above Delnabo. On the Gairnside moors he had the reputation of being the cheeriest of the party, and his geniality made the day enjoyable for all who served him. It amused him to use the speech of the locality, which he did with a faultless accent. On one occasion he noticed among the gillies, Peter Robertson, who for years had been his personal servant at Abergeldie Castle and had long retired. Delighted, he at once approached him and shaking his hand vigorously he exclaimed, 'Man, Peter, foo are ye?'

At the end of the shooting-season our friend, Donald Fraser, modest man, had to be sought out by the gentlemen who wished to show appreciation of his services; a keeper at Corndavon, on the contrary was known to hover in their vicinity with ready palm, and was open to receive tips of a different kind. He was rumoured to have considerable wealth because of his sound business acumen and his ability to invest his money profitably on the well-informed advice of some of his gentlemen. Another aspect of one of these shooting gentlemen is remembered. Mrs Beeton, in her bulky *Book of Household Management* advises the novice-mistress of a staff, 'We do not object to servants dressing as they please in their off-duty hours, or following their fancies in fashion at proper times and in proper places,' but this old gentleman, an upholder of Victorian tradition, did not leave such decisions to the mistress of the house though she was no novice. He took exception to the house-maids dressing in what he considered an unbecoming style for their station and, meeting two out for a Sunday walk near Delnabo, he sternly reprimanded one for wearing her 'pearls' and pink lace blouse.

With grouse-driving over, it was time for Glen farmers to think of the hairst. On some bigger farms bothy lads complained

Doon at Nether Dallochy there's neither watch nor nock,
Bit denner-time an' supper-time an' aye yoke, yoke!
It's hingin' in an' hingin' in a' day frae sax tae sax,
An' deil a meenit div ye get tae gie yersel' a rax.

The whole agricultural year led up to the hairst, which all agreed was 'the job tae gar ye pech'.

First, men had to scythe the inroads to the fields where the wind-ruffled corn changed colour with every breath.

Accommodation for reaping-machines was none too good on small farms; they had to take their chance for the greater part of the year in an open cartshed, the roosting-place of barnyard fowls, and were liable to suffer damage by having various oddments thrown on top of them, such as rakes, forks, and bags of lime. At the beginning of the season, therefore, a thorough cleaning and a few repairs were needed, before the horses harnessed to the reaper could be seen, with rippling muscles, moving round and round the field as the corn fell before the whirling blades. The early types of reapers were clumsy; they often broke down and had to be 'sorted', delaying the work and exasperating all who had to do with them.

My father was always ready to give a hand in the fields, on the peat-moss, or in the stack-yard, to repair a dyke, or to improve a path. He annually went to Corgarff to help his friend, the Rev. Archie Thomson, to harvest the corn on the Manse glebe; and we all turned out to give a hand in the fields at Ardoch, Tamnafeidh, or Balno, enjoying with the other workers the refreshment which the breaks at ten o'clock and four o'clock brought. Huge cans of tea were brought to the field, with batches of buttered scones in a white cloth. We drank the tea from mugs dipped in the can, and ate the scones in the shade of rustling stooks in a field shorn of its crop and carpeted in stubble that was prickly to the ankles. After a brief rest we returned to the making of bands, having earlier mastered the knack. The method was to take a handful of straw in each hand, cross the right hand over the left, give a twist to the crossed heads, turn them inwards, and lay the resulting band flat on the ground, positioned to receive the swathe. The two ends were then brought up and twisted together, and tucked neatly into the band. At the end of a day's continuous effort one's right thumb felt sprained. Gathering a swathe after a man with a scythe was not an easy business, but when horse-reapers came into use it was much easier to gather, because the reaper left behind, neatly spaced, the correct amount for a sheaf. It was team-work; one gathered the swathe and laid it on the band, another following on her heels tied up the sheaf, and a man came behind and stacked them in stooks. He could wax very sarcastic if the locked heads fell apart when he handled the sheaf, and a shame-faced bandster was given an on-the-spot demonstration on how to make bands.

Crops on crofts were at times poor and the grain inferior. The Year of the Short Corn (1868) was often recalled, when, it was said, not a shower of rain fell from seedtime to harvest; the ears never shot properly and, it was ruefully commented, 'the verra craws hid to get doon on their knees tae get at it'.

After another bad harvest in the Glen, the laird, Alexander Farquharson of Invercauld, in the following spring (1893) sent to every tenant on his estate a gift of seed-corn and my father wrote a letter of grateful thanks on behalf of them all.

'Stookie Sunday' explains itself, and it needs little imagi-nation to visualize the shorn fields; yet Harvest Thanks-giving, a Service held when all was 'safely gathered in, ere the winter's storms begin' was sometimes as late as the first of December.

Farmers tended to leave the corn longer in stook than they commonly do now, and sometimes left it too late. There was one field at Tamnafeidh which we knew well, where snowdrifts quickly gathered and lay deep and crisp and even. As we trudged to school or church, revelling in the sensation of treading hardened snow at dyke-level, we would sometimes stumble over the tops of stooks which had been out when the first snow fell. Normally, when a crop was dry, came the leading. One man or woman up on the cart tidily stacked the sheaves which another tossed up with a deft flick of the fork, the horse moving steadily from stook to stook, perhaps led by a mere child, and thence to the stack-yard. It was a matter of urgency to get on with the leading when the right time came, and eager and energetic farmers often carried on by the light of the Harvest Moon.

Part of the last sheaf to be brought in was nailed up in

the place of honour over the kitchen fireplace, there to remain till next year's harvest yielded a new one. One year, I remember, all the people who had worked in the harvest field at Ardoch were promised a dish of fro' milk, which to our surprise proved to be a delicacy with the flavour and consistency of whipped cream. The fro'ing stick had a wooden cross at one end, surrounded by a ring of cow's hair, the stick being turned about rapidly between the palms of the hands to beat the cream till it thickened. Mary Ann Hay, who had used the stick to good purpose, set a pint-sized basin of the luscious stuff before each harvester, and we consumed every spoonful with appreciative cries.

Kirn milk boiled with sourocks, mentioned by John Buchan in *Witchwood*, was not a Glen harvest dish, nor were there lavish Kirn Suppers and other Harvest Home celebrations which took place on large farms farther south.

We children had fine games of tig round the rucks which had been biggit in the stack-yard; they were allowed to sweat for a week or two before they could safely be thackit. In the meantime there was a job to be done in the barn, twinin' strae to secure the thack on the rucks. A man who had often done it as a boy described how his father sat at one end of the barn with a pile of drawn straw beside him, 'syne I twined wi' a thraw-crook, backin' awa' a' the time while he paid oot the strae; syne I gae'd forrit nice an' slow, keepin' the rape taut bit no' owre ticht, an' he'd be twinin' the rape intil a great big clew that I cud hardly lift!' There was also a method of making straw-ropes single-handed; Ellie and I used to watch from our nursery while an old man was so engaged in the barn opposite our window, on a wet day. On other days we saw him flailing grain, and once we witnessed the striking of a bargain between a farmer and a cattle-dealer over the sale of a cow. After much gesticulation and verbal fireworks the sale

o

was completed, each man spat on his right hand and the two struck hands, palm to palm, to seal the bargain.

Thatching of the stacks was an ancient craft which was carried out entirely by hand; now it can be done quickly, using machine-made matting when necessary, cutting out the risk of damage by weather.

Threshing was, of course, of the utmost importance; without it, neither man nor beast could be fed. At the time of my earliest recollections it was all done by a flail which consisted of two parts, the shaft and the souple, hinged with a piece of supple leather. It had to be used with discretion by the unskilled, for he could give himself 'a sair dunt on the heid, t' gar his lugs dirl' if he was not careful.

The shaft might last a lifetime, but a couple of hard winters' usage were enough to wear out the souple, and in the autumn men began to look around in the woods for a likely bit of stick to serve in the following season. The sheaves were laid on the barn-floor, four, six, or eight in a row, and the flail, swung high over the head in a tricky curve, brought the souple down, hitting the grain and causing it to fly out.

The threshing-machine which superseded the flail excited us by its noise and the bustle which accompanied its use. We would stand just inside the barn-door and watch the team at work. One forked up a sheaf, another cut the band with a sharp knife and fed the sheaf into the body of the mill. Down the chute rushed the golden straw and a third worker immediately forked it away to be built into a sugar-loaf stack. Meantime, we heard the grain come hissing down with a dry rattle and a swishing sound into the sack held ready to receive it. The sacks were later taken to the Mill o' Prony to be ground into meal to ensure an unfailing supply of porridge till next year's harvest came round. There used to be a number of water-mills in the Glen where the corn was ground with enormous stones which revolved as a huge driving wheel drove round and round. Now all are silent.

At the other side of the threshing-machine the chaff scattered and made the workers cough as the scaly husks flew about, but through the steady drone of the mill they laughed and shouted happily to each other. I recollect hearing of only one accident, when Jamie Ritchie, helping at the Shenval, caught his hand in the mill, and ran home to the Torran with mutilated fingers, dripping blood all the way.

Nowadays, in the cornfield, the giant combine devours the oats and threshes it as it lumbers on, straw gushing out behind, while grain pours into the collecting-bin.

When a roup, for one reason or another, became unavoidable, an announcement was made, but seldom was there issued a list of goods for sale, for, locally, everybody knew exactly what there was to offer in the way of stock, growing crops, and farm and household gear; so

The unctioneer cam' doon wi' verra sma' persuasion
Tae be in chairge o' the Occasion.

An occasion it certainly was, with the entire population present.

The departing tenant provided free an unlimited supply of home-brewed ale to encourage the bidding. It was skeachan, or treacle ale, made by the gallon from treacle, hops, and ginger, boiled in water with yeast added, and corked in gallon pigs till required. It was taken round the assembled buyers in zinc pails and served in oft-replenished mugs. For privileged buyers there was a taste of honey ale, made with honeycomb and yeast, which improved with keeping; and heather ale, which required a large quantity of heather in full bloom, with yeast and sugar added. Unlike honey ale, it was ready for use in a day or two. Bidding was speeded up, bidders became reckless and bought gear for which they had no apparent use, as, for example, Jamie McHardy, who became the owner of a plough. He had neither horse nor farm.

Woe betide the crofter in those days if winter should

overtake him with an insufficient supply of peat. The bleak moorlands were so exposed to bitter winds that work was rendered almost impossible if he was caught unprepared, as in the severe winter of 1895.

In the early summer, therefore, every man would depart with his family to the peat-moss, ablaze with spikes of golden asphodel, where he had inherited rights of cutting peat. His tools were few and simple, the most important being his spade with its longish, flat blade, and his peat-barra which had an upright front and no sides. Cutting took place any time from late spring to early summer, depending on the weather. Digging was gruelling work. It had to be done in a dry spell or they would have found themselves literally bogged down in soft brown peat. When the surface was dry it took the weight of a loaded barra, and peats dried quickly. The peat was cut from a vertical face which stood up like a miniature cliff from the already-cut part of the moss. It was light brown at the top and nearly black at the bottom. The top was poor quality, so the first job was to get it off, along with its covering of heather. For a week or two they worked away, slicing the peats and laying them flat on the ground, for they were too wet to handle. When the sun had dried them and they were reasonably firm, the children built them up into little stacks to let the wind get at them. There they stood all summer, rows and rows of black peats, gradually getting drier and lighter. In autumn the carts with clacking axles went to the hill and brought home the peats, and stacked them next to the house, where it was easy to run out on the darkest, wettest, windiest night and carry in an armful for the fire. In his early years at the Manse my father went himself to the peat-moss and did all the necessary work there, paying only for cartage. In later years he paid a farmer for a load or two. They were usually delivered in August and stacked away for the winter. Coal was seldom bought as the cost of carriage made the price prohibitive. It was always referred to in the plural . . . we filled the scuttle with coals, and put a shovelful of 'them' on the fire. A farmer occasionally agreed to fetch a sack or two of 'them' when his cart was not overladen with his own goods. My parents were total abstainers, but for hospitality's sake kept whisky in the sideboard, and the man who brought the coals was one of those who was pleased to accept a dram.

Stacking the peats was a job which could not be rushed; it needed skill and patience, for each peat had to be built separately into the stack. If the corners were not well tied-in the whole lot might collapse in the first blast of wind. Once built, rain might wet the outside, but within, the peats remained perfectly dry. The peat-stack was as necessary to the crofter as the roof over his head, and gave rise to those romantic pictures of thatched cottages in Hieland glens with blue reek rising from the lum. Another picture was of the gudewife smoorin' the fire before going to bed. This ceremony entailed her laying a couple of peats round a small core of fire, so building them that they did not burn themselves out but nursed the core till morning. The fire 'rested' and in the morning, surrounded by hot ash of purest white, would be the tiny core of fire ready with a strong puff of the bellows to set the fire ablaze again. The kettle would be humming on the swey, and often we heard the proud boast, 'Oor fire's niver been oot for fifty or sixty year, mebbe langer'.

In those days there were few blessings so comforting, so fragrant, and so free as a good peat-fire; now heather is growing over the old moss-roads into the hills. More convenient sources of heat have become available, and though electricity on the grid has not yet reached the Glen it is privately generated in a number of homesteads so that television and electric light may be enjoyed.

# CHAPTER ELEVEN

# RURAL EXCURSIONS

It was not that Nature had shed o'er the scene
Her purest of crystal and brightest of green;
  'Twas that friends, the beloved of my bosom, were near,
Who made every scene of enchantment more dear.

Thomas Moore

Looking back on childhood summers, my impression is that
we had tea in the summerhouse, or at the Milton, every day
in the fine sunny summers of long ago. We spent every
waking hour out-of-doors.

Our summerhouse in no way resembled that of Victorian
novelists, a spot for unchaperoned romances; it was a plain
structure of painted wood with one side open to the prospect
of the hills, within sound of the Gairn. It was furnished with
chairs and a bamboo table on which was spread a lace-edged
cloth. The bamboo cake-stand was placed at hand, and every
plate had a damask d'oyley trimmed with crochet or hair-
pin lace.

As a family we were very fond of picnics. We children
loved at all times to wade in the Gairn and in the tumbling

burns, feeling the smooth stones under our feet, and getting weed between our toes.

A favourite place was beside the chuckling water of the fern-fringed Milton Burn, where my father had built a rough stone fireplace, which other picnic-parties found useful when they chanced upon it.

As children, we were a mite resentful if we happened to arrive, carrying the big black kettle, and found strangers at Our Place by the pine tree, for there was no other place quite like it. On arrival we had to collect cowes and cones to make a fire, then we played in the burn making dams and waterfalls till the kettle boiled. My father was kettle-watcher and made a point of seeing that smoke did not enter the spout, for he, for one, did not relish smoked tea.

My mother spread a cloth under Our Tree, and we sat round it, with scalding cups of tea propped among the heather, tucking in to scones liberally spread with home-made jam, and returning to our paddling till, in the late afternoon when the shadows were lengthening, the midges came out to dance in clouds like wavering mist above our heads. They were a pest, and no so-called repellents had any effect on them. We packed up in a hurry and made for home.

Every summer my mother took our more active guests to the top of Maamie and Morven, and as soon as we were old enough, my sister and I went, too. Maamie was easy . . . grass, heather, and a few boulders; from the cairn we saw outspread the patchwork quilt-like pattern of the valley, varying shades of green, yellow, and golden-brown, with the silver ribbon of the Gairn thrown carelessly across it.

Morven was covered in smooth grass, and sheep grazed to the top of its rolling slopes, There was remarkably little heather on it. We followed the fence and arrived in good shape, being rewarded with a superb expanse of hills, and hills-behind-hills lost on the horizon, with Mount Keen, Lochnagar, the Hill of Fare, and Culblean brooding over all, and nearby, Glen Carvie where eagles once had their eyries. Not a sound could be heard save the cry of a hill-bird or the tremulous bleat of a yowe. Byron, an Aberdonian, for whom the mountain had a curious fascination, wrote from the farm at Ballat'rach where he stayed when a lad, of the time

> When I roved, a young Highlander, o'er the dark heath,
> And climbed thy steep summit, O Morven of snow!

Queen Victoria thought the view magnificent. 'Seas of mountains with blue lights', she wrote, 'and the colour wonderfully beautiful.' She was in residence at Balmoral for almost eight months in the year . . . 'only the winter fleggit her awa'' said the Glen folk.

On her Morven excursion she drove to the hill-foot, then she and her ladies mounted ponies and rode to the summit.

We foot-sloggers from the Manse had to tramp some miles over the moors to the base of Morven before we could start to climb, but it never failed to be an enjoyable jaunt.

There has long been a legend that on the summit of Lochnagar, looking down on Lochan-a-ghair, 'the noisy little loch', there may at times be seen a phantom white deer which roams there on moonlight nights. It is well known that a herd of wild goats feeds on the slopes above Lochnagar, and a large white solitary goat was seen above the Wells of Dee not so long ago. It is just possible that a similar large goat, with long, curving horns, seen at a distance may have been mistaken for a deer and given rise to the legend.

Queen Victoria made several ascents of Lochnagar. On the first occasion the Royal party spent a very disagreeable day on the mountain, for mist drifted in and hid everything, and the guides lost their way. Mr Gladstone went up twice . . . 'walked it all', he boasted. We, too, walked it all when we made the ascent, and on one occasion a great many years later, we, too, were caught in mist. A number of us, having gained the summit and been rewarded by the awe-inspiring panorama, as well as the sight of a golden eagle, a herd of deer, and the lochan lying darkly below, suddenly found ourselves enveloped in a thick, chilling blanket. There was deep silence and a sense of desolation. We sat still, afraid to move. When the mist lifted slightly we drew back in horror from the edge of a precipice, and started the descent, lost our way, and landed in sunshine at the head of Loch Muick on Royalty's private road. To make matters worse, we met the Royal Family out for a walk. A kilted Princess Mary and three of her brothers came swinging along, in a hurry to reach Glas-allt-shiel, where Meysie Anderson would be waiting with one of her famous teas, and perhaps intending to follow it with a walk to the Dubh Loch in a wild glen two miles beyond. Following staidly with some of her Balmoral guests came Queen Mary who, sensing our embarrassment as trespassers, gave us a gracious bow and an understanding smile. A few days later, when walking alone near home, I met a solitary gentleman in a shooting-brake, and had the presence of mind to curtsey as King George V drove by, receiving a Royal salute all to myself.

On another occasion we were at Rinloan when the Castle men-servants arrived to prepare a picnic tea on the grassy stretch in front of the house, closely followed by the children. Concealed behind lace curtains we observed them at play, frolicking in perfect freedom. Little Prince John was alive then and I chuckle when I remember how the eldest boy (the Duke of Windsor) put his little brother across his knee in mock severity, and brandishing the sticky circle from a jam-pot, called in glee to the others, 'Watch me rub John's face with strawberry jam!' But John's big sister came to the rescue; which quite irrelevantly reminds me of a Grand Bazaar which I attended with my parents, and was given half-a-crown to spend. The young Princes, Henry and George, were there in their kilts, accompanied by their tutor, the exacting Mr Hansell, and I was detailed to sell them post-cards. Then I decided to buy for my mother a bottle of scent which I saw on a stall, priced one shilling. Bazaars were fashionable occasions, the laden stalls were staffed by decorative society ladies in pretty dresses and smart hats, assisted by their sons and daughters, and a custom had been established that no change should be given. Gentlemen handed over a fiver with a flourish for goods priced at a much smaller figure, and nobody got change out of a sovereign. Unaware of this ruling, I tendered my half-crown and received my bottle of scent. 'No change!', said the smiling, Eton-collared young duke, who was the salesman. So there I was with no money to spend, and, to add to my discomfiture, the stopper came out of the bottle and drenched my velvet Dorothy bag. It must have been good scent, however, for the fragrance lingered for months!

Alexander Woolcott, at the age of fourteen, wrote in his diary, 'We enjoyed the ride very much. I ate a bag of candy, a bag of peanuts, two bars of popcorn, a glass of icecream soda, and a chocolate milk-shake. We had a lovely ride. We sang all the way.'

I remember such a ride in an open four-wheeled brake drawn by two horses. The coachman wore a top hat and a coat with silver buttons. He shook the reins lightly on the horses' rumps and we were off. Had Alexander been with us he would have been up on the box-seat beside the coachman, begging the honour of holding the whip which was lightly flicked round the horses' heads to keep off flies, but we were all girl-children and our mothers would have deemed it unladylike for us to sit beside the driver. He sat on the box alone, with a tarpaulin over his knees in case of rain. We passengers also had the protection of a tarpaulin lined with black and yellow tartan.

We were a merry party bound for the Linn of Dee, with my father feeding us with morsels of history and legend as we drove along. He knew something of interest about every place we passed, even about the inn at Coilacreich, where excellent whisky could be had at any hour for fifteen shillings a gallon, but that, he said, was a very long time ago.

When the white tower of Abergeldie Castle came in sight he drew our attention to the new bridge which the Queen had erected to replace the old contraption which used to be the only means of communication with the other side . . . a sort of cradle running on a rope suspended from posts on either bank of the Dee. It was a very precarious means of transport, and numerous accidents culminated in the death of a young couple on their wedding-day. A jealous lover was suspected of tampering with the rope, the cradle fell, and Babbie Brown, the bonny bride, and her newly-wed husband were both drowned.

Soon after passing Crathie Kirk my father pointed out the Cairn of Remembrance, a mere heap of stones within a clump of larches at the riverside. Cairnaqueen is the modern-ized version of the ancient Gaelic slogan of the Farquharsons, and this spot was their rallying-ground. They met there at the summons of their chief before a battle. Every man was told to bring a stone and lay it down a little way off. After the battle each survivor lifted a stone and carried it away. The stones that were left showed the number of the dead, and these were added to the cairn. This has been denounced as an incredible legend, but, in my childhood, the rude cairn was venerated and woe betide any sceptic who ventured to suggest that a single stone had been wantonly added to the heap. It is the only monument to those Jacobite clansmen who gave their lives in what they earnestly believed to be a wholly righteous cause.

Breathing in the rich, resinous scent of the pinewoods we drove on till Invercauld, stronghold of the Farquharsons since the early sixteenth century, was seen across the water. Our laird was Alexander Haldane Farquharson, a descendant of the great Finlaidh Mor, first of the Invercauld Far-quharsons, who was killed at the Battle of Pinkie in 1547.

Invercauld is, in its original Gaelic, Inver Challa, which means River-Mouth of the Defeat. This refers to a meeting with the Laird of Rothiemurchus, who laid claim to the estate. His men met in battle the men of Finlaidh Mor, and were defeated. The burn where the battle took place was afterwards known as Allt-a-Challa, and the mouth of the burn Inver-Challa.

We passed Old Mar Castle without a glimpse of the Princess Dolgorouki who made it her summer home. She was a very rich and hospitable woman whose husband, Prince Alexis Dolgorouki, was the youngest son of the Secretary of State and Privy Seal to the Tsar. When he was alive they entertained lavishly at the Castle, but after his death she spent the summer in complete retirement, with only the memories of her romantic youth. Through Inverey we trotted, the tiny clachan where John Lamont, the great astrologer, was born, passing the Gallows Tree, doleful reminder of days when a chief held the power of life and death over his clansmen. The mother of the last man to be hanged there, for sheep-stealing, put a sweeping curse on the chief and his family, prophesying that the tree would still stand when every man in the clan had died. That branch of the Farquharsons did become extinct, and the tree still stands, supported by wire struts.

At last we came to the Linn of Dee, where the river plunges through a rocky gorge only a few feet wide. Byron once had a lucky escape there; he tripped on a clump of heather and began to roll down towards the sheer rock-face to the torrent below, when a companion grabbed him just in time. Suitably impressed, we turned back to Braemar and tea; then, without Alexander's popcorn, icecream soda, and peanuts, like him we had a lovely ride home and sang all the way.

I never see a shooting-star without being reminded of the long walk home over the Glas-choille after fun and games at Corgarff Sunday School picnic, my father carrying Little Ellie on his back, I stumbling along at his side with my eyes on the stars.

On the outward trek, Ellie and I bounced along full of eager anticipation, sampling the ice-cold water at places where a large wooden tub fed by a spring was intended for the refreshment of thirsty horses on their long upward haul. We raced down the Corgarff side of the hill over the heathery short cut to the shakin' briggie which spanned the Don flowing at the foot of the minister's glebe. Before the picnic we had a short rest in Archie Thomson's doggie-scented living-room, and a game with his collies, Nero and Caesar, then away to the picnic field to take part in the races, the games, and the shots at Aunt Sally resplendent in a clerical coat green with age. After tea with baps, biscuits, and conversation lozenges, we had to take the road again and all bounce had gone out of us.

Many a year we came over the hill under a sunset sky of pale green barred with rose-pink, and soon a myriad stars overhead were indeed the Heavens' Embroidered Cloths. My mother and I tried to count the shooting-stars. What a number we used to see! We knew no superstition regarding them or the moon. We often saw the Aurora Borealis, or Northern Lights, filling the sky with a fantasy of colours. They lasted only a few minutes, but in that brief time all the colours of the rainbow flashed and changed shape till they flickered and died away. When the moon rose, diminishing the starlight, the hills on our right were solidly black, those on our left lay like crouching animals asleep.

We were not obliged to walk any great distance after Mr Thow retired to Torbeg and in his pony-phaeton drove us over the Stranyarroch to the Braemar Gathering and on many other excursions. He had been a postilion and out-rider in Queen Victoria's retinue in his young days, mine host at the well-known Inver Inn near Balmoral, and now was happy to put his phaeton at our disposal. He was a grand old man of striking appearance and personality, and his reminiscences of his youthful experiences at Windsor and Balmoral kept us enthralled and enlivened many a journey.

For the origin of Highland Gatherings we must go far

[211]

back to the days when Gaelic was the speech of the Highlands and the kilt was the dress for every day. It was to the advantage of every clan that its men should be fleet of foot and strong of arm, and any form of sport that strengthened these manly qualities was naturally encouraged. The Braemar Gathering was held in different spots before it found a permanent home in the lovely arena of the Princess Royal Park. On several occasions it was held at Balmoral and also in the Clunie Park near the Bridge of Dee. I recall a Gathering beneath the ancient walls of Old Mar Castle . . . a wild, wet, windy day, when spectators' umbrellas were blown inside out, and Little Ellie spent the afternoon in the sheltering folds of my mother's cloak.

In the obstacle race that day the competitors were obliged to wade through the shallows of the Dee, and a tipsy man took a sudden notion to join them. He flung himself into the river and floated down on his back, cheerfully protesting to his would-be rescuers, 'Never min' me, billies, never min' me!' He was hauled out, still full of good humour, shouting encouragement to the athletes.

One event of the early Games is no longer staged, the scaling of the rugged face of Craig Choinnich. This over-strenuous contest, inaugurated because of its traditional link with Malcolm Canmore, was discontinued at the express wish of Queen Victoria on account of the tremendous strain it imposed on the runners. There was another occasion, one of many, when she showed her great consideration for her people. When she inspected her Guard of Honour at Ballater in 1869, she noticed that the stiff material of the kilts was chafing the men's knees, and ordered that, in future, soft tartan was to be issued.

The March of the Clansmen used to be the great moment at the Braemar Gathering. As soon as Royalty had arrived and taken their seats in the rustic pavilion, the clansmen marched round the arena with banners flying, the sun glinting off axes and halberds. Nowhere else was it possible to see the mustering of three clans, and they made a glorious pageant. Each clan had its own standard-bearer and its own band of pipers, and all were natives of the surrounding glens, the young lad in his grand-da's kilt and the patriarch, alike. First came the Balmoral Highlanders in Royal Stewart tartan, bearing Lochaber battle-axes, their pipes playing 'Hieland Laddie'; next, the Farquharsons, to the 'Farquharson March', including men from Gairnside, wearing their own tartan and carrying basket-handled broadswords (sometimes erroneously called claymores, but these went out in the sixteenth century); then came the Duffs in vivid red Macduff tartan, shouldering their ancient pikes.

The last March of the Clansmen took place in 1936, and was replaced by a March Past of Massed Bands of Pipers. For the purposes of marching there is nothing so effective as pipes and drums . . . that is why the playing of the Massed Pipe Bands in the incomparable setting of the hills is so memorable.

Highland dancing goes back into the mists of antiquity, the steps requiring a high standard of grace, rhythm, and technique. One of the outstanding dances at Braemar is the Hullachan, which originated in this Valley of the Dee. The Ghillie Callum is a Dance of Victory handed down from earliest times when the victorious clansman danced over the sword of his foe with his own sword laid over it. The Highland Fling is the classic dance in the dancers' repertoire and is superbly executed by men whose training starts in early childhood. The Seann Truihbas (pronounced Shaun Trews) is performed in trews because it is believed to have had its origin after the '45 when the wearing of the kilt was a punishable offence.

Trees from the wood, smooth stones from the bed of the burn, hammers from the smiddy, all ancient ways of testing a young man's fitness, have their counterparts in the tests of strength in which the kilted giants, the Heavies, stars of all Highland Gatherings, take part. Tossing the caber (in Gaelic, the trunk of a tree) is one, and is supposed to have

[213]

been invented by men who had to toss the immense trees which they felled over the burns which flowed through the forest. The caber is a massive trunk raised by two men to the perpendicular. The athlete then lifts it, steadies it as it towers above him, staggers a little way with it, then throws it, not as *far* as he can but as *straight* as he can, a spectacular feat.

Putting the stone is popular among novices because it is comparatively easy to find a suitable stone with which to practise.

Throwing the hammer dates from the days when young men used to foregather of an evening at the smiddy, and compete with each other to see who could throw the smith's heavy hammer farthest by swinging it round and round above the head before releasing it.

In an old diary I read how, in September 1904, my parents, in their early forties, undertook a bicycling trip of several days. They set off one morning at dawn, my father on his new 'Raleigh' which had cost him nearly £4, my mother riding a 'Humber' Safety Bicycle with laced cords on the back wheel, which protected her long skirt of serviceable Scotch twill and prevented it from getting entangled in the spokes. Their machines lacked three-speed gears and many other modern amenities. They cycled through the Pass of Ballater, along the wooded Deeside road as far as Banchory, pausing at the Brig o' Feugh to gaze at the river foaming over the rocks, where earlier they might have glimpsed a salmon leap, a flash of silver and blue. They pedalled by Feughside to Glen Dye, facing a long steep climb, pushing their heavy machines up the Cairn o' Mount, and thankfully resting at the summit to enjoy the glorious view. The descent to the Clatterin' Brig had to be negotiated with care, for brakes were none too reliable and road surfaces poor. Their bikes with their cork handles, poorly-padded seats, and rat-trap pedals had no rubber suspension to cushion the bumps, nevertheless, the diary makes particular mention of their great enjoyment of the rare spin downhill.

[214]

On they went to visit my father's birthplace at Wyndford, and to Laurencekirk to see his parents and sisters. Aunt Mina walked with them as far as Marykirk, following the old country custom of walking a mile or two with friends to lessen by one's company the tedium of a long road. They continued their tour taking in Montrose, Brechin, Arbroath, and Stonehaven. Pushing their bikes over the Slug Road and up every steep hill they averaged seventy miles a day, arriving home saddle-sore and dog-tired but well content with their achievement.

On our walks to Ballater we shortened the journey considerably by using short cuts, first leaving the road below Culsh and taking a path through the broom past the home of our friends, the Christens, joining the main road at Brig o' Gairn. We then wandered along the Old Line, the route of the railway that was begun but never completed. It still makes a pleasant walk, much of it following the river.

Rodolphe Christen was an artist, a genial, dark-haired man with a bushy moustache. He and his wife always walked arm-in-arm along the country roads, he wearing a Panama hat at a jaunty angle and invariably smoking a cigar. When they first came to Deeside they were enchanted with the scenery and were resolved to make their home there. Eventually they found their ideal spot bounded on one side by the Gairn and sheltered by a clump of firs from northern blasts. There they built a house in the Swiss style, with a red roof, and called it St Imier, after Monsieur's birthplace in the Jura Mountains.

At the gate he had two cannons placed which he laughingly declared were to warn off besieging clergy. Hans, the brown-and-white collie, used to dash out and bark at everybody who passed, but was, in fact, a most affectionate animal. After many happy years, Monsieur one day severely injured his tongue by putting the glowing end of his cigar in his mouth while absorbed in painting. Before he had time to realize his mistake it burned a painful hole in his tongue, which caused him months of acute suffering before his death.

Madame was very fond of my mother. She enjoyed her company because she was a good listener, never interrupting the flow of reminiscences which were a relief to the childless widow whose whole life had been centred on her husband. There was a sort of musicians' gallery in the drawing-room which, like the other rooms, was full of Monsieur's paintings. Madame used to give us large folios of his sketches to examine while she and my mother continued their after-tea conversation.

When we acquired bicycles we often took friends to Loch Muick, beyond the Falls, where the river roars down a chasm of rock and fir, and usually stopped for a few minutes at Knock Castle, a ruined tower-house with a tragic story. The seven sons of the aged Laird of Knock were casting peats one day when a feudal enemy, Black Arthur Forbes of Strathgirnock, with his men surrounded them, and accusing them of trespassing on Forbes land, slew every one and stuck their heads on their flaughter spades in a row on the peat-moss. The servant who was sent with the young men's dinner came upon the dreadful sight and fled back to the Castle. When the old man heard the terrible news he fell backwards down the stone stairs and broke his neck. His heir, Gordon of Abergeldie, avenged his kinsmen by raiding Strathgirnock, slaying Black Arthur and seizing his lands. The grim story is typical of life on Deeside in those far-off days of clan warfare.

We often went to the place at the foot of Culblean where the Burn of the Vat, flowing towards Loch Kinord, falls over the rocks into a vat-shaped cave, sometimes erroneously called Rob Roy's Cave. Rob had not always been an outlaw; he was declared one when his lands were forfeited to the Duke of Montrose because of money he owed him; before that, Rob had prospered and become Chief of the Macgregors. He did visit his kinsmen on the Braes of

Cromar at the time of the '15 Rising, but the cave has no associations with him. Long before his time, Gilderoy, also a Macgregor and a freebooter, kept stolen cattle in the cavern and his name was given to it.

Nearby are two placid lochs, with beautiful reflections, which we admired in the late evening when we were cycling home. One is Davan, the other Kinord, both steeped in history. Relics of lake-dwellers were found here in bygone days and carefully preserved.

At a cottage by the wayside near the lochs there was a water-clock which intrigued us, but it, and the rustic museum where the prehistoric canoes were on view, have both disappeared.

# CHAPTER TWELVE

# HOLIDAYS

Bliss was it in that dawn to be alive,
But to be young was very heaven.
                              Wordsworth

When we burbled and boasted at school, 'We're going away', it meant we were going on our annual family holiday, which we took in early summer, and the very thought of it filled us with jubilation. There was no need for a great deal of planning, for when we were young our parents took us to stay with friends, who in turn spent holidays at the Manse; so no glossy brochures were consulted (I doubt if there were any in those days), only lavender-coloured penny time-tables, which, though usually out of date, never seemed to let us down.

My mother was a great one for preparing early; she began to pack days ahead, and the luggage was strapped the night before the journey, ready for an early start in a hired machine. We were astir at crack of dawn, and I remember the wonder of driving along the wooded road in the first clean magic of early morning when silver-wet cobwebs were laced between the grasses and glistening on the juniper bushes.

My father had a passion for punctuality and liked to arrive at the station a good half-hour before the train was due to depart. If there were unexpected delays on the road he fretted and fumed with anxiety. His personal luggage consisted of a Gladstone bag and another called a portmanteau, which was large and roomy and strengthened by two broad leather straps passed through steel slots in the framework. His staff and umbrella, and my mother's parasol, were rolled inside a bundle of travelling rugs and coats, held firmly in a monstrous sausage-shape by straps passed through a carrying-handle.

Everything about the railway-station excited me as a child . . . there was the small window at which my father had to stoop to peer in when buying the tickets, then the labelling of luggage; there were the trundling barrows laden with other people's luggage of all sizes and queer shapes, including Japanese hampers, which consisted of two deep basketwork oblongs, one slightly larger than the other. The smaller half could be packed to overflowing, then it was covered by the larger half, well pressed down and secured by two broad straps. It was possible to reserve a whole compartment but our parents never did this. The sight of a goggle-eyed child at each window was, as a rule, enough to ensure privacy on any journey. Families travelling with small children often resorted to this device. Other passengers could not face the prospect, if it could possibly be avoided, of occupying such a confined space on a long journey with a brood of restless children.

Train departure from Ballater was a fussy business. One of the two porters rang a large handbell to warn passengers to take their seats. We bairns were already in our corners with our noses glued to the pane. Friends said their final 'Good-bye, and be sure to write', the doors were slammed, (steam was up a while ago), the stationmaster blew a whistle and waved a green flag, and we were off.

Railway carriages were fitted then with fly-spotted mirrors, and faded photographs of noted castles and cathedrals, which were not necessarily part of the scene on that particular line. Every bit of the journey aroused our interest, aided and abetted by our parents who were eager that we should miss nothing. There was excitement at the first glimpse of the sea, the thrill of going through a tunnel, the noise and eerie darkness and the wonder of emerging into daylight again; even the cattle and horses in the fields looked different from those at home . . . we were ready to be amazed at everything we saw.

We were permitted to stand at the door of the compartment to view the passing scene and a firm grip was held on a handful of our bunched skirts lest the door fly open. The train seemed to go at such a speed, and there was no corridor between us and the outside world. When we holidayed in Stirling we enjoyed riding on the horse-drawn trams, for this was one of the last places to retain them for public transport, but we much preferred a ride in our uncle's trap with his brisk little pony known in the family as 'Papa's Johnny'. We clip-clopped along in fine style to Kippen and Drymen, wherever he had business calls to make, round by Cambuskenneth Abbey, and home to lunch on Waddell's sausages which we never had at home, or slicing sausage with a most delicious flavour.

Rolls, floury and warm from the oven, were delivered early each morning in a basket carried by a very small boy.

The shops had old-fashioned bells that rang to announce the entrance of a customer. Tea, sugar, rice, and other dry goods were ladled from large japanned canisters, weighed on brass scales, and made up into packages for each purchaser, and the goods were later delivered; it was unusual to see a lady carrying her purchases.

Every year I was taken to the hairdresser's salon to have my hair pointed and singed. With a flourish the hairdresser shook out a large white sheet in which he enveloped me, tucking it in at my neck. He had previously set me in a high chair which shot up when a lever was pressed. Some inches were cut off my long hair (this was pointing) and the hairdresser blew the surplus bits of hair off the nape of my neck. He then made a twist of each strand of my hair and passed a lighted taper up and down the spiral. Strand by strand was singed in this way, and my hair brushed and combed. Then the man, whose moustachio ends were twirled to point upwards in a most seductive way, took a fancy glass bottle of pleasantly-perfumed liquid and sprayed it over my head by pressing a rubber bulb, a refreshing experience.

We were impressed by the variety of carts that regularly came round from door to door. There was Jenkins, the red-bearded vegetable-man, who weighed potatoes in a huge balance which hung on the door of his cart; there was the milkman who poured the required quantity into the customer's china jug from an immense brass-bound churn, which sat on the tail of the cart, full of milk straight from the cow. He dispensed it from a tap, into pint and half-pint measures which, when not in use, hung on their sides on shining brass hooks. This was a big advance on the open pails of an earlier day, but still a long way from sealed bottles and cartons and milk from tested herds.

There was the coal-man who stood on his open dray which was drawn by a listless horse. As he went along he faced first the houses on one side then wheeled to face the other, ever on the alert for customers, shouting 'Coal!' at intervals in a resounding voice, while his horse, unheeding, continued to plod slowly along. Housewives ran out and bought a sack or two which he tipped into their cellars and then ran after his horse, vainly shouting 'Whoa!'

On hot days, pulled by another slow-moving horse, the watering-cart appeared, spraying from its rear cold jets to lay the white dust that covered the road. In its wake danced a happy gang of barefoot children.

Every day, on account of the number of horses, scaffies

[221]

with immense brushes and shovels went along sweeping
the streets.

Across the way from my aunt's house lived two little
girls with their widowed mother, a courageous woman, very
anxious to do her best for her children, and to bring them
up to be little ladies. They were always beautifully dressed,
kept themselves clean and tidy, were industrious at school,
and never played rough games. They were so prim and
proper my cousins and I found them insufferable. They
repeated to us what their ambitious mother had instilled
in them, 'What others can do, YOU can do!' and apparently
they could, without effort. They were forever being held up
to us as models of good behaviour and diligence . . . why,
they even practised their scales without a reminder! My
mother never failed to remind me of the day when she had
caught me romping in the playground in a most unladylike
manner, and urged me to imitate Gertrude and Muriel,
quoting their maxim, 'What others can do', but the charm
did not work . . . it was simply not in me to be neat, earnest,
and devoted to practising scales.

My first ride in a motor-car took place in Stirling in 1897,
when George Owen, one of those men who foresaw the
development of the motor industry, offered to take us for
an evening drive in his new motor-car. Like the Wright
Brothers, among others, he had been a bicycle-agent and
repairer. His garage was a converted bicycle-shop; his assis-
tants now wore overalls and were designated mechanics.

The taking out of a motor-car in those early days always contained an element of adventure. The drive in itself was sufficient object; only in later life did one drive to get somewhere.

When the open motor drew up at the front door it
appeared to be smaller than we had been led to expect.
It was not so big as a horse-drawn waggonette but it made
plenty of noise, and smoke and fumes drifted behind and
underneath it.

Snorting and vibrating it awaited our pleasure. George,

wearing goggles, and a large tweed cap, back to front so that the peak rested on his neck, invited us to take our places. With ill-concealed excitement we climbed in. The engine having ceased to vibrate, George stooped and wound the starting-handle vigorously, and after a series of loud crashes and explosions it again came to life; George climbed in hastily and took the wheel, which was like a monstrous piece of vegetation on a long stalk.

George and the passenger seated at his side sat high above the bonnet; there was no windscreen. We must have been among the first motorists who were able to travel without a flag. Since the Locomotives Act of 1896 it had no longer been the law that a man on foot carrying a red flag should precede a car along the highway.

As we drove along the roads outside the town the hedges were white with dust which rose in clouds. It was probably a dinful, bumpy ride but we were far from being critical; we were travelling on the level quite as fast as the horses we were accustomed to sit behind, from the engine came a curious new smell, and when we went downhill nothing could pass us.

We drove along the crown of the road, George, proudly, at all the corners, blowing his horn by pressing a large rubber bulb. We had several breakdowns on our short drive when George had to 'get out and get under'. The tools he required to adjust his taps and knobs and screws were kept in a box on which one of us was seated, the others occupying the recognized passenger-seats, including a dickey seat behind. We heard a variety of excuses for the delay . . . the engine was too hot, the engine was too cold, gadgets with strange-sounding names were giving trouble, but when the engine consented to go once more we were covering the ground at a good seven miles an hour. How far we actually travelled on that summer evening I never heard, but I know we arrived back full of exhilaration, feeling that we were upsides with the King who drove about in a 12 h.p. Daimler.

In the evenings in Stirling the grown-ups sat under the whiteness of incandescent gas-light in the sitting-room, with the dark-green Venetian blinds down, with acorns dangling on their cords. Gas-jets were mostly unshielded at that time. In our bedroom was a gas-bracket on which a naked blue flame without globe or mantle made a singing noise. Maggie Mason, the country lass who came with us on holiday, blew out the flame like a candle on her first evening in a town, and my mother came into the room just in time to save our lives. Maggie went for a walk one evening and was attracted by the sound of raucous music rising from a fair. In a murky yellow glow, swings rose and dipped to the blaring music, clanking steam-engines sprayed sparks and whiffs of hot oil as they drove the whirling roundabouts under the hissing naphtha flares. It was bewildering and fascinating. Maggie had never seen anything like it. She watched the young people having fun at the coconut shies, then turned her attention to the hobby-horses on the gaudily-striped Merry-Go-Round. When they stopped, she daringly took a seat, determined to have a go. It did not occur to her that there would be anything to pay, but when the man came round to collect the fares she produced a penny which she luckily had in her pocket, and that, it transpired, was adequate payment for her ride.

A well-known writer has declared that the view from the ramparts of Stirling Castle can hold its own with any in the world. We were taken up there many times, and to the Wallace Monument on the Abbey Craig, to see Wallace's mighty sword; and, of course, we were taken to the Field of Bannockburn on the outskirts of a very small village which has long since been swallowed up. The field was cultivated then, but a path led to the stone, with its socket covered with protective iron bars. In that socket, called the Borestone, the Scottish Standard was said to have been planted, and from its site on the hillside the lie of the battlefield could be made out. There is now a very imposing Memorial at Bannockburn.

[224]

Sunday in Stirling was very different from that at home. For one thing, we did not set out for church till all the church bells in the town began to ring. Our cousins wore pretty hats and dresses and, reaching to the calf of the leg, brown kid button-boots which had to be done up with a hook.

Ellie and I were dressed in the new clothes which had been bought the previous day. White piqué was popular for children's wear, and I remember my first 'peeky' dress, also a coat and skirt of white spotted duck, with collar and cuffs of broderie anglaise. That year we had frilly hats edged with such daintily-woven straw that, at first glance, everybody took it for lace. There was a full choir in the church with a precentor called Mr Dunsmore, who took his tuning-fork, ding-ed it on his knee and held it to his ear before giving the choir the keynote and leading them in the singing.

> And when at last the kirk has skailed,
> An' fowk hae gaen their ways,
> They micht forget the text an' prayer,
> But no' wha' leads the praise.

In the afternoon we went to Sunday School, and Mr Dunsmore was the Superintendent; again he used his tuning-fork and set us off in the opening hymn with a loud DOH.

Aeroplanes were still in their infancy, such a rare sight that crowds of people rose at dawn, we among them, to see a flying-machine land in the King's Park, I think the airman was Adolphe Pégoud, one of those

> Magnificent men in their flying-machines
> They go UP, tiddly up, and go DOWN, tiddly down.

He had just completed a stage of a test of skill and endurance, and was so weary that he snapped at the Provost who stepped forward to give him a civic welcome, 'Oh, you go to bed!'

Wherever we went on holiday, in Stirling and elsewhere, we were fascinated by the number of 'tastefully-designed drinking fountains' which were found in parks and public gardens and even by the wayside; it was a popular form of philanthropic gift to a town, or a memorial to a distinguished citizen. Every fountain was equipped with a metal cup which a thirsty passer-by could fill with water which spurted from a small gargoyle. It was fun to swing the heavy iron cup on its chain and dash it with a noisy chink against the imposing granite or marble edifice, but never, never, did we dare put our lips to the cup.

When I was seven we spent a holiday in Belford where Uncle George was parish minister, and lodged in a house with a butchery business attached. Cattle were actually pole-axed in the backyard. Once, I was horrified at the sight of a cow on its way to the slaughter-house, crazy with terror, held by ropes in the hands of yelling men.

A child's tricycle was hired and Ellie was given rides on it. I had a marvellous sense of adventure as I pedalled alone on the quiet road which was an extension of the long main street. Time makes places smaller and memories larger; when I passed through Belford many years later, the main street was no great length, and the leafy, tree-lined road of my memories was soon left behind.

Another year we went to Birkenhead to visit Old Uncle, a gentle soul with a neat, grey beard. Indoors he wore smoking-caps embroidered by loving hands, so that his hair should not smell of tobacco-smoke; one, of blue velvet embroidered in yellow had a tassel of yellow silk . . . another, like a scarlet fez, was covered with embroidery in gold thread, with a gold tassel.

Ellie was too young to leave my mother's side, so I went exploring alone. Old Uncle's house at the back overlooked the beautiful garden of a fine boys' school. One day we were invited to have tea with the wife of the Headmaster, who allowed me to wander round the garden and told me I could come and play there any day I wished. I took her at her word and went next day to drift round the grounds, half hoping to see again Fernando, a Spanish boy with dark, flashing eyes, whom we had met the previous day in the Head's house. He was a handsome youth with whom, we were told, no boy cared to quarrel, as he carried a knife which he was apt to produce at the first sign of disagreement. Evidently, confiscation in the interests of the community was not then practised. Alas! I was scolded for going to the garden without my mother's knowledge, and never went there again.

One year we stayed with a family in Montrose who lived in a flat over their draper's shop. My mother bought us lovely dresses, navy and scarlet, and 'crushed strawberry', with smocking; the scarlet ones had little pointed collars embroidered with leaves in gold thread, the prettiest dresses we ever possessed, with buttons like flower-heads.

Montrosians used to be known in neighbouring towns as 'Gable-endies', because many of its oldest houses had their gables on the street. Its port was then the centre of the fishing industry and most of the fisher folk lived in the village of Ferryden. We crossed the South Esk in a small rowing-boat to visit friends in Ferryden. While the grown-ups talked and talked, Ellie and I were sent out to play in the back garden which held nothing of interest. To overcome our boredom we rope-walked along a wooden edging to the borders, but were observed and sharply told to 'keep to the channel', the only time I heard that nautical term applied to a garden-path.

Some years before we had spent Christmas in Edinburgh. I was old enough to retain impressions of the gaily-decorated shops, and of the circus, carnival, and the pantomime. In those days the Big Top was everywhere at Christmas, not only big cities but smaller towns had circuses running for three or four winter months. Of my first circus no clear memories remain, blurred by the many acrobats, jugglers, and bareback riders in countless circuses since; but I have never forgotten the woman lion-tamer in the carnival in the Waverley Market, who put her head sideways into a lion's mouth and smiled reassuringly at us from under its

[227]

huge teeth. Nor have I forgotten the song-vendor bawling as he passed us where we stood in the queue for the early doors, 'All the Songs of the Pantymine! All the Pantymine Songs!' nor the comedian in that pantomime who sang (in Scotland's capital!) 'O what a happy land is England, Free from all sorrow, toil, and care!' amplifying this rash assertion in a number of verses, each ending in 'O what a happy race we are!'

Then there were the ghosts dressed in white sheeting, uninvited guests at a stage dinner-party, who glided in from opposite wings, a ghastly blue spot-light their sole illumination. They touched in turn the diners at the table, centre stage, and one by one the frightened figures fled. I had waited impatiently throughout the matinée performance for this ghostly act and went home much gratified, to a dreamless sleep.

There was also Poole's Novel Christmas Entertainment for Children in the Synod Hall, where a young man stood by the footlights and introduced the Myriorama. Massive paintings in vivid colours, mounted on rollers and controlled by mechanism, were moved across the stage to give the effect of scenery viewed from a wide railway-carriage window, and we were transported on a lightning world tour.

On Hogmanay night I was somewhat disturbed by the guisers who rang the bell for admission, then charged up the stairs with lowered heads, and at the door of the flat revealed soot-blackened features and masks called 'false faces'. Given pennies and sweeties, they clattered downstairs and on to the next block of flats. Watching from a window I often saw the lamplighter going from lamp to lamp in the street far below, touching each with a tiny flame flickering in the end of a pole which he thrust through a hole in the base, and magically the lamp lit up. I did not know then that Robert Louis Stevenson, as a boy, was enthralled by the same scene and wrote verses about it, but I was taught an old rhyme to chant as I watched the man each evening:

Leerie, Leerie, light the lamps,
Lang legs and crooked shanks.

This must have been a reference to the Daddy Long Legs shadow on the pavement as the man went about his work.

There were many mournful street-singers who picked our pennies off the cobbles and moved on; there was also a hurdy-gurdy man with a monkey, resplendent in a little blue jacket, red breeches, and a hat with a feather, which was sent up to the windows, climbing the rainwater pipes like a cat-burglar, sitting on the sills to collect the pennies. When the poor, shivering little thing had been up long enough, his master jerked the leash attached to his harness, and down came Jacko to hand over the coppers. Then the swarthy Italian with his curly black hair and permanent smile, would sweep off his wide-brimmed hat, bow, grinning towards the windows, and move away to do his organ-grinding in the next street.

There was a man with a street-piano which rattled out a series of popular tunes as long as he kept turning the handle. He made a regular round of visits, appearing in a certain district on the same day every week.

What a holiday that was! So many ferlies, so many delights . . . not least were rides on the tops of trams. It was a treat to be allowed to climb the winding iron stair, and to run to the front of the car to have a good view of the street ahead, sitting out on a little platform above the driver's head. There was a similar platform at the back of the car . . . sometimes the whole of the top was open. The bare, slatted, yellow-varnished wooden seats could be made to face in either direction merely by moving the back-support, so a party of four could sit facing each other. Trams were very noisy and went along with a great clanging of bells. An old country body described them as 'shoogly contraptions that fairly dunt up yer internals', but what a long ride you got for a penny!

A form of home entertainment which we met in

[229]

Edinburgh was a Zoetrope, or Wheel of Life, so called because it showed pictures of objects as if they were alive. It was cylindrical in shape and rotated on a stand. There were a number of three-inch slits at equal distance all round the circumference of the cylinder. Immediately below these slits a strip of paper had to be coiled. It was printed with a series of pictures depicting animals and people in action such as children skipping, couples dancing, horses or dogs racing, and so on, and when the wheel was spun and we looked through the slits the figures appeared to be moving at great speed.

Another home entertainment which was frequently pressed upon us was called a stereoscope, and was then considered to be the greatest novelty of all the visual inventions of the age. It was an easily-handled instrument with a velvet-covered eye-piece. Oblong cards with two identical pictures mounted side by side fitted into a frame. Through the viewer we saw, not two pictures but one, large and clear, a bold and third-dimensional picture. A box containing dozens and dozens of cards picturing Turkish dancers, the Crystal Palace, the Taj Mahal, battle scenes and other wonders kept us quietly fascinated for hours.

The delicate tinkle of the music-box was then a part of everyday life and we met it everywhere we went, in various shapes. We ourselves had one, a metal box about the size of a coffee-saucer, less than an inch deep, on which a beautifully-proportioned dancer in full Highland dress revolved in a characteristic Fling till the music stopped.

In Edinburgh we also saw a pianola, an instrument which could be attached to any piano. A large roll of paper perforated with a pattern of small holes was placed in a rack, and an operator, not necessarily one who could play a piano, was able to play tunes on the pianola by following the pattern of holes on the paper, partly on the keys and partly by pedalling.

The first gramophone I ever heard was a hired one at a recital of records in Glen Gairn school. The tin horn was the old 'His Master's Voice' type, and the records were wax cylinders which slid like a cuff on to an arm-like projection. The music was tinny, but everybody thought it astounding. The gramophone had to be wound by hand for every record, and made a painful noise when it ran down. Later, at the age of nine, I heard a similar gramophone concert in the open air at Leazes Park, Newcastle-upon-Tyne. We were staying in Leazes Park Terrace and heard the records from our windows. They were mostly the songs of Harry Lauder, who made his first appearance in London in 1900, and 'Roamin' in the Gloamin'' was all the rage. Gramophones were still a novelty to me when I went to boarding-school. A senior girl brought back from her holiday a box of records, each of which was introduced by a pompous nasal voice which announced dramatically 'EDISON-BELL-RECORD!' Among them were John Philip Sousa's spirited marches, 'Washington Post', 'El Capitan', and 'Liberty Bell', the soldiers' chorus from 'Faust', and 'Floradora'. Betty played them in the dormitory when opportunity offered, till the Voice of Authority said 'Stop'; so the gramophone with its green and gold horn and its metallic sound-box was silent for the remainder of the term.

Throughout the ages it has been the habit of an older generation to be slightly shocked and pained by the type of modern music beloved by the younger. I have read that the waltzes of Strauss at first met with strong disapproval from those who had been brought up on the dignified airs of the minuet, and I know that when 'Alexander's Ragtime Band' was first played in the 1900s there were many who condemned it, but by 1905 it was sweeping the country. We heard it in Newcastle-upon-Tyne when it was very new . . . we came to know all the popular songs of the day . . . 'Navaho', 'Whistling Rufus' and many others. We actually saw a One Man Band with his complicated assortment of instruments playing at the kerbside, and a German Band, skilled performers on brass instruments, which were then a familiar sight in the streets of all big cities.

I was taken to Marks and Spencer's Penny Bazaar, then an unspectacular place consisting of one long ill-lit room with trestle-tables down the middle and sides of the building. These were laden with small household articles, packets of pink, scented writing-paper with envelopes to match, pens and pencils, and a bewildering array of games and toys to dazzle a wide-eyed country child. The Bazaar lived up to its name; nothing cost more than a penny. You could buy a box of assorted beads, or tiny pearly shells, or balls of coloured glass and make your own necklace. I bought a box of stamp-sized pasteboard letters of the alphabet with which we played 'Word Making and Word Taking' on winter evenings for many years. Penny Bazaars vanished in the upheaval of the First World War, and their successors, the Sixpenny Bazaars and the Multiple Stores, never recaptured the glamour of the gas-jets and the semi-darkness. In a waxworks show we saw a tableau of a bit of Scottish history. There stood a terror-stricken Catherine Douglas with her arm thrust through the iron bar of the door to keep out the Scottish nobles, who had entered the Dominican Priory in Perth to murder King James I; but we know it was all in vain, they forced their way in, Catherine's arm was broken and she went down in history as Kate Bar-Lass.

As we came out of the waxworks, and into the brightly-lit streets, we noticed a blind girl in a straw boater, dark glasses, neat short jacket and long skirt. She had been singing in the street and had stopped to appeal to passers-by to protect her from a man who was following and pestering her. I could not get her out of my thoughts for a long time.

In the shops, overhead railways carried cash from any part of the store to a concealed cash-desk, and presently returned the container to the correct department with a customer's change and cash-slip. There was a considerable rattle overhead as the railways functioned.

We went on to Harrogate where we stayed in a fine hotel

as guests of a great-aunt. We took the waters, attended concerts in the Kursaal, and went for bracing walks in the parks, where I remember seeing a bevy of girls in riding-habits dart across the grass, and, holding up their skirts, climb an outside staircase on their return to school from their morning ride.

In the summer of 1904 when I was eleven, we holidayed in Stonehaven and took rooms in Cameron Street with a crippled lady, Miss Edwards, who sat all day in her chair doing crochet work which, with the letting of rooms to summer visitors, was her only means of livelihood. Most afternoons I was directed to take a long ramble with her brother, an elderly silent man. We sauntered along the cliff-tops, or explored the shore, scrambling over rocks encrusted with limpets and hung with bright green slimy weed. We gathered shells and seaweed, the feathery dark crimson fronds that spread like lace in the clear pools left by the tide. Sometimes we collected dulse, an edible seaweed which Mr Edwards ate just as it came off the rocks, folding the water-beetles inside the slippery strands and cramming the whole lot into his mouth. We lingered often by the harbour wall where the gulls wheeled and screeched and squabbled over the bits of bread thrown to them by loiterers like ourselves. Once we trudged as far as Dunnottar Castle, over six centuries old, perched high on a rock and all but surrounded by sea. Over sixty years later it was to see the romantic open-air wedding of a young Nor' East couple who had done their courting among the ruins. As the bride moved along the windswept aisle it is unlikely that she gave a thought to the ghosts of William the Lion, William Wallace, Sir Walter Scott, and members of families with ancient family names, who had walked there at some time in its turbulent history, not forgetting Mrs Granger, the wife of the minister of Kinneff, who smuggled out the Scottish Regalia . . . sword, sceptre, and all, and kept them safe for posterity.

Having climbed to the Castle, explored the acres of

ground up there, and gazed awestruck at the wild sea foaming on the rocks below, I must have been weary as we tackled the long walk home. Doubtless I slept soundly that night with the smell of the sea in my nostrils and the cry of seagulls in my ears.

There were striped machines on wheels, known as bathing-coaches, which were pulled down to the water's edge by tired old horses, and left there till it was time to fetch them back beyond the reach of the tide. They were like little houses with painted roofs, and had steps leading down to the water. For bathing, women wore tunics and baggy bloomers trimmed with white braid, and mob caps with elastic inserted to make them cling to the head. Little girls, with their frocks crammed into the waistband of their knickers which were rolled above the knee as high as possible, splashed in the sea. My mother would not have dreamed of letting us make such an exhibition of ourselves, so we walked demurely on the Esplanade with our parents, in our kilted skirts, our blouses with sailor collars, and our round straw hats, watching other children paddling and building sandcastles. We were not envious; we realized that such ploys were not for us.

At intervals the fishing-boats put out to sea, not with a putt-putt-putt as nowadays, but silently slipping out of the harbour and away beyond the horizon.

There were no overwhelming crowds of holidaymakers, no ice-cream barrows, no candy floss, hot dogs, or transistors. Instead of fun fairs and funny hats there were the 'peeroes' in white overblouses with black pom-poms down the front, baggy trousers, and dunce's hats topped with a pom-pom; and there were donkey rides. The donkeys trotted along but could not be persuaded to go a yard beyond the regulation length of the ride. Ellie lay along her donkey's back, clinging with both arms, while laughter was jerked out of her in bumpy shrieks.

I have a clear recollection of seeing every day a well-dressed, quiet young woman who frequented the beach shelter and sat for long periods doing some simple stitchery, but every time a personable man came by she threw aside her needlework, left her little pile of coloured silks, and followed him. People round us thought it very amusing to see her antics and her gentle pestering. She was known to all regular frequenters of the beach, but appeared to have no companions. Nowadays, such a girl with her sweet, vacant smile and obsession with men, would be looked after for her own sake and that of the community, but in those days, poor girl, she was a laughing-stock, and nobody realized that she had a sick mind.

Another holiday I remember was spent on a large farm in East Lothian, where our host rode on horseback round his fertile acres, looking every inch the Gentleman-Farmer in his hard riding-hat, well-cut tweeds, and burnished leggings. We young people ambled along the country roads in a governess-cart drawn by a fat pony. Sometimes a groom took the reins, sometimes a daughter of the house. We drove to Gifford and Haddington, and went to Cockenzie for a beach picnic. It was delightfully secluded in those days; we were the only picnickers there that afternoon.

We had great capacity for enjoyment when we were young; no matter where our holidays were spent we retained happy memories of them, but were equally happy to return home. I recall

> The slow and drowsy journey in the rattling train,
> The station there to welcome us again;
> The little dog-cart bowling us along
> The winding lanes, the green and summer song
> Of meadows rich with flowers, the smell of hay,
> The skylarks singing through each golden day,
> And then, as now, the sudden warm content
> Caught in the fragrant honeysuckle's scent.

'Ah well', said my mother, 'back to porridge and old clothes!' a saying not to be taken too literally, but we knew what she meant!

# SOME BOOKS CONSULTED

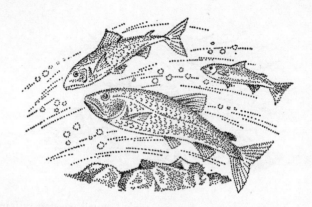

*The Deeside Guide*, Lewis Smith & Son, Aberdeen, 1891.

MACINTOSH, JOHN, *History of the Valley of the Dee*, Taylor & Henderson, Aberdeen, 1895.

MICHIE, JOHN, *Deeside Tales*, D. Wylie & Son, Aberdeen, 1908.

*The New Deeside Guide*, Lewis Smith & Son, Aberdeen, 1832, revised edition 1849.

QUEEN VICTORIA, *Leaves from the Journal of Our Life in the Highlands*, Smith, Elder & Co., London, 1868.

TAYLOR, ELIZABETH, *Braemar Highlands*, William P. Nimmo, Edinburgh, 1869.

# GLOSSARY

*ahint*, behind
*appleringie*, southernwood
*ashet*, oval meat-dish
*backet*, small shallow tub
*barm*, yeast
*birl*, to turn round rapidly
*black sugar*, liquorice
*bodach*, old man
*bosie*, bosom
*bowie*, tub-like small barrel with open end
*braws*, fine clothing
*browst*, a brewing (of illicit whisky)
*busses*, bushes
*caff*, chaff
*cailleach*, old woman
*canny*, shrewd
*carvies*, carraway seeds
*cast* (snow or peat), to dig
*claik*, chatter
*clash*, gossip
*clew*, ball
*clout*, cloth
*clype*, to carry tales

*cogie*, small wooden milking-pail
*coorie*, nestle, crouch
*couldna win*, could not go
*coupit*, upset, overturned
*couthie*, cosy, welcoming
*craw plantit*, crow planted
*creepie*, three-legged stool
*dander*, dawdle
*deen*, done
*dicht*, wipe
*dinna*, do not
*dirl*, throb, vibrate
*dochter*, daughter
*douce*, sober, sedate
*dowie*, depressed
*duinewasal*, laird of small estate
*eggeree*, scrambled eggs
*fair forfochan*, tired out
*fan*, when
*far*, where
*ferlies*, things to excite wonder, fairings
*fit*, what

*fleggit*, frightened
*fly cup*, a quickly served cup
*forenicht*, evening
*fushionless*, tasteless
*galluses*, braces
*gar*, compel
*gaun aboot bodies*, wanderers, tramps
*gey*, very
*gird*, iron hoop
*graip*, garden fork
*grat*, wept
*hairst*, corn harvest
*halflin*, young lad
*hap*, wrap, cover
*hingin' in*, working steadily
*hurll*, a ride in any vehicle
*ingans*, onions
*jalouse*, to suppose or guess
*kail-yaird*, vegetable-garden
*keek*, peep
*kep*, catch
*kist*, chest (box)
*lad o' pairts*, lad endowed with recognized abilities
*larach*, ruined homestead
*littlins*, little ones
*loup*, leap
*lowe*, a flame
*lowsin'*, unyoking
*lum*, chimney
*maskin' o' tea*, sufficient tea for an infusion
*moose*, mouse
*muggins*, knitted leggings
*nae mows*, not very wise
*neeps*, turnips
*nock*, clock
*ootbye*, outside, beyond the home environment
*orra loon*, odd-job man
*oxter*, armpit
*pech*, to pant

*peer*, poor (peer stock! poor old man!)
*piece*, sandwich, packed lunch
*pirns*, reels of cotton
*pokes*, paper-bags
*potty*, putty
*preens*, pins
*press*, wall-cupboard
*puckle*, a small quantity
*quate*, quiet
*queyns* (quines), girls
*rashes*, rushes
*rax*, stretch
*reek*, smoke
*roared an' grat*, wept noisily
*roch*, rough
*roup*, sale by auction
*row* (like hap), to wrap
*rozzen*, resin
*ruckle*, heap
*rugging*, tugging
*sark*, chemise, shirt
*saut*, salt
*scaffie*, scavenger, street-sweeper
*scuttering*, scurrying
*scunnert*, disgusted
*shargar*, undersized fellow
*sheen*, shoes
*skailed*, emptied
*skelp*, slap
*sneck*, simple door latch
*soos and coos*, pigs and cows
*softie*, a type of roll
*sowans*, a dish made from inner husks of oat-grains
*speen*, spoon
*spier*, enquire
*stirk*, young heifer or bullock
*stot*, an ox; also, to bounce a ball
*swack*, nimble, sure-footed

GLOSSARY

*sweirt*, unwilling
*teem*, empty
*theevil*, spurtle, porridge-
   stick
*thole*, to bear pain
*thrawn*, stubborn
*tither*, the other

*trauchled*, weary
*unco'*, very
*unctioneer*, auctioneer
*wale*, choose
*wyvin'*, knitting (derived
   from weaving)
*yowe*, ewe

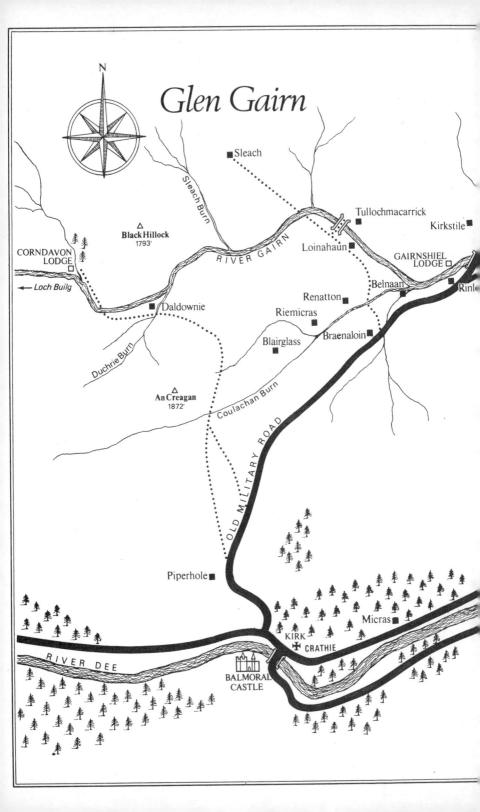